# POVERTY

*Explanations of Social Deprivation*

# POVERTY

*Explanations of Social Deprivation*

Robert Holman

Martin Robertson

First published in 1978 by Martin Robertson & Company Ltd., 17 Quick Street, London N1 8HL

ISBN 0 85520 175 4 (paperback)
ISBN 0 85520 176 2 (cased)

Printed by Richard Clay Ltd., The Chaucer Press, Bungay, Suffolk.

# CONTENTS

# Contents

# Preface

The subject of poverty has concerned me for much of my life. As a boy, my father constantly impressed upon me the importance of gaining a secure 'white collar' job in order to avoid his experiences in the 1930s. He was a most intelligent man and even then I could not but reflect upon the injustices of a system which robbed him of the opportunities to develop and use his talents. Subsequently, as a local authority child care officer, my caseload included families whose lives had been broken by social deprivations.

Following the social work experience, I spent ten years in academic life. Consequently, I had time to study, reflect upon and teach about explanations of poverty. Now I have returned to field work as a community social worker and am in daily contact with the low-paid, the unemployed and those wholly dependent upon social security payments. The pattern of my life has been such that it has been impossible not to observe and think about the nature of social deprivation.

Much of the planning behind this book was undertaken while still an academic. The bulk of the writing, however, has been completed during the last fifteen months while engaged in full-time social, youth and community work. It therefore suffers from having been written in short spells, often in spare minutes between seeing people in the community. On the other hand, I have had the advantage of reflecting on poverty immediately after helping a neighbour with a social security problem, accompanying an unemployed youngster in a job search or seeing the despair of a family carrying considerable fuel and housing debts.

Many people contribute to an author's work. My thanks are due to all those students with whom I have discussed poverty and to my friends and neighbours who teach me from their first hand experiences. I wish to thank Audrey Browne for typing much of the manuscript and for the good humour

with which she puts up with the man she calls 'Mr Forgetful'.
I want to acknowledge the part played by Edward Elgar for
it was his enthusiasm for the book which made me place it
with Martin Robertson. Above all, my gratitude and love go
to my wife, Annette, and my children, Ruth and David. They
put up with a home often filled with people or littered with
papers. I am happy that they too look to a day when a
more determined effort is made to deal with the distress and
injustice created by poverty.

*Bob Holman*
*November, 1977*

*to Annette*

# CHAPTER 1

# The Meaning of Poverty

The subject of poverty is sometimes brought to public notice by a revealing or unexpected piece of research. In Victorian times, Charles Booth's *Life and Labour of the People* provoked some surprised reactions with the assertion that a third of Londoners were in poverty.[1] In 1965, Townsend and Abel-Smith's *The Poor and the Poorest* met a similar response.[2] Even prior to this, in the USA, Harrington had published his *The Other America* and in so doing sparked off a poverty literature which eventually contributed to the establishment of a number of poverty programmes.[3] At the inception of these programmes in 1964, President Johnson called for '. . . a national war on poverty. Our objective—total victory . . .'.[4]

Research studies, including those just mentioned, have usually concentrated on establishing the extent and range of poverty. Less attention is devoted to considering the explanation of poverty. Sometimes the categories used to describe the poor are taken to be the cause. For instance, Charles Booth, and later Seebohm Rowntree, identified unemployment and low pay as both categories and causes of poverty. More recently, the poor have been divided into groupings such as one-parent families or immigrants as though their very grouping explained their low income. But the categories do not explain why there is unemployment or low pay or why one-parent families or immigrants should be more liable to poverty than other groupings in society. They describe the expression of rather than the explanation of poverty.

This book is concerned with explanations. It cannot claim to be a comprehensive review of all theories of poverty. Marxists and political liberals, for instance, may well complain that whole chapters should be devoted to Marx or Galbraith. Instead, an attempt has been made to identify the explanations which have informed recent writings and policies. In chapters 2, 3 and 4, these explanations are separated, described and evaluated. Then drawing upon some fifteen years' experience of studying poverty and working directly with the poor, the writer presents the explanation which makes most sense to him. A final chapter considers some implications for action to counter poverty.

Before explanations can be discussed, it is necessary to ponder the meaning of poverty. Chapter 1, therefore, will examine the definition of poverty, will assess its extent, will identify the persons most likely to experience it, and will look at the meaning of social deprivation. In the course of this, some leads about the causes of poverty will be noted for subsequent debate.

### SUBSISTENCE POVERTY

Observations about the poor are as old as history. Within the Bible, the Old Testament places numerous injunctions upon the Jews to make provision for those in greatest need.[5] In Britain, the concern created by poverty was most clearly expressed in the establishment of the Elizabethan Poor Law, the influence of which has lasted until modern times.[6] In 1797, Sir Frederic Eden published a remarkable book (re-issued in 1928).[7] Apart from an introductory history of the poor, Eden provided a mass of figures on the wages of labourers, the cost of food, and conditions in workhouses. Despite its many statistics, Eden's work did not provide a satisfactory definition or estimate of poverty. During the succeeding century, a number of literary revelations of poverty and government reports on housing and health conditions came to public notice. However, it was not until near the end of the nineteenth century that a major contribution to definition and measurement was made. It came from the efforts of a Liverpool businessman, Charles Booth.[8]

### *Charles Booth*

Booth was originally moved to mount a scientific investigation into poverty in order to disprove the claim, made in a series of articles in the *Pall Mall Gazette*, that one in four, or a million, Londoners were in poverty. He found abundant sources of material about East London in the reports of London School Board Visitors, Poor Law statistics and police records of registered lodging houses. In addition, he needed a definition of poverty. Booth explained:

> by the word 'poor' I mean to describe those who have a sufficiently regular though bare income, such as 18s to 21s per week for a moderate family, and by 'very poor' those who from any cause fall much below this standard. The 'poor' are those whose means may be sufficient but are barely sufficient for decent independent life, the 'very poor' those whose means are insufficient for this according to the usual standard of life in this country. My 'poor' may be described as living under a struggle to obtain the necessaries of life and make both ends meet, while the 'very poor' live in a state of chronic want.[9]

How did Booth hit upon the figures of 18 to 21 shillings? They appear to emerge from the average expenditure of thirty families on food, rent and clothes.[10] Booth added that the poor would survive on these incomes only if they lived frugal and self-disciplined lives and if they met no major personal disasters.

Booth's work was first published in 1899 under the title *Life and Labour of the People*. It included a detailed house-to-house investigation of the poor, a study of their trades, and chapters on such subjects as the Jewish community and the 'sweating' system of labour. Interestingly, parts were contributed by an assistant, Beatrice Potter, whose later writings, as Beatrice Webb, contain some interesting comments about Booth.[11] A major finding of the book was that in East London, 35 per cent, that is 314,000 were 'poor' and of these 110,000, or 12½ per cent, were 'very poor'. Subsequently, Booth enlarged his survey to the rest of London and the succeeding volumes were entitled *Life and Labour of the People of London*. He had expected less poverty in these parts but, in all, 30.7 per cent of Londoners were rated as 'poor'. Oddly enough, Booth finished up by showing that the *Pall Mall Gazette* figures were too small.

The contribution of Charles Booth was immense. Raymond Williams says: 'What Booth did that was new was not only to continue the inquiry on a large scale, but to introduce and formalise a method of impersonal inquiries ....'[12] But the impersonal inquiry finally ran to seventeen volumes. It was not the size nor the style to catch the public imagination. Strangely enough, it was another Booth, General William Booth of the Salvation Army, who was to supply the popular work. His *In Darkest England and the Way Out* opens with a colourful chart stating that in London there were 300,000 'starving' people, 220,000 'near to starving' and 387,000 'very poor'. These figures, it is subsequently shown, were derived and projected from Charles Booth's calculations.[13] The General's vivid approach and proposed practical solutions made such an impact that 200,000 copies were sold within a year. The extent of Victorian poverty was no longer a secret.

## Seebohm Rowntree

Charles Booth's method of investigating poverty became a starting point for others concerned with the subject. One such was the Quaker, Seebohm Rowntree, who declared:

> Booth's *Life and Labour* made a profound impression upon me ... but I thought to myself, 'Well, one knows there is a great deal of poverty in the East End of London but I wonder whether there is in provincial cities. Why not investigate York?'[14]

He decided that 'nothing short of a house-to-house inquiry extending to the whole of the working class population of the city would suffice.'[15] By 'working class', he meant those families who did not keep servants. He thereafter obtained particulars regarding 11,560 families or 46,754 persons. Astonishingly, most of the work was carried out by one investigator in a few months in 1899. The sheet or schedule he used to note down information is reproduced in Rowntree's first volume and covers income, rent, housing conditions and occupants.

But which residents should be deemed as poor? Rowntree started by making an initial distinction between primary and secondary poverty.

(a) Families whose total earnings are insufficient to obtain the minimum necessaries for the maintenance of merely physical efficiency. Poverty falling under this head I have described as 'primary' poverty.

(b) Families whose total earnings would be sufficient for the maintenance of merely physical efficiency were it not that some portion of them is absorbed by other expenditure, either useful or wasteful. Poverty falling under this head is described as 'secondary' poverty.[16]

As it turned out, Rowntree gave little attention to secondary poverty in this or subsequent surveys.

Booth's poor were those unable to afford the 'necessaries of life'. Rowntree was more precise and pinpointed an income necessary for 'physical efficiency' as the dividing line between poverty and non-poverty. He then went further by attempting to assess exactly how much cash was required to ensure physical efficiency. To do this he had to know how much food was required and in order to make this calculation he turned to the work of two nutritionists, Atwater in the USA and Dunlop in Scotland. Both scientists had carried out experiments with convicts to establish how many calories were needed to keep a man working efficiently. Rowntree accepted Atwater's figure that 3,500 calories per day were required for men with 'moderate muscular work'.[17] The next step was to compile a diet which contained sufficient protein to provide 3,500 calories. Using the diets of workhouses (but excluding meat which he considered too expensive), Rowntree listed a menu which would yield 137 protein grams of 3,560 calories.[18] Next, he priced the items at the cheapest shops in York and concluded that a man needed 3s 3d, a woman (whose calorie needs were less) 2s 9d and children between 2s 7d and 2s 1d a week.

Rowntree then conceded that the maintenance of physical efficiency also required shelter and certain household sundries. For shelter, he added the average rent which his investigator found was being paid. Under household sundries, Rowntree considered, for example, that a couple with three children would need per week 2s 3d for clothing, 1s 10d for fuel and 10d for other items.[19]

By adding the three categories together, Rowntree now had his poverty line. For a three-child family, the necessary income was food = 12s 9d, rent = 4s, and household sundries = 4s 11d, a total of 21s 8d per week. For two parents and one child, it came to 14s 6d. Three-child families with incomes below 21s 8d per week were poor, and so on according to family size.[20] Rowntree then proceeded:

> Let us now see what was the result of this examination. No less than 1,465 families, comprising 7,230 persons, were living in 'primary' poverty. *This is equal to 15.46 per cent of the wage earning class in York, and to 9.19 per cent of the whole population of the city.* [Rowntree's italics][21]

These results, published in 1901, were seen as a confirmation of Booth's claim that poverty afflicted substantial numbers in Britain.

Rowntree's work did not finish in 1901. In 1936, he studied 16,362 families in York excluding, this time, not those with servants but those with an annual income of over £250. He also raised his poverty line to 43s 6d for a family of five (two parents and three children). The sum allowed for food was calculated according to the recommendations of a Committee of the British Medical Association which had determined the '. . . minimum weekly expenditure on food stuffs which must be incurred by families of varying size if health and working capacity are to be maintained.'[22] Rowntree also lengthened the list of necessities to be paid for and included compulsory insurance, travelling expenses to work, and trade union subscriptions. He also added a few luxuries such as a newspaper. The results were not published until 1941. If Rowntree had simply updated his 1899 measure, allowing for price increases, then in 1936 6.8 per cent of the working class or 3.9 per cent of the total population would have been in poverty. But Rowntree had changed his measure to include extra items and had thus raised his poverty line. By this measure, 31.1 per cent of the working class or 17.7 per cent of the population of York were in poverty.[23]

In 1950, Rowntree—now nearing eighty years of age—completed his third survey of York. It differed in having a co-author, G. R. Lavers, and in taking a sample of families instead of the whole population. In other respects the approach was similar to his previous work. The diet of 1936 was slightly modified and the estimates for clothing, fuel, light and extras were altered. The poverty line was set at 100s 2d for the family of five. The result published in 1951, showed only 2.77 per cent of the working class and 1.66 per cent of the total population in poverty.[24]

Rowntree's contribution to the study of poverty was immense. His biographer, Asa Briggs, called his first survey a '. . . kind of modern social Domesday Book'.[25] More concise than Charles Booth's seventeen volumes, more reputable than William Booth's clarion cry, its '. . . conclusions were taken seriously by people of quite different religious and political persuasions'.[26] Rowntree had not only demonstrated its existence, he had established a means of measuring and conceptualising poverty which endured throughout his lifetime. A number of other surveys were executed in Britain in the first half of the twentieth century. Sheffield, Bristol, Liverpool, Plymouth, Southampton, Northampton, Warrington, Stanley, Reading and Bolton, all came under the investigator.[27] They tended to come to similar conclusions for they had adopted Rowntree's approach.

Rowntree's—and Booth's—concept of poverty has been called subsistence or absolute poverty. Three elements can be identified. Firstly, the poverty line is set at just that level which allows people to be physically efficient. Enjoyment of life or the development of intellectual capacities are not involved. The level is simply enough to subsist on. All below are in poverty. Rowntree stated: 'My primary poverty line represented the minimum sum on which physical efficiency could be maintained. It was a standard of bare subsistence rather than living.'[28] It is assumed that people's requirements to subsist, to be physically able to work, will be the same in any age or any country. Thus, sometimes the concept is called the absolute concept of poverty to reflect the universality of its application (allowing for price changes) throughout time and distance. Secondly, the concept involves the utmost stringency both in its calculations and in the mode of life it implies. Booth considered his poor only those whose incomes entailed '. . . a struggle to obtain the necessaries of life'. Rowntree's standards in 1899 were more harsh than those of the Poor Law. For his 1936 survey, he allowed some increases but still noted: 'My cost of living standard only allows for the maintenance of a fully furnished house. It allows nothing for the purchase of furniture and bedding, or for other similar expenditure of a non-recurring nature.'[29]

Moreover, his outlay on food allowed for no increases save that accounted for by rising prices. His diets originated and continued as minimum not optimum feeding. Thirdly, the subsistence concept is not related to the incomes of society as a whole. Booth and Rowntree excluded all considerations of the incomes and expenditure of people who were not working-class. The subsistence approach involves, not comparison between people, but comparison between people and what is seen as an objective yardstick, a yardstick which can differentiate between subsistence and an inability to carry on working in a proper manner.

## The Attack on the Concept

The subsistence concept of poverty has had enormous influence in Britain. Townsend states that 'The sociological study and measurement of poverty in this country dates from the pioneering work of Charles Booth and B. Seebohm Rowntree at the end of the last century.'[30] It has influenced social policy as well as research. Its ideology was incorporated into the public assistance system in the USA as well as in Britain. But since the 1950s its dominance has been increasingly under attack, an attack spearheaded by Townsend himself.

The subsistence concept is presented as taking into account the needs of individuals. In fact, its methods of construction involve a degree of inflexibility which does just the opposite. In calculating how much money families need, the pioneers often worked from the average of the lowest. For instance, Booth, in justifying his poverty line, revealed that he had examined one week's expenditure of thirty families. Obviously, such a number is far too small to be representative, yet from these thirty he then determined the average expenditure of the poorest on food, rent and clothes.[31] It was then assumed that all families above this figure should be able to cope. This reasoning has a twofold danger. It ignores the probability that the financial needs of some families are so great as to be above the average. Further, it takes for granted that the families studied were coping. Oddly enough, Booth admits they were not. It was not only that, in times of crisis, they had to hold back the rent or go short on food, but also that '. . . in almost all the poorer cases the admitted expenditure exceeds the supposed income'.[32] There seems little doubt that some families above Booth's poverty level did not have sufficient for '. . . decent independent life'.

Rowntree followed a similar inflexible course when calculating nutrition and thereby cash requirements. As mentioned, he accepted Atwater's estimates, derived from studying convicts, that a man doing moderate muscular work needed 3,500 calories. He chose 3,500 because it came between Atwater's figures of 2,700 for a man with little physical exercise and 4,500 for a man with active muscular work.[33] Yet, no doubt, many working men in York had occupations whose heavy work demanded a high calorie intake. By insisting on a middle figure, Rowntree allowed them less than they required. The approach is also inflexible in that, for instance, it takes no account of the needs of an unhealthy indoor worker whose special dietary needs might be more expensive than those of a healthy outdoor worker. Even more fundamental, it is doubtful whether the calorific intake of convicts working a restricted eight-hour day with no domestic responsibilities could be applied to men who do overtime work and then have activities within their own homes.

The inflexibility of Booth and Rowntree's subsistence measure is also revealed in their acceptance of its universality. Booth believed his East End cash level applied to all London. Rowntree made a very dubious assumption that York was a 'representative' or typical town.[34] They therefore acted as though the cash needs of the East London and York residents were those of people elsewhere. Yet food and other prices are known to vary markedly between regions and districts. What is sufficient income in one place may be insufficient elsewhere. Further, the need for extra clothing or food might well be greater in colder parts of the country; the cost of housing higher in other parts.

The inflexibility of the system might have been acceptable if its figures originally erred on the side of generosity. But rather they stressed stringency. Consequently, those individuals whose cash needs did not fit into the average of the lowest or whose nutritional requirements were higher than that of the moderate muscular worker would be in poverty although recorded as above the line.

The stringency of the subsistence measure, then, was joined by inflexibility. Consequently, even families above the poverty line might be expected to survive on minimum incomes. Yet to do so required the parents to select the most nutritious foods (ignoring likes and dislikes) at the lowest prices. Even a highly trained expert might have difficulty in doing so. Rowntree admitted as much: 'It must also be remembered that at present the poor do not possess knowledge which would enable them to select a diet that is at once as nutritious and economic as that which is here adopted as the standard.'[35] As Townsend aptly commented: 'If, indeed, few working class families attain this standard, then it may not be a practicable one to use in measuring poverty.'[36]

The use of dietary tables and calories has given the impression that the subsistence concept involves an objective, scientific measure. Yet a reading of Booth's and Rowntree's methodology shows it littered with subjective, even arbitrary judgements which were never justified. As mentioned, in 1936 Rowntree added to his list of necessities such items as compulsory insurance contributions, trade union subscriptions and a newspaper. But why these and not, as Townsend asks, the cost of laundry, handkerchiefs, contraceptives and haircuts.[37] Also in 1936, Rowntree changed the dietary requirements to meet the recommendations of a committee of the British Medical Association—recommendations which were themselves heavily criticised.[38] But even within this, Rowntree substituted condensed skimmed milk for fresh milk and argued that all bread could be baked at home. These arbitrary decisions did not reflect how people in York (let alone elsewhere) actually lived.

Much of the arbitrary nature and inflexibility might have been avoided if Booth and Rowntree had started by examining how the majority of working-class people actually did spend their money instead of investigating how much they earned and then saying how it should have been spent. Townsend points out that in the 1930s Rowntree assumed that families should spend 58 per cent of their incomes on food and 42 per cent on all other items. Yet surveys of actual consumption patterns of that time revealed 41 per cent spent on food and 59 per cent on other items.[39] The extent to which Rowntree ignored the way people actually lived is shown in his decision to include all the earned income of children (including older children who went out to work) as part of the disposable total family income.[40] Yet obviously the children would have kept some for their own leisure and, more importantly, would have made savings for their own marriages. Consequently, their income was not wholly available for food, rent and household sundries. Further, low-income families did feel compelled to buy items not in Rowntree's calculations. The result was that although some would be above his poverty line, they would not have sufficient to spend on food and rent. As Townsend says,

> The main fault in the standards used has been their lack of relation to the budgets and customs of life of working people. Many who are considered to be above the poverty line because their income exceeds the total cost of meeting basic needs, do, in fact, spend less on the individual items included in the standard—food, clothing, fuel and light and household sundries—simply because they spend money on other things.[41]

The failure of the subsistence concept to consider how families actually spent money reflects a failure to admit that humans are moulded by psychological, social and cultural factors as well as by a physical one. The concept of subsistence poverty, as Booth and Rowntree made plain, allowed expenditure only on the food, shelter and basic household implements necessary to keep people in physical order. Rowntree said his concept was based upon the premise that a family

> ... must never purchase a half penny newspaper or spend a penny to buy a ticket for a popular concert. They must write no letters to absent children for they cannot afford to pay the postage. They must never contribute anything to their church or chapel, or give any help to a neighbour which costs them money ... the children

must have no pocket money for dolls, marbles or sweets. The
father must smoke no tobacco and must drink no beer.[42]

One wonders what Rowntree expected the families to do if
they needed to spend a penny to go to the lavatory! But
men and women are not just physical beings. They are also
psychological and social beings who possess personalities and
who live within communities. Consequently, they will spend
money to meet needs engendered by these aspects of their lives.
Consider clothing. In 1899 Rowntree stated that a woman could
suffice with a pair of boots, a secondhand dress, a skirt made
from an old dress, two pairs of stockings and a few under-
clothes.[43] Yet women, particularly young women, would have
experienced social pressures to wear attractive up-to-date clothing.
Similarly, families have a psychological need for leisure, and
research shows that they will cut expenditure on food '...
in order not to forego an occasional visit to a cinema or
football match'.[44] More recently, Marsden in his study of low-
income mothers, reported that they felt social pressures to maintain their homes to something like '... the standard set by
the rest of the community'[45] even if this entailed cutting down
on physical essentials.

The needs and therefore spending habits are shaped by local
conventions and nationally approved social standards. These
conventions and standards, being socially imposed, will change.
For instance, today working-class parents are expected to spend
on the educational encouragement of their children—books, uni-
forms, school trips—in a way unknown seventy-five years ago.
Similarly, pressures now exist to possess television, which technological advancement has made an integral part of modern life.
The spending needs of contemporary families are therefore
greater. But a subsistence concept which accepts only unchanged
physical requirements will not be prepared to incorporate such
developments. It is true that later Rowntree did acknowledge
the existence of social needs and countenanced the buying of
a newspaper. But it was a reluctant concession and he preferred
to argue that the working class should abandon their customs
and social standards and should concentrate on physical needs.
Writing of his nutritional plans, he says: '... the adoption
of such a diet would require considerable changes in established

customs, and many prejudices would have to be uprooted.'[46] The subsistence concept as formulated by Rowntree contains the demand that the poor should change their customs. It is not flexible enough to incorporate the fact that changing social patterns alter needs and hence spending requirements.

The criticisms of the subsistence concept do not imply the judgement that Booth and Rowntree were inhumane. On the contrary, both of them wanted to alleviate poverty and made a number of proposals for doing so. Both admitted that their definition of poverty was harsh. But this was a deliberate step, for they wanted to show that poverty was extensive even within a stringent measure. Notwithstanding, Rowntree was still accused by Mrs Helen Bosanquet and the Charity Organisation Society of adopting too high a standard.[47] The accusation did not stick and the subsistence measure held sway for over half a century.

Yet admiration for Booth and Rowntree should not be used to cloak the disadvantages of their approach. Its inflexibility meant that some individuals would be assessed as above the poverty line when, in fact, their income did not meet even their needs for food, shelter and sundries. In short, the subsistence measure did not meet its own claim to uphold physical efficiency. Further, the concept entailed working-class persons possessing such extensive and expert knowledge of nutrition that it just was not practical or realistic. The use of arbitrary decisions by Booth and Rowntree meant that the so-called objective measure really depended upon subjective judgements. Not least, the measure ignored the social, psychological and cultural needs of persons. This criticism is the most fundamental of all. The subsistence concept rested on the assumption that poverty means simply a lack of money to meet physical needs. It crumbles under the discovery that humans are as strongly motivated to meet other needs of a more social nature.

RELATIVE POVERTY

The inadequacies of the subsistence concept have contributed to the formulation of an alternative—the concept of relative poverty. From this perspective, the poor are not defined as those who fall below a fixed subsistence level but as those whose incomes are considered too far removed from the rest of the society in which they live. In short, the poor are identified in relation to or relative to other people. Lafitte defines poverty as 'a level of income sufficiently low to be generally regarded as creating hardship, in terms of the community's prevailing living standards, and so requiring remedial action on the part of public social policy.'[48] This approach could be used to claim that the majority of people are relatively poor compared with a minority. For instance, it might be shown that in Britain ten per cent of the population own over two-thirds of all wealth and that, therefore, 90 per cent of the population is poor by comparison. In practice, however, the concept is used to compare a minority with the position of the majority or the average. Thus, the incomes of the bottom five per cent might be at such a distance from the remainder of the population that they are considered poor in that they cannot meet the social needs judged as essential to social living by society at that time. The Social Science Research Council stresses the distance of the minority from the average in its definition of poverty: 'It is therefore the continually moving *average* standards of that community that are the starting points for an assessment of its poverty, and the poor are those who fall sufficiently far below these average standards.'[49]

A perusal of the above definitions reveals four main elements within the relative concept. It involves comparisons with other persons; it is concerned with standards within a contemporary social environment; it talks of the gap or distance or, to use another word, the inequality between different sections of society; and it depends upon value judgements as to what is right or wrong.

*Comparisons with Other Persons*

The relative definition of poverty is concerned with the lowest incomes being too far removed from those of the rest of the community, i.e. with the people who make up the community.

For instance, in Britain people would survive if they did not wear shoes and socks. But few would disagree that it is socially necessary to have footwear. Those who cannot afford shoes will be considered poor relative to those persons who can. This approach contrasts with the subsistence measurement where comparison was made with an alleged line of physical efficiency rather than with other persons.

## The Contemporary Environment

Relative poverty, Lafitte pointed out, has to be assessed in the context of 'the community's prevailing living standards'. In other words, it is related to the person's immediate environment or community and to the prevailing or contemporary standards of the time. The concept, it follows, is distinguished from the subsistence one in important ways. It is not tied to comparisons with past ages or with other societies. It is able to incorporate changing expectations.

The subsistence measurement assumes that the definition of poverty does not change over time because the same nutritional intake will always uphold physical efficiency. This has led to a popular belief that poverty no longer exists because, in real terms, the incomes of all workers have risen since the nineteenth century and all must enjoy a better diet. According to the relative concept, by contrast, poverty still exists if there is hardship by comparison with other people in today's society. As Runciman makes clear, people evaluate themselves and others in terms of what happens around them now, not in terms of past Victorian events.[50] In industry, sport, politics and all other aspects of life, judgements are continually being brought up to date. The relative concept does the same for poverty, ensuring that the lowest incomes are assessed against those of living members of today's society rather than against the dead of a bygone age.

Similarly, within the relative concept it is not legitimate to assess a people's poverty by unfavourable comparison with another culture or society. It is sometimes claimed that there can be no poverty in Britain because the lowest incomes here compare favourably with the subsistence incomes in Asia. But this is to miss the point of the relative concept of poverty. It looks at poverty within the standards, norms and conditions of a person's immediate environment. Their income and therefore the question of their poverty, to quote Berthoud, '... is to be evaluated in terms of what is usual in the society in which the subject is living.'[51]

The subsistence concept of poverty, it was explained, is unchanging. The relative concept accepts the influence of environment and the social standards and expectations within it. But these factors are subject to change and the relative concept can change with it. For example, 200 years ago it was not expected that all parents should buy birthday and Christmas presents for their children, take them on holiday, put sheets on their beds. Today there are strong social sanctions which demand conformity to the practice of children being so provided. Parents who lack the money to conform will now be considered poor if they cannot ensure a style of life considered normal. It follows that there can be no once-and-for-all specification of poverty but that it must change with societies' changing expectations and norms.

*Inequality*

In their studies, Booth and Rowntree excluded any consideration of the incomes of the affluent or the middle class. The subsistence concept is concerned only with the relationship between the lowest income recipients and their capacity to survive physically. By contrast, the relative concept—by virtue of examining these recipients within a social context—looks at the relationship between them and other sections of society. It is, therefore, concerned with the gap or distance between the lowest and the average or normal standards. It follows that relative poverty is closely allied with another concept, that of inequality. Berthoud, in his study of inequality, states simply that '... inequality is concerned with some people having less than others, the others being either the average or the comparatively rich. The reference point is other members of the same society.'[52]

In order not to repeat continually the same terms, the words 'poverty' and 'inequality' will often be used interchangeably in this book. But there is a difference. For instance, university lecturers may have incomes unequal with those of High Court Judges. Nobody would argue that the former are poor, although some might argue that the degree of difference between the two occupations is too great. On the other hand, within the relative framework, the poor are always unequal if their poverty rests not on the lack of any absolute amount of cash but on unacceptable differences between their incomes and those of the rest of the population, which means that they cannot attain standards or conditions deemed essential to decent living. Berthoud puts it much more succinctly: '... poverty might be considered as that part of inequality which is unnecessary, and consequently unfair.'[53]

The association of relative poverty with inequality has some significant implications. It means that a general improvement in the standards of living of a society does not necessarily entail a reduction in poverty if all sections benefit to the same extent. Such an improvement will not reduce the gap, the inequality, between them. Further, policies aimed at reducing poverty will involve reducing inequality and will therefore affect the position of the non-poor. As Mencher put it, the proof of the lessening of relative poverty '... relies on the demonstration of relatively greater additions to lower incomes at the expense of upper incomes.'[54]

Such actions would no doubt require profound legislative changes. Poverty is thereby taken into the world of political conflict. Again, a contrast is made with the implications of the subsistence concept. William Beveridge, author of the Beveridge Report[55] which laid the foundations of much welfare legislation, was strongly influenced by Booth and Rowntree. He therefore considered that poverty could be solved without '... taking money from the rich to give it to the poor'. Instead, it would be achieved by the poor being made to save more.[56] Not surprisingly, his proposals led to little political controversy compared with more direct recommendations to reduce relative poverty.

*Value Judgements*

Lafitte said that relative poverty occurred when the gap between the lowest and others created 'hardship'. The Social Science Research Council report stated that it occurred when the lowest fell 'sufficiently' far below others. Elsewhere their style of life is termed not 'acceptable' or 'decent', it is 'unfair' or 'unnecessary' when compared with the rest of the population. Each of these terms implies some kind of value, something which is held up to individuals or society as worth pursuing. A value judgement is being made when it is said that the standards of life of the majority are acceptable and that those whose incomes exclude them from it should be enabled to enjoy the same.

But who decides what is 'hardship', 'sufficient', 'acceptable', etc.? Two kinds of decisions are being made. One concerns the kind of life which all people should enjoy. The other concerns how great a distance can be allowed between what standards people do attain and what they should. In identifying who makes the judgements, it is useful to distinguish between those who may be vulnerable to poverty and those who are not.

In a well-known study of relative poverty (or relative deprivation),* Runciman discusses the extent to which those with the lowest incomes actually regard themselves as poor. He argues that relative poverty occurs when (i) person A does not have income X; (ii) A sees other persons as having X; (iii) A wants X; (iv) A sees it as feasible that he should have X. The key points turn on if and when the low-paid see others as having X, whether they want it, and whether they think it possible to obtain it. In Runciman's view, these decisions depend on whether they

> ... have been led to see as a possible goal the relative prosperity of some more fortunate community with which they can directly compare themselves, then they will remain discontented with their lot until they have succeeded in catching up.[57]

---

* He talks of relative deprivation which includes relative poverty. Later in this chapter the concept of poverty as income deprivation is broadened to cover other forms of deprivation.

In other words, they would judge themselves to be poor if they use as what Runciman calls a 'reference group', a section of society which they feel it is possible and right to emulate. He demonstrates that the recipients of low pay are themselves a group who may make judgements about the existence of poverty. It follows that any study of poverty must examine the role played by the poor in shaping social judgements and decisions.

In practice, public debate about poverty is dominated, not by the value judgements of those with low incomes but by politicians, academics, journalists and social commentators. These public figures made a notable contribution in the 1960s when academics such as Abel-Smith and Townsend, politicians such as Meacher and pressure groups such as the Child Poverty Action Group, began to publicise the notion of a relative concept of poverty. Townsend argued that the prevailing views on poverty did not sufficiently allow for the social necessities of life.[58] Meacher argued that the post-tax differential between top and bottom incomes was too great at 20 : 1 and recommended it be reduced to 7 : 1—a ratio which Baroness Wootton would reduce to $2\frac{1}{2}$ : 1.[59] These well-known people were making judgements about what should or should not happen in society. Their judgements stemmed from their own values, which in turn were derived from certain humanitarian, religious and political beliefs. Unlike the low-paid, any desire to abolish poverty sprang not from direct experience of it but rather because its existence was at variance with their own beliefs.

Value judgements cannot be separated from any definition of poverty. Even if it is decided that poverty means starvation and if it is further decided that the poor should be allowed to die, a value judgement is still being made, namely that poverty entails extreme suffering and death. Further, because value judgements are involved, any estimates of the extent of poverty will depend on which groupings—be they the low-paid, politicians of whatever hue, pressure groups, academics—have sufficient public influence to determine what is an acceptable standard of living and so what constitutes the poverty line. The implication is that poverty, its definition and alleviation, is connected with the question of which groupings hold power in our society.

Relative poverty has now been explained. It involves four major elements—comparisons with other persons, standards within a contemporary environment, the distance between different groups, and value judgements. A discussion of these revealed that poverty is also concerned with decisions made by the poor themselves, with the distribution of power and with political action. The relative concept has the advantage of being adaptable to changing social standards and expectations. Nonetheless, as this book proceeds to discuss current explanations of poverty, it will be seen that, although the relative concept has gained ground, the subsistence measure is still influential.

## THE EXTENT OF POVERTY IN BRITAIN

Within the relative concept, the poor are regarded as those whose incomes are so far removed from the rest of the population that they cannot attain the mode of life considered acceptable in society. The advantage of this concept is that it allows room to encompass changing social needs and expectations. Its difficulty is that it depends on judgements about the meaning of 'acceptable', on which there may be no consensus within society. It is appropriate, therefore, to consider which judgements and measurements have received at least some recognition in post-war Britain. It will then be possible to offer some indications of the extent of poverty. Before proceeding to quantify the extent of poverty, a cautionary note must be made. The data which is presented is drawn from sources which for three main reasons are not completely satisfactory. Firstly, poverty statistics are frequently culled from surveys or investigations which were not specifically designed to measure the extent of poverty. For instance, on previous occasions the present writer has drawn upon the General Household Survey, the Family Expenditure Survey, the New Earnings Survey, the Census and the reports of the Department of Health and Social Security (DHSS). Yet none of these are concerned solely to collect comprehensive incomes data on all members of the population. Secondly, there are differences as to the definition of income. For instance, fringe benefits and perks are sometimes excluded. Yet it is estimated that they add thirty-one per cent to the salaries of the highest income earners.[60] Again, capital gains may or may not be counted as income. The overall effect is that the various studies are not always directly comparable. Thirdly, and arising from the varied purpose of the investigations, there is a lack of uniformity about the unit being measured. For instance, in some surveys the family is taken as the basic unit of income receipt, in others the individual, in others the householder. Some studies will include just the income of the head of the household, others will take into account the incomes of other members of the same household. In making any estimates of the extent of poverty, the limitations of the data must always be held in mind.[61]

## Official Poverty

How does the government define and measure poverty? Persons without means of support are eligible for financial help from the Supplementary Benefits Commission, more commonly known as Social Security. The scale rates of supplementary benefit are, according to its booklet, intended to cover '... all normal needs which can be foreseen, including food, fuel and light, the normal repair and replacement of clothing, household sundries ... and provisions for amenities such as newspapers, entertainment and radio and television licences....'[62] The latest scale rates at the time of writing (November 1977), to which rent and rates would be added, are for a married couple £23.55, for a single householder £14.50, and for dependent children between £4.10 and £8.90 according to age. Obviously the rates are stringent and it is believed when first instituted—as national assistance—they were based on Rowntree's calculations. In this sense they might be regarded as the subsistence minimum which just allows physical efficiency to be maintained. Yet it is noticeable that, over time, changing social needs have been acknowledged with allowances for radio and TV licences. Despite this acknowledgement, it is also noticeable that the ratio between supplementary benefit levels and average earnings has altered but little.

The scale rates for a married couple in 1974 were 39 per cent of average net earnings compared with 42 per cent in 1967.[63] In 1975 the ratio to the average earnings of male manual workers was almost exactly the same as in 1948.[64]

At the end of 1975, 2,891,000 persons were receiving supplementary benefit in the United Kingdom out of a total population of 56,000,000. The numbers had risen from 1,902,000 in 1961.[65] Of course, the number of persons dependent on benefit was greater, since some of the payments would be made to persons in respect of their dependants.

The figures just presented enumerate the persons receiving supplementary benefit, not the numbers whose incomes fall below its basic rates. For if the government regards the scale rates as sufficient for all normal needs, it is only those *below* who are in poverty. Certainly, the government's own publication *Circumstances of Families* in 1967 did work on this definition of poverty.[66] The relevant question then becomes: how many persons in Britain have incomes below the scale rates?

A number of investigations have used the official poverty line as a level for their calculations. Abel-Smith and Townsend estimated that for the year 1960 between three and four per cent of the population were in this position.[67] In 1963, Gough and Stark concluded a figure of 9.4 per cent.[68] Three years later, Atkinson put it at 3.7 per cent.[69] The findings vary, partly because they were made in different years but probably more so because of the varying sources of information they were employing. Even so, it can be said that at any one time between $1\frac{1}{2}$ and $5\frac{1}{2}$ million persons were in poverty. More recently, the DHSS, drawing upon the Family Expenditure Survey, estimated that in December 1974 1,410,000 persons (drawn from 920,000 families) were dependent upon incomes below the supplementary benefit minimum rates.[70] By the end of 1975, the Child Poverty Action Group stated that the number had increased to two million.[71]

The official measure of poverty has the advantage of being easily operationalised. But it has been subjected to some severe criticism. It is often pointed out that no justification has ever been given for the original rates adopted by government at the installation of national assistance (supplementary benefit as it is now called). These rates have remained the base for periodical upgradings as wages and prices have risen. The national assistance rates were drawn from the recommendations of the Beveridge report which in turn were alleged to have been based on the work of Rowntree.[72] But this process made the dubious assumption that Rowntree had devised an adequate measure of poverty. As explained earlier, his concept of poverty is no longer considered defensible.

As well as setting particular rates of benefit for individuals, supplementary benefit also involves the setting of two kinds of ratio. There is the ratio between supplementary benefit rates and average earnings. As shown, this ratio has been maintained fairly constantly over the years. Yet what is its justification? It does not appear based on any calculation of how average earners and low earners actually do spend money and whether this expenditure is sufficient to avoid hardship.[73] In addition, supplementary benefit sets a ratio between different categories of persons. Thus Atkinson explains that if a single person's entitlement is taken as 100 per cent, then a couple receive 164 per cent, a youth aged sixteen to seventeen receives 58 per cent, and so on down to a child under five who gets 29 per cent.[74] No explanation for this ratio is offered. Yet some continental countries use different ratios, some of which are much more generous towards children.[75]

Even more pointedly, there is the criticism that a reasonable life cannot be maintained on the basic supplementary benefit rates. Surprisingly few studies have been made of how low-income families actually cope financially. However, an important investigation has been completed by Evason and her findings can now be summarised.[76] Taking the basic supplementary benefit rates as 100 per cent, Evason divided a sample of households into income bands of below 100 per cent, 100–110 per cent, and 110–140 per cent. Amongst households in the level below 100 per cent, i.e. those in official poverty, Evason distinguished between large (four or more children) and small families. The former simply did not have sufficient income to spend on food, clothes, heat and light. There was little waste or expenditure on non-essentials, but they still faced constant financial crises and debts. Having no financial reserves, an unexpected bill could mean disaster. Small families survived without extensive debts by cutting expenditure to the minimum. They would never use public transport, would make do with secondhand clothes, would never buy bedding, would never take holidays, and so on. Both kinds of families had a diet consisting mainly of bread and potatoes with '... significant deficiencies in the consumption of milk and meat'.[77] Over half the parents stated that their poverty put strains on their marriage.

Households in the 100–110-per-cent band were mainly those receiving the basic supplementary benefit rates. They consisted predominantly of older persons with no dependent children, or younger couples with children under five years of age. The former generally avoided falling into debt by concentrating their spending on rent, fuel and food. Consequently, there was little left for clothes, leisure activities or savings. The latter, typically in their first years of marriage, had taken on hire-purchase commitments prior to the man losing his job. Where young children were involved—unless relatives were able to help—the families were likely to be behind on electricity bills, to go short on clothing, furniture and food, and to experience deficiencies in milk consumption.

Households with incomes in the 110–140-per-cent range, i.e. 10–40 per cent above basic scale rates, were usually headed by an adult in full-time work. Even amongst these, some considerable hardship was identified. Those in the bracket 110–120 per cent with school-age children were likely to have life styles equivalent to poorer families. Large families above the 120-per-cent level were also likely to be in difficulties.

By examining the way various kinds of households actually managed, Evason produced empirical evidence of the standards of living achieved at different income levels. Her main conclusion is that not only do families below the official poverty line experience hardship, but so do large families or families with young children whose incomes are somewhat above this level. The life style they have to adopt entails a lack of new clothing, an embargo on regular leisure activities, and a vulnerability to debt. Indeed, at times the choice could be between buying food or going into debt. In Evason's judgement, this standard is not consistent with a decent or reasonable way of life.

Evason's arguments are supported by a similar study conducted by Church. In September 1975, supplementary benefit rates for children on a daily basis were 30p for those under five years,

47p for 5–11-year-olds, 58p for 11–13-year-olds and 71p for
13–16-year-olds. As the amount had to cover all expenses—food,
clothing, shoes, toys, etc.—Church reckoned that at the very
most 75 per cent of this daily allowance could be spent on
food (although most families spent about 33 per cent on food).
He then asked a group of unsupported mothers to record how
they spent 30p on children's food and subsequently calculated
the energy value of the purchase. Comparing with nationally
recommended figures, he found that '. . . only the most efficient
mothers, with the smallest children, could even hope to provide
enough energy for their children . . . .' Further, he concluded
that the allowance for 5–10-year-olds was '. . . totally inadequate
to provide enough food, even if as much as 75 per cent of
the benefit is spent on food in the most efficient fashion.'
Even the efficient shoppers had to reduce the amount spent
on food if an outlay had to be made on some other expensive
item such as shoes or a winter coat.[78]

A major deduction to be drawn from the work of Evason
and Church is that poverty is experienced by persons in receipt
of supplementary benefit as well as those receiving incomes
below the basic rate. Drawing on data from the Family Expenditure Survey, Berthoud explains that there is little evidence to
support the claim that those with low incomes are extravagant
in their expenditure. Yet '. . . it appears that about half of
all supplementary benefit dependents are in debt to formal credi-
tors . . . .'[79] Similarly, there is evidence that persons with incomes
at these levels have great difficulty in meeting fuel bills.[80] With
no extra to spare, an accident or an illness or a breakage
can be a disaster that entails money being taken from food,
clothes, or rent.[81] The implication is that the basic supplementary
benefit rates are not an adequate measure of poverty. The
standard of life achieved at this level can mean great hardship
and, in the eyes of researchers, is too far removed from that
of the rest of the population.


## A Percentage above the Supplementary Benefit Rates

The hardship experienced by persons living on incomes above
the official poverty line has led some writers to argue that

the poverty line be re-cast as a small percentage above the basic supplementary benefit rates. An additional argument is that as numbers of claimants receive more than the basic rates—because of the disregarded earnings rule or the granting of small additional allowances—the effective minimal rate is frequently above the actual scale rates. The implication is that the government is here recognising that the basic rates are not sufficient. Noticeably, the DHSS now publishes figures for the numbers of persons whose net income (less housing costs and work expenses) is less than 20 per cent above the supplementary benefit entitlement (120 per cent if 100 per cent represents the basic rates). In 1975, 8,880,000 persons were so placed, compared with 7,300,000 in 1974.[82] Some researchers have settled on a figure slightly higher at 40 per cent above the rates (140 per cent if 100 per cent is the basic rates). How many persons experience an income below this poverty level? Drawing upon Inland Revenue data, Gough and Stark estimated that in 1959 18.1 per cent of the population were in this position.[83] For 1960, Abel-Smith and Townsend calculated 14.2 per cent.[84] According to these estimates, there would be between seven and eleven million people in poverty in the United Kingdom. Parker's figures for 1970 come to between eight and nine million people '. . . living below or around the supplementary benefit level . . .'.[85] By 1974, the Child Poverty Action Group claimed that thirteen million people were living on incomes not more than 40 per cent above the basic rates.[86]

## A Percentage of Average Wage

The above measures of poverty depend on the value judgements that an income of under 120 or 140 per cent gives rise to a life style which is too far removed from the rest of the population. It will be remembered that another perspective of poverty was to examine the gap or distance between low incomes and average or median incomes. The advantage of this measure, according to Berthoud, is that those persons on low incomes are likely to judge their own position by comparison with the average.[87]

But what distance from the average is considered poor? In

1975 the average household income in the United Kingdom was £72.87 per week. 3.7 per cent of households had an income range of under £15 per week and most people would accept that they were in poverty. But fewer people, no doubt, would have agreed that the 16.1 per cent in the range £40–60 could be so classified. And what of those in between, the 7.0 per cent with £15–20, the 9.7 per cent with £20–30 and the 7.4 per cent with £30–40?[88] Researchers who prefer this comparison with average wage as a measure of poverty, find their numbers by selecting a percentage below the average wage and taking all below this line to be poor. For instance, if all households with incomes less than 40 per cent of the average (less than about £30 per week) is taken as the line, then about 20 per cent of all households would be counted as the poor. Other writers take a similar approach but use a percentage of average earnings of male workers (although such figures do not include people who are not earning, nor the incomes of other members of their families). For instance, Trinder and the Low Pay Unit accept as in poverty all those with '. . . earnings less than two thirds of average (median) earnings for all adult men working full time'.[89] In April 1974 there were 1,200,000 plus their dependants beneath this level. It is interesting to note that the relative distance between the lowest-paid and the median has changed little since the last century. In 1886, the lowest decile of manual workers earned 68.6 per cent of the median manual wage. In other words, the lowest tenth earned just over two-thirds of the median. By 1975 they were earning an average 69.2 per cent, which the year before had been exactly the same as for 1886, namely 68.6 per cent.[90]

Whichever definition of poverty is used—below supplementary benefit rates, a percentage just above them, below two-thirds of average earnings, etc.—the conclusion is still that the numbers in poverty are to be counted in hundreds of thousands or millions rather than hundreds. Moreover, the relative distance between lowest incomes and the rest of society appears to have been maintained over a long period. As Berthoud summarises, '. . . it is difficult to argue that there is any basic effective trend towards greater equality between the poorest and those average families with whom they will compare themselves.'[91]

In order to put this conclusion into perspective, three points must be made. Firstly, as already said, it is not disputed that, in general, standards of living have improved for all people. Secondly, the persistence of the gap between lowest incomes and others does not imply that changes have not occurred in the relationship between other income groups, for instance between average incomes and top incomes. Thirdly, it is clear that society cannot be divided between the poor working class and the prosperous middle class. Even the estimates which put the poor at thirteen million did not make them even a half of the population. The poor are a minority even within what is usually called the working class. Despite these qualifications, the over-riding conclusion is that the poor are a substantial number, and further information about them is required.

## WHO ARE THE POOR?

The numbers in poverty appear to make up a sizeable minority of the population. Who are they? Have they any common characteristic apart from a low income? Abel-Smith and Townsend's seminal investigation offers some pointers. Of those classified as poor in 1960, they found that about a third were mainly dependent upon a pension while over a third were in full-time work.[92] In other words, the plight of the elderly and low wage earners stood out. Following their study, the work of other researchers has identified six main groupings as being more liable to low incomes than other sections of the population.

Firstly, the *elderly*. In the United Kingdom, at the end of 1975, of 2,891,000 persons receiving supplementary benefit, 1,739,000 were of retirement age.[93] Further, the DHSS, in calculating numbers in Great Britain with low resources, records that in December 1974 550,000 persons of pensionable age had incomes below supplementary benefit levels, 2,130,000 were at these levels while 1,360,000 had incomes of less than 120 per cent.[94]

The elderly make up such a substantial proportion of the poor that the question is posed whether poverty can be explained as the problem of old age. Should theory and action concentrate on the old? The answer must be a negative one. Many of the poor are not old. Abel-Smith and Townsend established that 30 per cent of the poor were children, and their number, 2,225,000, made up 17 per cent of the child population.[95] The DHSS estimate of numbers with incomes below the 120-per-cent line showed 3,260,000 persons who were not retired.[96] Even more important, as Atkinson points out, the elderly poor probably do not find poverty a new experience.[97] They face poverty in old age because their incomes in youth and middle age did not allow them to accumulate the kind of occupational pensions, investments and possessions which would keep them in comfort in old age. Poverty is not a condition which suddenly arrives at a certain age.

Secondly, the *unemployed*. When Abel-Smith and Townsend published their study, Britain was enjoying a period of high employment. By July 1976, however, 1,463,500 persons were unemployed in the United Kingdom, 6.3 per cent of the working population.[98] Increases in the numbers in poverty are not necessarily the same as increases in the numbers unemployed. Some may have been in poverty while they were employed. Others may be unemployed but not poor in that their national insurance benefits, redundancy payments and private incomes continue to keep them above the poverty line. Nonetheless, figures published by the DHSS showed that in December 1974 510,000 persons were dependent on the incomes of persons who had been unemployed for at least three months and whose incomes were below the 120-per-cent level.[99]

Thirdly, the *sick and disabled*. In 1975, 255,000 sick and disabled persons were receiving supplementary benefit in the United Kingdom. Others were at work but apparently in low-wage occupations. In all, at the end of 1974, some 570,000 sick and disabled persons (and their dependants) were living below 120 per cent of the supplementary benefit basic rates.[100]

Fourthly, *one-parent families*. In 1971, 1,227,000 households consisted of a lone parent with children, being 6.7 per cent of all households.[101] The lone parent is predominantly, although not exclusively, female. In common with other women, they are less likely to have qualified, through their work record, for the higher national insurance benefits for the unemployed and are more likely to be in disadvantaged positions on the job market when available for work.[102] Their weak position is indicated by the fact that nearly half the families drawing Family Income Supplement—the government benefit for families with low earnings—were one-parent families. In December 1975, 32,300 one-parent families, caring for 53,000 children, were in receipt of FIS.[103] Many more are dependent upon supplementary benefit. In 1975, in the United Kingdom, 281,000 one-parent families were drawing such benefit compared with 78,000 in 1961.[104] Taking, again, below 120 per cent as the poverty line, then in 1974 some 300,000 one-parent families, involving 890,000 persons, were in poverty.[105]

Fifthly, *low wage earners.* Perhaps the finding that caused most surprise in the Abel-Smith and Townsend research, was that a third of the poor were in full-time work. As Atkinson points out, the figure bears comparison with that recorded by Rowntree in 1936.[106] Eventually, the government did introduce the measure mentioned above, the Family Income Supplement, specifically to help the working poor. By the end of 1975 it was being received by 67,000 families with 163,800 children in the United Kingdom.[107] However, the benefit does not necessarily take them out of poverty. In 1974, in Britain, 270,000 families, involving 890,000 persons, were dependent upon full-time workers' earnings which were not sufficient to take them above the 120-per-cent level.[108]

It will be realised that the above categories are not exclusive. There may well be considerable overlap, with some people being both unemployed and disabled or both low wage earners and lone parents. Further, membership of these groups does not necessarily entail poverty. The Queen Mother may be elderly but she is not poor. Vanessa Redgrave may be a lone parent but her earnings are doubtless well above the 120- or 140-per-cent levels. However, research does show that these groups are more likely than others to experience low incomes. In short, they are particularly vulnerable to poverty. The same could be said for the sixth grouping, *ethnic minorities.*

For the years 1974–5, it was estimated that 3.3 per cent of the population of Great Britain were of New Commonwealth and Pakistani ethnic origin.[109] Census returns show that members of these ethnic minorities are more likely than others to be in low-paid manual occupations and less likely to be in supervisory, managerial or professional positions.[110] A study by Political and Economic Planning further established that their earnings are often lower than those of white men of comparable age and occupational level.[111] As Parker states, 'Employment seems to be the area in which race, or at any rate a coloured skin, is associated with the most serious disadvantages.'[112] Being liable to manual occupations means not only lower pay but also increased job insecurity and greater possibilities of unemployment. In turn, chances of re-employment seem less. Black youngsters are clearly at much greater risk of not obtaining a job or of getting a low-paid one even when their qualifications are similar to their white counterparts'.[113]

Again, the overlap with other groupings must be stressed. Some persons will be both black and elderly or black and lone parents. Yet membership of these groups does not automatically imply poverty. Some members of ethnic minorities are affluent. Nonetheless, the evidence does suggest that being a member makes one more open to the experience of poverty.

Many of the poor are found amongst the elderly, the unemployed, sick and disabled, lone-parent families, low wage earners and ethnic minorities. Is there then no unifying factor? Berthoud shows that the risk of poverty is predominantly '... amongst those of low social status'.[114] Whatever the categories as outlined above, the members are also likely to have been at the bottom of the *social-class* structure. This point will be mentioned again in the following section and enlarged on in chapter 5.

## SOCIAL DEPRIVATION

So far, poverty has been examined in terms of income—or lack of it—with the implication that a certain amount of money is required to purchase the goods necessary for a reasonable life. But income is not the only factor making for such a life. This reason caused Abel-Smith and Townsend to be dissatisfied with their own definition of poverty. Poverty, they contended, really

... refers to a variety of conditions involving differences in home environment, material possessions and educational and occupational resources as well as financial resources ... we need to develop other indicators of the command of individuals and families over resources.[115]

Their plea has been taken up by subsequent researchers, who have made two major points. Firstly, in our society the social distance or gap between different individuals and different sections of the population involves not just income but factors such as housing conditions, job security and educational opportunity. Secondly, a mere raising of income in itself may not be sufficient to change the conditions which persons experience. For instance, a person's income may be raised to just above the 120-per-cent level. However, the increase may not be sufficient to improve his housing conditions or his job prospects.

Some members of society, then, are lacking not just income but the conditions, opportunities and educational resources, etc., enjoyed by others. The term 'social deprivation' has been employed to describe this position. Berthoud defined a deprivation shortly as '... a lack of something other people have ...'.[116] Later he expanded his version to say: 'Deprivations might therefore be considered to be those aspects of inequality that are avoidable.'[117] The present writer suggested that a social deprivation is '... a condition in which there is a failure to attain certain social norms to which existing social policies are apparently intended to provide access.'[118]

Leaving aside the semantic distinction between a privation (something which has never been had) and a deprivation (something which has been lost), it will be realised that social deprivation, like poverty, can also be regarded as an absolute or as a relative concept. For instance, an individual could be so completely deprived of adequate housing that his physical efficiency is destroyed. He would be relatively deprived when his housing conditions are considered too far removed from society's accepted standards. Taking up the relative concept, it follows that the same question of value judgements is raised. Who decides the standard? Who says when the gap is too far removed? Who determines which factors are included within the list of deprivations?

There is no consensus of opinion in reply to the questions. Nonetheless, Parliament, government departments and local authorities, as well as independent researchers, have identified certain social conditions or standards which they feel the population should enjoy. Further, they have devised measurements and cutting-off points to distinguish between the deprived and others. Here mention will be made of just a few social deprivations. A more detailed exposition can be found in the specialist literature.[119]

## Housing

Central and local government spend substantial amounts on housing. In the United Kingdom in 1974–5, their current expenditure on housing was £1,190 million while tax relief on private mortgages amounted to £770 million.[120] Clearly, government accepts that adequate accommodation is a vital social need and has devised some means of ascertaining the extent of housing deprivation. In general, it is taken that houses should be structurally fit, that they should possess certain basic amenities and that they should not be overcrowded. Undoubtedly, as Willmott makes clear, housing conditions have improved dramatically in the last century.[121] Yet a significant minority of persons are still in conditions which the government recognises as unreasonable. Thus, in 1971, 1,244,000 dwellings in England and Wales, i.e. seven per cent of all dwellings, were officially considered unfit for human habitation yet were still in use.[122] The situation is revealed as even more severe when the numbers without basic amenities are taken into consideration. In 1971, 11.5 per cent of all households in Britain lacked an indoor water closet, 9.1 per cent lacked a fixed bath and 6.5 per cent a hot-water tap.[123] According to the Sample Census of 1966, 1.6 per cent of all households were overcrowded in that their density of population was over an average of 1½ persons per room.[124] Not least, the existence of these measures implies that people should have somewhere to live. Yet the number of homeless families—that is, those living in local authority temporary accommodation—has risen. In March 1966, the number of homeless

persons in England and Wales was 13,031, by 1971 it was
28,879 and figures for 1975 indicate that the tide has not
turned.[125]

It is worth noticing the distribution of housing tenure. At
the end of 1971, in Britain 50 per cent of dwellings were
owner-occupied, 31 per cent rented from local authorities or
New Town corporations and 14 per cent were privately rented.[126]
Privately rented dwellings are the type of tenure most likely
to be deficient.[127] It is also the sector of the housing market
which has experienced a marked decline in numbers in recent
years. The decline has meant a drop in the number of dwellings
which possess socially depriving conditions. It has also reduced
a source of housing to that section of the population which
cannot afford to buy a house and may not yet qualify for
a council tenancy. Paradoxically, therefore, the decline of one
form of housing deprivation may have contributed to another—
homelessness.

## Health

Parker explains that health, or ill-health, is '. . . a matter of
crucial importance . . .' both for the nation and individuals.
For the state, illness and incapacity can impose an economic
cost through loss of production and through increased demands
on medical resources. The individual deprived of sound health
may be unable to function on a par with his or her contempor-
aries.[128] Most people appear to enjoy good health but, at any
one time, numbers are in hospital or ill at home. Thus during
1975, hospitals in the United Kingdom had an average of 396,000
occupied beds each day. In addition, there were around 100,000
residents in mental hospitals.[129] Three million people in Britain
report a long-standing illness which limits their activities.[130]
A national survey of children found that 6.2 per cent had
a history of stammering or stuttering while 4.9 per cent had
some degree of hearing impairment.[131] Minorities of adults are
also handicapped by bronchitis, pneumonia and impaired
vision.[132] These examples show that a minority of the population
do suffer health deprivations, often of a long-term or permanent
nature.

*Education*

Education is awarded a prominent place in our society. The age at which children commence formal education, the type of school they attend, the attainments they reach and the higher education they pursue, are all accorded weighty concern by Parliament and the press. Yet amongst children there are wide variations in the type of schooling they receive and the educational levels they attain. A minority of two- to four-year-old children are fortunate enough to obtain some form of organised education.[133] A small number eventually proceed to higher education. In between, most children gain some 'A' levels, 'O' levels or CSE (grades 2–5) examinations.[134] But a small number fare badly. A national survey of seven-year-olds found that 27.8 per cent of boys and 15.8 per cent of girls were poor readers while 3.1 and 1.4 per cent were non-readers. Similar minorities were also rated as far below average on number and oral work.[135] There can be little doubt that many of these children will be amongst those who leave school without any qualifications at all. Relative to other children they are educationally deprived.

The evidence reveals that numbers of persons experience inferior housing conditions, health and educational attainments when compared with the bulk of the population. These are just three indicators of social deprivation. Some persons are deprived of access to the health and social services which they need. Conditions of work in terms of health hazards, security of employment, holidays, perks and occupational pensions also show enormous differences.[136] Consideration might also be given to the possession or lack of a car, a garden, or play space. Further examples could be listed but the point is clear. In Britain, some sections of the population are considered socially deprived in that their conditions, lack of access to certain services or absence of amenities places them at an unacceptable distance from the majority.

## MULTIPLE SOCIAL DEPRIVATION

Social deprivations might be easier to bear if they occurred singly. That is, they would be more tolerable if one person experienced poor housing conditions and a different person had ill-health, if one person lacked money and another educational attainment. However, investigations suggest a tendency for deprivations to occur together, to be in multiples. The trend can be illustrated by studies identifying a relationship between two or more deprivations, by looking at what are called socially deprived areas, and by recalling the categories of the poor to see if they also endure other deprivations.

## Multiple Social Deprivations

Research workers have frequently pinpointed the association between low incomes and housing deprivation. According to The General Household Survey, less than one per cent of the highest income group were without a bath but 25 per cent of the lowest. Similarly, less than one per cent of the former lacked an indoor lavatory compared with 22 per cent of the latter.[137] The connection is obviously related to the advantage higher income groups have in securing owner-occupied accommodation—the form of tenure most likely to possess housing advantages. Those with low incomes are much more likely to have to rely on privately rented dwellings, the tenure most linked with overcrowding, lack of amenities and other unsatisfactory conditions.[138] However, it should be noted that low-income residents may be eligible for local-authority housing. Consequently, as Willmott and Aiach point out, in districts where there is a high concentration of council housing some of the poorest inhabitants may be in good-quality accommodation.[139] Despite these exceptions, there is still a general tendency for those with housing deprivations to be also deprived in terms of income.

Recent publications also show the likelihood of a pairing between persons suffering unsatisfactory housing conditions and ill-health, between low income and under-achievement at school, and between overcrowding and poor educational performance.[140] Other studies go beyond pairings and note a constellation of deprivations. A national study of eleven-year-olds found that six per cent endured unsatisfactory housing conditions, received low incomes and were also in households which either had only one parent or had four or more siblings. The children were far more likely than others to suffer a serious illness, such as rheumatic fever, and to have difficulties in hearing. The same children were liable to score badly on reading and mathematics tests and to need special educational help.[141] It is not claimed that social deprivations always occur in multiples, nor that the existence of a pair (or more) implies a causal relationship. The point is that some individuals are deprived on a variety of indices.

## Socially Deprived Areas

The multiple aspect of social deprivation is also shown in a concentration of many deprived persons in geographical locations which can themselves be termed deprived. It has long been recognised that regions differ markedly not only in the occurrence of slums, unemployment and health risks but also in their resources in terms of rateable value, the quality of their hospitals and schools, and their numbers of doctors and teachers. Similarly, within the same regions, it is known that towns differ markedly. Towns also differ within themselves, and frequently even prosperous cities may contain areas of intense deprivation. In the late 1960s, the present writer collated census material for a number of wards in the largest British cities. Certain wards were identified, on a variety of indices, as being far more disadvantaged than the majority. For instance, Woodside Ward in Glasgow had 21.5 per cent of its households overcrowded, compared with 11.8 per cent in Glasgow and 1.6 per cent in Britain. In addition, 54.9 per cent had no hot-water tap and 76.9 per cent no fixed bath. Such wards also tend to be those with populations with greater than usual social needs. Soho Ward in Birmingham had 13.9 per cent of its population aged 0–4 years compared with 8.9 per cent in Birmingham and 8.6 per cent in Britain. Further, 12.9 per cent of the households contained six or more persons while 21.3 per cent were born in the New Commonwealth. The conclusion was that such deprived areas are characterised by inferior housing conditions; higher than average proportions of unskilled workers, persons in poverty, large families and one-parent families; a lack of play and recreational facilities; a high incidence of child deprivation and delinquency; and poorer health than is found in the population as a whole.[142] Although the areas are typically found in the inner rings of industrial cities, they are also met on outlying council estates. The location of the socially deprived is not the result of random distribution. Many who are deprived of adequate income, health and education will find themselves living in districts which lack the amenities and advantages enjoyed elsewhere. Their deprivations are thereby intensified:

Work on the geography of poverty has been extended by Holtermann, who has now compared 85,578 urban enumeration districts (which, on average, contain 163 households or 470 persons).[143] Initially, she took a number of indicators of social deprivation and recorded their occurrence. Here mention can be made just of housing deprivation and unemployment. She recorded that, on average, the enumeration districts had 20.2 per cent of households lacking a basic housing amenity. But a mere one per cent of the districts had 92.3 per cent lacking an amenity. The mean rate of unemployment was 5.8 per cent of active males. Again, the average was misleading, for the worst one per cent of the districts had over 24 per cent of their men unemployed. Holtermann then examined the overlap between housing deprivation and unemployment. She discovered a core of 2,415 enumeration districts which were simultaneously the most deprived in respect of unemployment and lack of amenities and overcrowding. Such overlap districts were most numerous in Glasgow, where 18.9 per cent of the total population lived in them, followed by Birmingham, Edinburgh, Manchester, Bradford, Dundee and Islington. Interestingly, she added that although much multiple deprivation is found '... in the inner ring areas dominated by private rental accommodation ...', it is also found in council estates '... where problems of unemployment and overcrowding can occur on a scale at least as bad as in private rented housing.'[144]

The conclusion is that many deprived persons will find themselves living amongst concentrations of other deprived persons and in the midst of deprived physical locations. But a word of caution must be interjected. The fact that social deprivation is often concentrated within small geographical districts does not mean that all or even most deprived persons live there. For instance, Holtermann did find that a mere five per cent of the enumeration districts contained 33 per cent of the over-crowded households. Nonetheless, it will be realised that the majority of overcrowded households—67 per cent—lived else-where. Similar findings were recorded for unemployment and lack of amenities. The picture that emerges is of high concentrations of persons suffering multiple deprivations within small areas, along with a larger number scattered amongst the bulk of the enumeration districts.

## Groupings of the Deprived

Earlier, six main groupings of persons vulnerable to income deprivation were identified—the elderly, the unemployed, the sick and disabled, one-parent families, low wage earners and ethnic minorities. In addition, the poor were said to be predominantly found amongst members of the lowest social class. The question then arises: are these groupings also likely to experience other social deprivations? Here, attention will be given to the elderly, one-parent families, ethnic minorities and social class. However, similar points could be made about the other groupings and the reader is referred to the research by Hill, Harrison and Sergeant[145] and by Daniel[146] on the unemployed, by Harris, Smith and Head[147] on the disabled, and the Low Pay Unit on low wage earners.

The elderly, not surprisingly, are also liable to problems of ill-health and disability. Although they constitute 13 per cent of the population, they suffer 37 per cent of the chronic illnesses, 60 per cent of physical handicaps and 75 per cent of very severe handicaps. Similarly, small, elderly households and single old persons account for 52 per cent of the homes with no baths and 49 per cent of those without an indoor lavatory.[148]

Lone parents, particularly lone mothers, are likely to face a whole range of social deprivations. Marsden found that 40 per cent of those in his sample did not have the exclusive use of hot-water taps, indoor water closets and fixed baths. He also noted that over half were overcrowded to some degree.[149] Marsden's sample was restricted to mothers dependent upon supplementary benefit but Hunt, Fox and Morgan's study of working as well as non-working mothers agrees that they are in a very weak position in the housing market.[150] Their investigation also confirms the smaller and earlier one by the present writer that lone mothers have difficulties in getting access to adequate day-care facilities in order to free themselves for employment.[151] Further, there is evidence to suggest that illegitimate children who remain with their mothers tend to under-achieve at school.[152] The national study of children at the age of seven, states that 38 per cent of those with no father were poor readers compared with under 30 per cent of the total population, that 30 per cent were below average on oral ability compared with 22 per cent, and 32 per cent were poor at arithmetic compared with 29 per cent.[153] It should be added that subsequent research emphasises that these educational limitations were related to their other social deprivations rather than to the sole fact of living with a lone parent.[154] Lastly, George and Wilding's study of lone fathers found them to be less liable to overcrowding than lone mothers but more so than the population at large.[155]

Turning to ethnic minorities, there is now strong evidence that not only are they vulnerable to low incomes but also to inferior housing. The General Household Survey recorded that 23 per cent of 'coloured' households were overcrowded as against six per cent of white households (although the difference was partly due to the larger average size of the coloured households).[156] Further, although in 1973 the proportions lacking a bath and water closet were identical, 20 per cent of the coloured households shared a bath and toilet compared with only three per cent of white households.[157] Even where black families are granted access to council housing, there is evidence that many receive lower-quality accommodation than their white counterparts.[158]

The above six groupings, it was shown, were themselves frequently found within one other category; they were likely to be members of the lowest social class. It can be anticipated, therefore, that other social deprivations will also be located here. In chapter 5 the definition of social class will be discussed. Here it suffices to say that the Registrar-General's socio-economic classification will be used. Are the socially deprived disproportionately found in the lowest social class, the unskilled manual workers (social class v)? To take housing tenure, members of the lowest class are much more likely to use private rented accommodation, that tenure type most associated with housing deprivation.[159] A high proportion of this class lack sufficient bedrooms, an internal toilet or a fixed bath.[160] For example, 21 per cent of this class have insufficient housing amenities as against three per cent of social class I.[161]

The lowest social class also contains the members most likely to be at the bottom of educational ratings. Proportionately fewer of their children attend day nurseries and nursery schools.[162] Their children are far less likely to be achieving well at school at the age of seven.[163] After compulsory school-leaving age, only 32 per cent of children of manual workers continue in full-time education compared with 60 per cent of those of other families.[164] Halsey points out that these differences hold even when intelligence is constant.[165] Of course, more children from the lowest class now go to university or college than fifty years ago. But children from other classes have gained even more. Parker summarises the evidence:

> Although a higher proportion of children from all social backgrounds now have a university education, the chances of those from unskilled backgrounds as compared with those from the professional classes have actually worsened.[166]

In short, the educational distance between these sections of the population has not lessened.

The low-social-class connection is particularly obvious in regard to ill-health. Social class v, and to a certain extent social class IV, are much more likely than other classes to have members suffering from arthritis, rheumatism, bronchitis and mental disorder.[167] Willmott reviews the evidence found within the General Household Survey:

> Unskilled men of working age, says the Report, are three times

as likely to say that they suffer from chronic sickness as professional
men of the same age group. Furthermore, *younger unskilled men
are more often than professional men sufferers at middle age.* The
unskilled are three times as likely as the professional class to suffer
from arthritis and rheumatism; and even that condition most associated with an 'executive' style of life—heart disease—is still *more
often* a cause of long standing illness for the unskilled. [Willmott's
italics][168]

Class differences are even revealed in the final deprivation—death.
Infant mortality rates are highest amongst lower-class families.
Most remarkably, not only are general mortality rates highest
amongst social class v but '. . . the differences between the
classes . . . have actually increased over the past forty years.'[169]

Lastly, Berthoud has calculated the average number of deprivations—counting lack of housing, education, health, employment
and capital—across the five social classes. He records that social
class v had an average of 2.22 deprivations. The figure then
steadily decreased, with social class i having an average of
only 0.47.[170]

### *Implications*

These sections have now established both the extent of and
nature of social deprivation in Britain. There is no doubt that
gaps exist between different sections of the population in regard
not only to income but to housing, health, education and
other factors. The persons concerned may be considered poor
in that they are deprived of housing, health, etc., to a degree
thought to be unreasonable in comparison with the rest of
society. It was further shown that frequently (but not inevitably)
persons suffer from more than one form of deprivation. Some
have the additional handicap of residing in deprived areas. Certain
groupings of the poor—identified by their age, lack of a partner,
colour, etc.—are also known to be vulnerable to multiple deprivations. Not least, it was established that social deprivations are
not randomly distributed across social classes but occur proportionately more amongst the lowest social class.

Of course, it is not maintained that these are the only deprivations in society. Runciman, for instance, argues that people may be deprived of economic advantage, status and power.[171] However, it is maintained that the social deprivations which have been discussed (and they would fit into Runciman's first category) are so extensive as to warrant an examination of the reasons for their existence. Eventually, it may be that the explanation requires a consideration of the other two types of deprivation listed by Runciman.

The findings about the nature of deprivation have a major implication. The concept of poverty is widened. The social deprivations not only make for further unacceptable conditions in society, they are also frequently linked with a lack of income. The concept of poverty has to be enlarged, and Townsend now states,

> Individuals and families whose financial resources and/or whose other resources including their educational and occupational skills, the condition of their environment at home and at work and their material possessions fall seriously below those commanded by the average person or family in society may be said to be in poverty.[172]

From now on in this book, the term 'social deprivation' will be used interchangeably with poverty (and with inequality). Further, in discussing explanations of poverty, attention must be focussed on accounting not just for a lack of income but also for a lack of housing, health, educational attainments and other factors which are deemed essential to a normal life.

## THE ACKNOWLEDGEMENT OF POVERTY

Investigations may establish the existence of poverty according to the research criteria. But this is not to say that the government or the public also recognise it as a feature of society. It is of interest to trace briefly the prevailing belief about its existence. During the immediate post-war years, there was a strong assumption that poverty was an ill of the past. In a popular textbook of 1952, Hall took it that as this social problem was now

virtually solved, social reformers could concentrate on more
urgent problems such as,

> ... the increasing number of marriage breakdowns, the spread of
> juvenile delinquency, and the dissatisfaction and sense of frustration
> of the worker in spite of improved pay and conditions—that is,
> problems of psychological maladjustment rather than material
> need.[173]

So much was poverty considered a thing of the past that,
in 1957, the catch-phrase of the prime minister Harold Macmillan,
'You've never had it so good', seemed to stand for the belief
that affluence for all had taken its place.[174] Galbraith could
write of these years: '... few things are more evident in modern
social history than the decline of interest in inequality as an
economic issue ....'[175]

Why did poverty receive so little public recognition during
these years? One reason concerned the definition of poverty.
Rowntree's subsistence concept continued to hold sway and
it appeared obvious that rising standards had almost abolished
any prospect of not being physically efficient. Further, the 1950s
witnessed the start of a boom in the British economy accompanied
by full employment. The contrast with the austerity of the
war and the stagnation of the 1930s could hardly have been
greater. In fact, the relative differences between the average
and lowest incomes were changing but little. Yet Runciman
concludes that those on low incomes were not concerned, at
this time, about comparisons with the average or the affluent.
They '... were much more likely to compare their lot with
that of themselves and their parents during the Depression,
and by this comparison to count themselves fortunate.'[176] Consequently, they were unlikely to see themselves as poor and unlikely
to draw public attention to their position. Next, during these
years, the Labour Party established itself first as a government
and later as the major party in opposition. In both activities
it received support from the trade unions. To many of the
lowest-paid it might have appeared that these bodies were capable
of dealing with any problems of social deprivation. Lastly, it
was popularly accepted that the creation of the modern welfare
state constituted an effective defence against poverty and inequa-

lity. A number of critics thought the swing had gone too far and an influential book of 1949 by Lewis and Maude complained of a '. . . huge redistribution of wealth . . .' brought about by the welfare state.[177] Berthoud summarises:

> Certainly, the 1950s, and the dawn of the so-called 'Affluent Society', showed a marked decline in concern for the underprivileged, on the assumption that a booming economy and the welfare state had solved the problems of the 'people as a whole'.[178]

The doublefold assumption—that poverty was abolished and that Britain was a more equal society—did not go unchallenged. As the 1960s proceeded the challengers gained ground. Titmuss and his colleagues contested the conventional view that taxation and the social services were redistributing income and wealth.[179] As already explained, Townsend and others demonstrated the inadequacies of the subsistence concept. They adopted different measures of poverty which revealed substantial numbers as poor. As time progressed, it may have been that fewer low-income families compared themselves with the depression but, bombarded by television and mass media coverage, examined their lot against that of more favoured groups. Consequently, discontent about social deprivation was more likely to be expressed. A vehicle for its communication was found in the Child Poverty Action Group—soon joined by other pressure groups—which skilfully attempted to publicise the existence of poverty. The impact of their statistics and case studies was reinforced in the early and mid-1970s by the return of large-scale unemployment and a rapid rise in the numbers dependent upon supplementary benefit. Both major political parties now openly admitted the fact and the seriousness of poverty and made some indications that forms of intervention were required.

The political acknowledgement that poverty remains confirms the desirability of some discussion of the explanations of social deprivation. In addition, the acknowledgement implies a recognition that social policies—and, within them, the social services—have not as yet countered poverty. At this juncture, it is worth recording Warham's conclusion that social policy covers

. . . a range of processes (in the form of policies) and of institutions

(in the form of services) which are collectively created and maintained
in response to social problems and socially defined needs, and to
serve social as distinct from economic purposes.[180]

Now, if governments perceive a relationship between poverty
and social policy, then any discussion of explanations must
take this into account. It must consider what are the aims
of social policy in regard to poverty. Political parties may now
recognise poverty, but are their policies intended to abolish
it? If so, is the failure due to the limitations of the social
services? Certainly, the social services—including those with a
major social-work element, usually called the personal social
services—will receive a great deal of attention in this study.

## THE EXPERIENCE OF POVERTY

Poverty has so far been discussed in terms of definition, numbers
and public recognition. But, as anyone who has made personal
relationships with the poor will know, poverty entails more
than statistics. It also concerns personal experiences, feelings
and attitudes. As Raymond Williams wrote, in an introduction
to Charles Booth's work, we '. . . need to consider being poor
as a whole experience, in men and women like ourselves, and
not only as a problem for investigation, classification and
report.'[181]

The understanding of personal experiences poses difficulties
for research workers. A number of autobiographies by the poor
have been published.[182] These do reveal the route by which
some individuals move into poverty and how they react to
it. But autobiographies cannot be considered as representative.
Fortunately, other studies have examined in depth the behaviour
and opinions of a sample of poor families.[183] From these,
it is possible to identify something of what social deprivation
means to its recipients.

Poverty does seem to entail a restricted life style. Evason
points out, and other research confirms her findings, that the
poor frequently depend on borrowing money and using second-

hand clothes.[184] Despite popular stereotypes to the contrary, it appears that most socially deprived families do not take holidays and do not pursue regular leisure activities.[185] Their life style is different from most other families. Further, poverty can involve frequent crises. As Berthoud says, the poor face housekeeping problems not faced by most other people. A small drop in income, an illness, a rise in prices, a breakage of a household item, can spell debt and disaster.[186] The restricted mode of life and the financial crises are the harder to bear because often the efforts of the poor to escape their plight and to take on a new pattern of living seem unavailing.

The experiences are associated with certain feelings. The poor may well see themselves, and be seen by others, as inferior to or more lowly than the rest of society. Anxiety and worry about their ability to survive has also been observed. Feelings of inferiority and anxiety may also be joined by a sense of inability to change circumstances or even to contribute significantly to society. Townsend believes this sense is the more humiliating when individuals feel they cannot participate properly in the mutual giving and taking of family and community life.[187]

The above experiences and feelings—and they are only a selection—are associated with poverty. They may contribute to the causes of social deprivation or they may be a part of its consequences, an expression of poverty. If they are significant the question arises: to what extent are these experiences and feelings stimulated by or modified by popular attitudes, by the social services and by other institutions outside of the poor? The point being made is that social deprivation cannot be studied just by examining broad trends in the numbers in and out of poverty. The study must also ponder individual feelings and behaviour, it must consider what poverty means to the poor.

This introductory chapter commenced by debating the concepts of subsistence and relative poverty. Within these frameworks the extent of poverty within contemporary Britain was charted. But poverty, referring just to a lack of sufficient income, was considered too restrictive and its meaning was extended to include a number of social deprivations. Poverty, in this wider sense, is now recognised as a feature of society which justifies some form of government intervention in order to alleviate its incidence or consequences.

The discussion has raised a number of pointers which can later be followed up in considering explanations of social deprivation. For instance, certain categories or groupings of persons were identified as particularly vulnerable to poverty. Indeed, some were also vulnerable to multiple deprivations. The question, then, is posed: is there anything about these groupings and the individuals within them which accounts for their poverty? Or is the answer to be found in the depriving environments which make up the places of residence for many of the poor? Statutory bodies have devised social policies and established social services. Yet poverty remains, and so the relationship between social agencies and poverty must be explored. The poor, it was detected, are disproportionately found amongst the lower social class. Is this because its members possess certain inherited traits or behavioural patterns which push them into poverty, or does class membership itself dispose them towards poverty, irrespective of personal qualities? Lastly, attention was drawn to poverty as a personal experience. Do the experiences and feelings of the poor add up to a culture which makes poverty an acceptable and inevitable way of life for a section of the population or do they entail the responses of individuals who are striving to escape from their circumstances? These leads will be incorporated into succeeding chapters as explanations are studied with reference to individuals, patterns of family behaviour, social agencies and social structures.

REFERENCES

1 C. Booth *Life and Labour of the People* vol. I, Williams and Norgate (1889)
2 B. Abel-Smith and P. Townsend *The Poor and the Poorest* Bell (1965)
3 M. Harrington *The Other America* Collier-Macmillan (1962)
4 Cited in E. James *America Against Poverty* Routledge (1970) p. 65
5 e.g. Deuteronomy xv, 1–12 and xxiv, 19–22
6 For an historical account see B. Rodgers *The Battle Against Poverty* 2 vols., Routledge (1969)
7 A. Roger (ed.), Sir Frederic Eden *The State of the Poor* Routledge (1928)

8 See T. and B. Simey *Charles Booth* Oxford University Press (1960)
9 A. Fried and R. Elman (eds) *Charles Booth's London. A Portrait of the Poor at the Turn of the Century Drawn from his 'Life and Labour of the People of London'* Hutchinson (1969)
10 *ibid.* p. 44
11 B. Webb *My Apprenticeship* Longmans (1926). See also M. Cole *Beatrice Webb* Longmans (2nd imp. 1946) ch. 3
12 R. Williams in Fried and Elman *op. cit.* p. xi
13 W. Booth *In Darkest England and the Way Out* International Headquarters of the Salvation Army (1890) pp. 21–2
14 Cited in A. Briggs *Seebohm Rowntree* Longmans (1961) p. 17
15 B. S. Rowntree *Poverty: A Study of Town Life* Macmillan (1901); 2nd edn Longmans (1922) repr. Howard Fertig (1971) p. xviii
16 *ibid.* p. xix
17 *ibid.* p. 123
18 *ibid.* pp. 130–5
19 *ibid.* p. 142
20 *ibid.* p. 143
21 *ibid.* pp. 143–4
22 Cited in Briggs *op. cit.* p. 296
23 B. S. Rowntree *Poverty and Progress, A Second Social Survey of York* Longmans (1941)
24 B. S. Rowntree and G. Lavers *Poverty and the Welfare State* Longmans (1951) pp. 30–2
25 Briggs *op. cit.* p. 30
26 *ibid.*
27 See P. Hall *The Social Services of Modern Britain* Routledge (6th edn 1963) pp. 17–20
28 Rowntree, *Poverty and Progress* pp. 102–3
29 Cited in Briggs *op. cit.* p. 296
30 P. Townsend *The Social Minority* Allen Lane (1973) p. 25
31 Fried and Elman *op. cit.* p. 44
32 *ibid.* p. 45
33 Rowntree *Poverty: A Study of Town Life* p. 123
34 *ibid.* p. xvii
35 *ibid.* p. 137
36 Townsend *op cit.* p. 28
37 *ibid.* p. 26
38 Briggs *op. cit.* p. 297
39 Townsend *op. cit.* p. 28
40 Rowntree *Poverty: A Study of Town Life* pp. 55–6
41 Townsend *op. cit.* p. 28
42 Cited in Briggs *op. cit.* p. 38
43 Listed in P. Townsend 'Poverty and Relative Deprivation' in D. Wedderburn (ed) *Poverty, Inequality and Class Structure* Cambridge University Press (1974) p. 28
44 Townsend *The Social Minority* p. 29
45 D. Marsden *Mothers Alone* Penguin Books (1973) p. 299
46 B. S. Rowntree *Poverty: A Study of Town Life* p. 137
47 Briggs *op. cit.* pp. 33–6
48 F. Lafitte, 'Income Deprivation' in R. Holman (ed.) *Socially Deprived Families in Britain* Bedford Square Press (1970) p. 7
49 Cited in Lafitte *op. cit.*

50 W. G. Runciman *Relative Deprivation and Social Justice* Penguin Books (1972)
51 R. Berthoud *The Disadvantages of Inequality* Macdonald and Jane's (1976) p. 20
52 *ibid.* p. 18
53 *ibid.* p. 42
54 S. Mencher 'The Problem of Measuring Poverty' *British Journal of Sociology* vol. 18, no. 1 (1967)
55 W. Beveridge *Report on Social Insurance and the Allied Services* HMSO Cmd. 6404 (1942)
56 J. Beveridge *Beveridge And His Plan* Hodder and Stoughton (1954) pp. 107–8
57 Runciman *op. cit.* p. 10
58 Townsend *The Social Minority* chs 1–3
59 B. Wootton *In Pursuit of Equality* Fabian Society (1976) p. 11
60 See J. Parker *Social Policy and Citizenship* Macmillan (1975) p. 58
61 For a fuller discussion of the difficulties see A. Atkinson 'Poverty and Income Inequality in Britain' in Wedderburn *op. cit.*
62 *The Supplementary Benefit Handbook* HMSO (1972) para. 37
63 Central Statistical Office (CSO) *Social Trends* no. 6 HMSO (1975) p. 117
64 Berthoud *op. cit.* p. 55
65 CSO *Social Trends* no. 7, HMSO (1976) table 5.23, p. 120
66 Ministry of Social Security *Circumstances of Families* HMSO (1967)
67 Abel-Smith and Townsend *op. cit.* p. 58
68 I. Gough and T. Stark 'Low Incomes in the United Kingdom' cited by Atkinson *op. cit.* p. 58
69 *ibid.* p. 58
70 CSO *Social Trends* no. 7, table 5.31, p. 124
71 F. Field cited in the *Guardian* 2 Dec. 1976
72 Atkinson *op. cit.* p. 48
73 *ibid.* pp. 56–7
74 *ibid.* p. 49
75 see M. Wynn *Family Policy* Penguin Books (1970)
76 E. Evason 'Measuring Family Poverty' *Social Work Today* vol. 4, no. 3 (3 May 1973)
77 *ibid.*
78 M. Church 'Can Mothers Manage on Supplementary Benefit?' *Poverty* no. 33 (1975/6)
79 Berthoud *op. cit.* pp. 65 and 68
80 Survey by Research Institute for Consumer Affairs reported in the *Guardian* 18 July 1974
81 Berthoud *op. cit.* pp. 63 and 65
82 CSO *Social Trends* no. 7, table 5.29, p. 123
83 Gough and Stark *op. cit.* p. 58
84 Abel-Smith and Townsend *op. cit.* ch. 4
85 Parker *op. cit.* p. 176
86 Field *op. cit.*
87 Berthoud *op. cit.* pp. 29–30
88 CSO *Social Trends* no. 7, table 5.10, p. 112
89 C. Trinder 'The Social Contract and the Low Paid' in P. Willmott (ed.) *Sharing Inflation?* Temple Smith (1976) p. 24
90 CSO *Social Trends* no. 6, p. 108, and no. 7, table 5.15, p. 116
91 Berthoud *op. cit.* p. 34. For further discussion, see pp. 33–5
92 Abel-Smith and Townsend *op. cit.* table 18, p. 42

93 cso *Social Trends* no. 7, table 5.23, p. 120
94 *ibid.* table 5.31, p. 124
95 Abel-Smith and Townsend *op. cit.* table 17, p. 41
96 cso *Social Trends* no. 7
97 A. Atkinson 'Who Are The Poorest' *New Society* vol. 23, no. 543 (1 March 1973)
98 cso *Social Trends* no. 7, table 4.17, p. 102
99 Cited in Willmott *op. cit.* p. 62
100 *ibid.*
101 cso *Social Trends* no. 7, table 2.1, p. 73
102 See A. Hunt, J. Fox and M. Morgan *Families and Their Needs* 2 vols. hmso (1973)
103 cso *Social Trends* no. 7, table 5.26, p. 121
104 *ibid.* table 5.23, p. 120
105 *ibid.* table 5.31, p. 124
106 Atkinson *op. cit.*
107 cso *Social Trends* no. 7, table 5.26, p. 126
108 Cited in Willmott *op. cit.* p. 62
109 cso *Social Trends*, no. 7, table 1.20, p. 71
110 Parker *op. cit.* pp. 34–5
111 D. Smith *The Facts of Racial Disadvantage* pep broadsheet no. 560 (1976)
112 Parker *op. cit.* p. 34
113 For a discussion, see *The Struggle For Equal Opportunities—Strategies for Social Welfare Action* National Council of Social Service (1976) ch. 3
114 Berthoud *op. cit.* p. 179
115 Abel-Smith and Townsend *op. cit.* p. 63
116 Berthoud *op. cit.* p. 12
117 *ibid.* p. 168
118 R. Holman 'Unmarried Mothers, Social Deprivation and Child Separation', *Policy and Politics* vol. 3, no. 4 (1975)
119 See Berthoud *op. cit.*; and Holman (ed.) *Socially Deprived Families in Britain*
120 cso *Social Trends* no. 7, tables 8.19 and 8.20, p. 158
121 P. Willmott 'Housing' in M. Young *Poverty Report 1974* Temple Smith (1974) pp. 133–4
122 Parker *op. cit.* table 7.1, p. 108
123 cso *Social Trends* no. 7, table 8.6, p. 152
124 Holman (ed.) *Socially Deprived Families in Britain* table 3, p. 210
125 K. Spencer 'Housing Deprivation': supplement to R. Holman (ed.), *Socially Deprived Families in Britain* Bedford Square Press 2nd edn (1973) p. 3
126 Parker *op. cit.* p. 109
127 Berthoud *op. cit.* p. 93; and Parker *op. cit.* pp. 108–12
128 Parker *op. cit.* p. 71
129 cso *Social Trends* no. 7, tables 7.9 and 7.12, pp. 139–40
130 Berthoud *op. cit.* p. 173
131 M. Kellmer Pringle, N. Butler and R. Davie *11,000 Seven Year Olds* Longmans (1966) table 18, p. 59; table 25, p. 66
132 T. Arie 'Class and Disease' *New Society* vol. 7, no. 174 (27 Jan. 1966)
133 cso *Social Trends* no. 7, tables 3.4 and 3.5, p. 88
134 *ibid.* chart 3.9 and table 3.10, p. 90
135 Kellmer Pringle, Butler and Davie *op. cit.* table 7, pp. 28, 30–4
136 Wedderburn (ed.) *op. cit.* ch. 7
137 Cited in Parker *op. cit.* p. 110

138 cso *Social Trends* no. 7, chart 8.11, p. 154
139 P. Willmott and P. Aiach 'Deprivation in Paris and London', in Willmott (ed.) *op. cit.*
140 R. Davie, N. Butler and H. Goldstein *From Birth to 7* Longman (1972) pp. 54–7
141 Cited in Berthoud *op. cit.* p. 120–3
142 Holman (ed.) *op. cit.* pp. 155–6 and appendix B
143 S. Holtermann 'Areas of Urban Deprivation in Great Britain: an Analysis of 1971 Census Data', in cso *Social Trends* no. 6
144 *ibid.* p. 44
145 M. Hill, R. Harrison and A. Sergeant *Men Out of Work* Cambridge University Press (1973)
146 W. Daniel *A National Survey of the Unemployed* PEP broadsheet (1974)
147 A. Harris, C. Smith and E. Head *Income and Entitlement to Supplementary Benefit of Impaired People in Great Britain* (Part III of *Handicapped and Impaired in Great Britain*) HMSO (1972)
148 Berthoud *op. cit.* p. 176
149 Marsden *op. cit.* ch. 2
150 A. Hunt, J. Fox and M. Morgan *Families and Their Needs* 2 vols, HMSO (1973)
151 R. Holman *Unsupported Mothers and the Care of Their Children* Mothers in Action (1970)
152 E. Crellin, M. Kellmer Pringle and P. West *Born Illegitimate* National Foundation for Educational Research (1971)
153 Cited in cso *Social Trends* no. 6, p. 23
154 National Children's Bureau *Growing Up in a One Parent Family* National Foundation for Educational Research (1976) pp. 119, 140–6
155 V. George and P. Wilding *Motherless Families* Routledge (1972) table 10, p. 31
156 Cited in Parker *op. cit.* p. 113
157 cso *Social Trends* no. 7, table 8.7, p. 152
158 See *Runnymede Trust Bulletin* no. 76 (May 1976)
159 Berthoud *op. cit.* table 11, p. 47; table 2.5, p. 102
160 *ibid.* table 25, p. 102
161 *ibid.* table 40, p. 178
162 cso *Social Trends* no. 7, chart 3.2, p. 87
163 Kellmer Pringle, Butler and Davie, *11,000 Seven Year Olds* pp. 114–20
164 cso *Social Trends* no. 7, p. 90
165 Cited by Parker *op. cit.* n. 14, p. 105
166 *ibid.* p. 100
167 Office of Population Censuses and Surveys *The General Household Survey* HMSO (1973) table 8.13
168 Willmott 'Health and Welfare' in Young *op. cit.* p. 199
169 Parker *op. cit.* pp. 73–4
170 Berthoud *op. cit.* table 41, p. 185
171 Runciman *op. cit.* pp. 44–8
172 Townsend *op. cit.* p. 57
173 Cited by B. Wootton *Social Science and Social Pathology* Allen and Unwin (1959) p. 269
174 See A. Sampson *Macmillan* Allen Lane (1967)
175 J. Galbraith *The Affluent Society* Penguin Books (1970)
176 Runciman *op. cit.* p. 107
177 R. Lewis and A. Maude *The English Middle Classes* Penguin Books (1949) p. 24

178 Berthoud *op. cit.* p. 9
179 R. Titmuss *Income Distribution and Social Change* Allen and Unwin (1962)
180 J. Warham 'Social Policy and Social Services' Unit Two of Open University *Social Work, Community Work and Society* (1977) p. 13
181 Williams in Fried and Elman *op. cit.* p. xii
182 e.g. J. Colin *Never Had It So Good* Gollancz (1974); and P. Chapman and L. Berg *The Train Back* Allen Lane (1972)
183 e.g. Marsden *op. cit.*; and H. Wilson 'Parenting in Poverty' *British Journal of Social Work* vol. 4, no. 3 (1974)
184 Evason *op. cit.*
185 See Social Tourism Study Group Report cited in the *Guardian* 19 August 1975
186 Berthoud *op. cit.* pp. 63–5
187 Townsend *op. cit.* p. 17

# CHAPTER 2

# Individuals and Poverty

Charles Booth believed that many people could not be blamed for their plight. But he also identified the '. . . lowest class, which consists of some occasional labourers, street sellers, criminals, and semi-criminals'.[1] He dismissed its members in scathing terms referring to their vices of drink, laziness and bad company.[2] Booth held these paupers to be individually responsible for their position. Seebohm Rowntree continued the refrain by describing, amongst those in secondary poverty, persons whose income should have been sufficient had they not wasted it.[3] In regarding certain individuals as personally responsible for their poverty, Booth and Rowntree were voicing an explanation which has always held much popular support. The explanation is based on the belief—deeply rooted in our society—that individuals are self-determining beings able to control their own environments and destinies. It follows that they are individuals who are wholly responsible for their behaviour, morals and conditions. Consequently, their poverty is explained in terms of individual failure. The emphasis on individualism was expressed again in the early days of the post-war welfare state, when it was assumed that welfare provisions made it possible for 'normal' people to avoid social deprivations if they so chose. The lack of individual normality of the poor was reflected in Stephens' description of them as '. . . the misfits who failed to benefit from the provisions which suffice for average people'.[4] Pearson summed up the prevailing ideology of the period as '. . . the idea that social problems—including unemployment, crime, material hardship, homelessness—were caused by individual pathologies, or by inadequate problem families . . .'.[5]

The present chapter will draw attention to three explanations which emphasise the relationship between individuals and poverty. The analyses do not necessarily allocate blame to individuals who are poor, but they do regard poverty as stemming from the limitations, maladjustments or deficiencies of individuals. The explanations are those which look at individuals in terms of their biological endowments, their economic capacities, and their psychological qualities. Although each variation has considerable popular appeal, they frequently lack specific exposition and appear within the context of studies whose main purpose is not geared towards poverty. The genetic theory of poverty is found within studies mainly concerned with the debate about the nature of intelligence. The economic explanation tends to occur within publications primarily arguing the case for selective rather than universal social services. The psychological emphasis appears most strongly within treatises attempting to establish the existence of 'problem families'. In response, the form of this chapter will be to identify and isolate the explanations, to state them and to evaluate them critically.

GENETIC MAN

The belief that the behaviour and social position of individuals are directly and primarily attributable to the biological inheritance of certain traits and characteristics appears to command considerable popular sway. Social workers are used to hearing a person's promiscuity or laziness attributed to his parents with the words 'it's in the blood'. At the other end of the social scale, Sir Douglas Allen, the former head of the civil service, has suggested that the continuing preponderance of public-school and Oxbridge persons in the highest posts, is due to the biological inheritance of talent.[6]

Whatever the popular views about biological influences, many social scientists have been sceptical about them as major determinants of behaviour. As Meade and Parkes put it to a symposium of the Council of the Eugenics Society,

The rather naive enthusiasms of some of the early social Darwinists, together with the fearful crimes committed allegedly for eugenic purposes, have undoubtedly made many students consciously or unconsciously reluctant to consider the genetic element in social situations.[7]

But Meade and Parkes were speaking in the early 1960s. Today the genetic element is more widely considered. It cannot now be seriously disputed that biologically inherited factors mould certain physical capacities such as the ability to perceive colours or the extent of early oral sucking movements. In short, behaviour is directly influenced. Further, academic institutions have become the forum for public debate of opposing views on the alleged genetic differences between races. Not surprisingly, therefore, greater attention has been given to the relationship between genetics and poverty.

Explanations which do attribute poverty directly to the inherited capacities of individuals are of three kinds. Firstly, those that consider that some inadequacy or pauper syndrome is biologically transmitted through the genes of one person to another. Penrose has pointed to the complete lack of justification for regarding conditions of this nature as approximating to a specific gene.[8] Of course, such a belief may have popular currency but the actual merit of the claim need not be discussed further at this point. Secondly, those explanations that claim that intelligence determines income and that intelligence is a largely inherited attribute. Thirdly, those that regard mental illness or unstable temperament as inherited incapacities which precipitate individuals towards social deprivation.

*Intelligence and Poverty*

The strongest case for a biological and individual explanation of poverty rests on three interlocking planks, namely that

    intelligence is measured by IQ tests

    intelligence is largely determined by biological inheritance

    intelligence determines individuals' level of educational attainment, occupation, income and social-class position.

The case has been most forcibly articulated by Herrnstein who starts with a syllogism,

    1. If differences in mental abilities are inherited, and

2. If success requires those abilities, and

3. If earnings and prestige depend on success,

4. Then social standing (which reflects earnings and prestige) will be based to some extent on inherited differences among people.[9]

Herrnstein then attempts to remove the 'ifs' and, indeed, to demonstrate that income and success depend mainly and increasingly on inherited differences.

Drawing upon the work of Jensen—which, in turn, relied heavily on that of Cyril Burt—Herrnstein accepts that the genetic contribution to IQ is between 80 and 87 per cent.[10] Children with high IQs then succeed at school. 'Those with higher intellectual endowments have tended to persevere in school and have earned better grades along the way.'[11] The innately favoured ones then succeed in the world, for 'Occupational success is correlated with IQ.'[12] The intelligent thus move into the upper class. Overall, those who inherit high IQs will be successful in terms of prestige and earnings, those endowed with low intelligence will receive low pay or be unemployed, they will be the poor.

Herrnstein then proceeds to argue that the influence of genes is increasing. Welfare services, the provision of universal education, the effects of progressive taxation, have reduced, he believes, if not abolished the differing effects of environment on the development of intelligence. Working-class children have been enabled to develop their capacities and have been free to move up the social scale. Once in the upper class they marry spouses of similar intelligence, for 'People tend to marry within their class, and by doing so, they pair off corresponding genetic endowments'.[13] Such couples then produce children of high intelligence who will themselves be successful at school and work. By contrast, the lower class will have lost its able members and, by intermarriage, will perpetuate a class of low-intelligence, poorly paid members. Herrnstein states: 'Whatever else this accomplishes, it will also increase the IQ (hence, the genetic) gap between upper and lower classes, making the social ladder even steeper for those left at the bottom.'[14] Genetic factors, in Herrnstein's view, are creating a rigidly divided society and point to a future '. . . in which social classes not only continue

but become ever more solidly built on inborn differences'.[15]
As technological advance makes occupations even more dependent upon skills and intelligence, the prospects for those at
the bottom become even more gloomy. He identifies '. . . a stra-
tum that is unable to master the common occupations, cannot
compete for success and achievement and is most likely to
be born to parents who have similarly failed'.[16] Failure, low
income, poverty can be attributed to biological inheritance, and
the situation will build up so that '. . . the tendency to be
unemployed may run in the genes of a family about as certainly
as the IQ does now.'[17]

In Britain, Rhodes Boyson MP and his colleagues write from
a more overtly political platform than Herrnstein. They appear
to have used and applied some of his work. Thus they agree
that intelligence is largely inherited while educational opportunities have enabled the intelligent working-class persons to move
up the social scale. The result is a shrinking of the gene pool
of natural ability within the working class. Social classes thus
correspond to IQ levels and, as biological transmission will only
increase the ability gaps, the prospect is of a 'static social
system' with birth determining wealth and poverty not by the
inheritance of capital but by the inheritance of genes.[18]

Eysenck, while agreeing with the main thrusts of the above
analysis, presents an account which is more modified than Herrnstein's and more humane than Boyson's. Accepting that intelligence owes about 80 per cent to genetic influences, he also
sees IQ as largely determining success or failure at school which,
in turn, shapes access to job opportunities and levels of income.
Eysenck perceives a very close relationship between differing
occupations and differing IQs and produces a table showing
that higher professional people such as top civil servants, profes-
sors and research scientists have IQs of about 140, as against
labourers, gardeners, etc., with IQs of around 90. In turn, the
occupations fit into different social-class categories. As he puts
it, success '. . . defined either in terms of income or social prestige
. . . correlates quite well with IQ'.[19] In Eysenck's view, then,
intelligence remains the key to worldly success or failure while
intelligence is largely derived from biological transmission.

  The attempt to explain poverty as the result of genetic endow-

ment rests mainly upon the alleged relationship between poverty
and inherited intelligence. Several strong criticisms can be made
of this explanation. One attempt to remove the foundation
of the case is the claim that IQ tests do not adequately measure
intelligence (some writers even question the very concept of
intelligence). Kogan argues that the tests often measure factors
which are not to do with intellectual functioning. In a paper
published in 1973 he demonstrates that the questions used draw
out cultural or class differences which are then taken to be
differences in individual ability. He also shows that children
from socially deprived backgrounds are slower in attaining
'. . . basic cognitive competence'. They do catch up but by this
time have already been graded as 'low IQ', a figure which
tends to stay with them. Kogan would thus dismiss as unreliable
the present use of IQ tests and with them the arguments built
up about the causal relationship between intelligence and
poverty.[20]

Another fundamental attack questions the credibility of Burt's
published research. Jensen, Herrnstein and Eysenck all draw
heavily (but not exclusively) on original figures supplied by
Burt in order to argue the innate nature of intelligence. The
accusations that Burt's figures were at best unreliable and at
worst fraudulent are detailed by Kamin while Burt's defenders
expressed their side in an acid correspondence in *The Times*.[21]

Leaving aside the dispute about the validity of IQ tests and
Burt's work, the next criticism of the genetic explanation seeks
to emphasise the part played by environmental factors in forming
intelligence. The theme is that if intelligence does determine
poverty, then environmental influences play a significant part
in determining intelligence. Much of the evidence for the influence
of environment comes from studies of children raised in different
kinds of circumstances. Children bred under conditions of severe
privation are very likely to suffer serious intellectual impairment.
The point has been made so often that Rutter and Madge
state that '. . . the findings are not in dispute'.[22] Adoptive studies
provide further material on the impact of social and physical
surroundings. Skodak and Skeels studied children taken mainly
from parents in unskilled occupations and placed with those
of a higher class. At the age of thirteen, their mean IQ was

some twenty points above that of their natural mothers.[23] Similar findings were recorded by Seglow, Kellmer Pringle and Wedge in a subsequent and larger study.[24] Even more recently, Tizard has studied samples of children coming into public care who were then placed in various forms of environment. She found that although the children came from different kinds of social-class background, the important element in developing their intellectual skills was the quality and nature of the residential setting into which they were placed. From further material, she established that children placed with adoptive parents, who tended to be affluent and to possess high occupational status, scored higher than similar children restored to poorer natural parents or left in institutions. She concluded: '. . . we could find no evidence that genetic factors were responsible for these IQ differences.'[25]

Summarising their review of the research literature, Rutter and Madge wrote: 'It may be concluded from these (and other) studies that social circumstances can and do influence children's intellectual development. . . .'[26] They add that—contrary to Jensen's assertion—not only do environmental handicaps depress IQ scores but favourable circumstances increase them.[27] Intellectual development may be impaired by overcrowded housing conditions, lack of amenities and poor nutrition.[28,29] It may be increased by an abundance of stimulating experiences, by the material supports which allow opportunities to study, and even by extensive coaching.[30]

There can be no doubt that intelligence is not wholly inherited. The extent to which it is open to environmental influences is now the point at issue. Jencks and his colleagues calculate that hereditary factors make up only 45 per cent of intelligence, environmental ones 35 per cent and co-variance 20 per cent. Co-variance refers to the fact that bright parents may have children who are both genetically advantaged and advantaged by a stimulating environment. Conversely, dull children may have a double disadvantage.[31] If intelligence is closely related to poverty, then the environmental influence (which could bridge the gap between low and average intelligence) can be crucial and genes alone cannot be isolated as the explanation of poverty.

Before leaving the subject of genetics and intelligence, one further observation must be made. Genetic factors do not always favour the offspring of bright parents or work against those of dull parents. It is generally thought that genetic factors play a large part in perpetuating very low IQs. It might then be considered that the intermarriage of two 'feeble-minded' persons within poor environments should invariably produce very-low-intelligence children. Yet, as Eysenck points out, frequently their offspring have IQs of over 90.[32] The reason is not—in Eysenck's view—that environmental forces are at work but that genetic transmission is as likely to produce differences as similarities. It should not even be assumed that an aggregate or category of similar persons will produce an aggregate of identical persons. Gibson and Young have drawn attention to the tendency by which the IQs of children whose parents fall in the extreme groups '. . . regress from the extreme towards the mean of the general population. Fathers (or mothers) with mean IQs of about 84 or 140, have children with IQs of about 92, or 120, respectively.'[33] Eysenck also gives prominence to the same phenomenon:

> Children of fathers in the higher professions show the greatest decline; children of the unskilled workers show the greatest increase in score. It almost seems as if there were a deity watching over our affairs, determined to reduce the differences in IQ which at present exist between different occupations and classes.[34]

This regression to the mean, as it is called, has a direct bearing on any biological explanation of poverty. For over time the intelligence and thereby the capacity to avoid or fall into poverty, will change significantly. It follows that poverty would not simply run from one family to the next by such mechanisms. Herrnstein underplayed this aspect of genetics, and his pronouncement that unemployment will run in the genes of families can be dismissed as certainly as that of Boyson that the working-class gene pool of natural ability is shrinking. The influence of genetic factors on intelligence has been overemphasised but even where they do operate, they do not separate out a biologically self-perpetuating class of paupers.

The above discussion has assumed that intelligence does determine level of income but has disputed the part played by genetics. The next criticism challenges the view that intelligence —no matter how it is initially formed—is the sole or all-important determinant of a person's social position, affluence or poverty. The challenge can be pursued by examining the relation-ship, firstly between intelligence and education, secondly between intelligence and occupation, and thirdly between intelligence and social class.

If an individual's intelligence determines his educational success (and the monetary rewards that follow), then children with high IQs should achieve well at school and proceed to higher education. Certainly, and expectedly, there is a strong trend in this direction. But substantial exceptions are most marked. Take entrance to selective secondary schools. The work of Douglas and his colleagues established that for children of the very highest intelligence there were opportunities to enter. But middle-class children of 'good' ability were much more likely than working-class children of similar ability to obtain places.[35] Similarly, access to prestigious public schools appears to depend heavily on previous family connections with the schools.[36] Turn-ing to performance at school, '. . . at all levels of ability the working class child was more likely to leave school early and less likely to gain good certificates. Even after equating for intellectual grading at age 11 years, more middle class children than working class children gain qualifications for higher educa-tion.'[37] The Crowther Report of 1959 found that, amongst the sons of manual workers, the vast majority in the highest ability groups left school at sixteen years or earlier.[38] Movement to higher education reveals comparable findings. The Robbins Report calculated that amongst children with IQs over 130, 72 per cent of manual workers' children did not reach univer-sity.[39] In the USA, Riessman records that a majority of children from low-income homes did not go to college although their IQs were sufficient.[40] In all cases, children of comparable intelli-gence but from more advantageous backgrounds were much more likely to gain places at university or college. Intelligence is not the only determinant of educational success. Intelligence is partially shaped by environment. But even amongst those with the same IQs, social circumstances enable some children to receive educational benefits while holding back others. Herrn-stein's claim that environmental influences have been evened out by welfare provisions is not supported.

What of the link between intelligence and occupation? Studies, not unexpectedly, reveal a close association. But it is by no means complete. For instance, as will be expanded in chapter 5, in Britain the top 24,000 posts in banking, the armed forces, the judiciary, etc., are disproportionately distributed amongst persons whose fathers held such posts. This trend continues despite the phenomenon of the regression to the mean and despite the fact that more able persons could certainly be found amongst the other fifty-five million people in the United Kingdom. That the 24,000 are more intelligent than most other people is not in dispute. The point is that some other individuals are likely to be of higher intelligence than those members who seem to succeed their fathers whilst the former do not obtain the position. In the USA, Jencks explains that although intelligence frequently does shape occupational status, it is not the sole force. Indeed, he estimates that intellectual abilities and educational attainment do not explain 35 per cent of the differences in occupational status.[41]

Intelligence was also claimed to determine levels of income by selecting persons for social classes. If the views of Herrnstein and Boyson are correct, then amongst the present population the highest IQs will be in social class I and receiving the highest incomes while the lowest will be in social class V receiving the least. If regression to the mean is taken into consideration, however, and if intelligence is the deciding factor then some interchange between social classes will be expected as generation succeeds generation. After examining the evidence, Rutter and Madge declare that '. . . the correlation between IQ and social class is only moderate (about 0.5) and leaves much of the variance unexplained.'[42] Burt, using a sixfold classification of social class, admitted that workers in the lowest class were sometimes more intelligent than those in higher classes.[43] Indeed, the range within each class is greater than that between classes.[44] Eysenck, after regrouping Burt's categories into three main classes, established that '. . . only 55 per cent of the population could be regarded as correctly placed if intelligence were the only criterion: nearly 23 per cent are in a class too high . . . 22 per cent are in a class too low.'[45] Turning to movement between classes (and more will be said in chapter 5), there is less traffic out of and into the top and bottom than would be expected if the transmission of genetic *differences* were allowed to operate unhindered.[46] Intelligence alone does not determine social-class position while factors other than biological ones must be used to explain the lack of social mobility.

This section has been dealing with the proposition that poverty can be explained by individual differences of inherited intelligence. In response, it has not been argued that biological transmission plays no part in the formation of intelligence. Nor is it argued that IQ tests can play no part in predicting educational or occupational levels. However, it has been shown not only that intelligence is shaped by a mixture of influences but that high intelligence does not necessarily lead to educational success, the best-paid occupations or high social class. The general arguments, the trends, the figures can all be called upon to show that inherited intelligence is not the cause of poverty. However, they do not illustrate in any detailed or personal way how social factors can inhibit the development of an intelligent person. For a graphic example of such an individual, reference should be made to the autobiography of Pat Chapman. A talented and persistent woman, she yet lived a life of poverty and suffering. Denied educational opportunities, she fought for the chance both to express her creativity and to maintain her family unit. Refused access to an occupation with an adequate income, she also met rebuffs from lawyers and doctors who channelled her into a servile position. At times, she began to accept that she was inadequate, unable to contribute to life or to care for her family. Of Pat Chapman's intelligence—as revealed in her writings—there can be little doubt, but it was not enough to save her from social deprivations. Faced with social pressures that demanded she see herself as 'a failure', she found it almost impossible to break free.[47]

Both personal autobiographies and large-scale studies make reference to the social factors which help to promote or hinder intelligence, educational success, occupation and social-class position. What are these factors? Here mention must be limited to two which are awarded some prominence by recent authors. Firstly, inherited wealth. Atkinson has assayed to document the extent of inherited wealth and income in our society,[48] while Giddens has shown that—despite popular notions about self-made men—most wealthy people have achieved their position through being left money.[49] It follows that persons of limited intelligence may maintain a position of affluence despite their lack of ability. To cite Rutter and Madge again,

> Inherited wealth, property or business are protection against downward social mobility. An individual may inherit resources which give him a socially prestigious position which, on the basis of his own abilities and interests, he would not otherwise have attained.[50]

Secondly, social class. Once again, members of the lowest social class appear in a particularly disadvantageous position. Insofar as intelligence is developed by environment, they frequently lack the amenities, possessions, housing conditions and experiences which increase IQ scores. But even where their intelligence is comparable with that of members of other classes they still have less chance of attaining the education and occupations which can remove them from the threat of poverty. Accordingly, any explanations of poverty must consider these wide-ranging general economic and social tendencies which work for some sections of the population but against others.

## Genetic Mental Disorder

Although not to the same volume, voices are occasionally heard claiming that poverty occurs in individuals unfortunate enough to inherit biologically certain mental or psychiatric disorders. Apparently, the disorders make the individuals unfit for normal occupations and they sink to a life of poverty.

The debate over the genesis of psychiatric illness has raged as fiercely as that over intelligence and has similarly divided along nature-versus-nurture lines. It is impossible to summarise adequately the various views in a short space. Nonetheless, it is fair to say that few writers would now claim that it can be fully attributed to either biological transmission or environmental pressures. There is strong evidence that genetic factors do contribute to schizophrenia and psychopathy, and possibly some indications of a genetic component to neuroticism. Biological links with other mental disorders are less likely.[51] However, it should be added that schizophrenia and psychopathy also occur where, apparently, there is no genetic link. Further, it may take certain environmental stresses to trigger off disorders.[52]

Whatever the genetic element in psychiatric disorders, no studies establish that such disorders are the cause of poverty. They may make their victims more vulnerable to social distress, and there is some suggestion that inner-ring deprived areas attract a high proportion of schizophrenics. But, although some mentally ill persons may be poor, there is no evidence that the poor are predominantly schizophrenic or psychopathic. Further, it appears that other mentally disordered persons avoid poverty. Indeed, the drive and obsessive qualities of some disorders may actually favour the accumulation of wealth. Poverty cannot be attributed to genetically inherited psychiatric illness.

### Poverty and Genetics

This section has considered the premise that poverty arises because some individuals biologically inherit weaknesses or limitations. Certainly, there is a genetic element in intelligence and some mental disorders but for three main reasons this does not constitute an explanation of poverty. Firstly, biological mechanisms promote differences as well as similarities. Secondly, even if genetics do predispose individuals towards poverty, they do not explain why poverty is tolerated by society. Eysenck—who leans heavily towards biological accounts—discusses a range of social interventions designed to save from poverty those whose own limitations propel them towards it.[53] Yet society has not made such interventions. Why? The question calls for a societal rather than an individual explanation. Thirdly, genetics cannot be used to account wholly for intelligence and psychiatric disorders. They are also moulded by outside pressures. Indeed, it may be a false distraction to talk continually of nature and nurture as separate entities. Thoday points out that every human characteristic depends initially on having the '... necessary genetic endowment ...' and on the environmental stimulus to develop it or to allow it to function.[54] Understanding of poverty must be pursued by asking why the stimuli are provided for some sections of society, but not others.

## Economic Man

An influential contribution to the discussion of the causes of social deprivation derives from a school of writers who emphasise the role of individuals in the free market system of economic life. 'Free' is used in the sense of freedom from state control of production, buying and selling. The features of this free or capitalist system were particularly identified during the eighteenth and nineteenth centuries when more rapid industrialisation led to an advanced division of labour and the formation of large-scale private enterprise. Amongst the more important features were:

(a) competition in the 'market place' between various sellers and buyers. The competition stimulated further specialisation in manufacture and distribution in order to improve efficiency in the struggle for success.

(b) the existence of the 'cash nexus' as the means through which competitors related to each other and the market. In short, the determining factor in obtaining goods was not need or altruism but price.

(c) the acceptance of the 'laws' of demand and supply as determining not only prices of goods but also the supply of land, labour and capital.

### The Free Market and the Individual

A number of notable authors, particularly Hayek,[55] Friedman[56] and Lees,[57] have written persuasively of the advantages of the free market economy as against a planned or state-controlled one. They argue that private firms functioning within the framework of supply and demand lead to greater *efficiency*. Lees believes that this system provides both consumer goods and welfare goods (such as pensions and health care) more cheaply and more capably than other economic systems. Explaining its merits, Lees states,

> Suppliers would be more responsive to wishes of consumers. Competition would tend to reduce costs. Dispersion of decision making power would enable more effective use to be made of existing

knowledge and give greater scope for experiment and innovation.[58]

Thus, under the demands of competition, manufacturers of both welfare and consumer goods are provoked to higher standards while inefficient organisations go to the wall.

As well as being more efficient, the advocates of the free market believe it supports certain *freedoms*. Initially, there is the freedom of firms to produce as they wish and of consumers to choose what they wish. If goods and wages are priced and made available through the almost untrammelled operation of the laws of supply and demand then, it is argued, the consumer is king and can decide his own wants simply by his choice whether to buy a certain good or not. Lees puts it thus: 'Logic and experience alike tell us that it is only in competitive markets, working through prices determined by supply and demand, that consumers call the tune.'[59] Such arguments are applied not only to consumer goods but also to welfare goods and services. If these are also supplied by private firms in competition with each other, then the consumer is free to choose the hospital, doctor, school, etc., which suits his desires.

The economic freedom of the consumer is then equated with political and social freedom. If consumers and firms are not free from the state, then it is argued that the way is open for the state to control other aspects of their lives. Friedman links the free market system to a movement or philosophy of freedom:

> ... in the late eighteenth century and early nineteenth centuries, the intellectual movement that went under the name of liberalism emphasised freedom as the ultimate goal and the individual as the ultimate entity in the society. It supported laissez-faire at home as a means of reducing the role of the state in economic affairs and thereby enlarging the role of the individual.[60]

Thus, economic freedom is seen as a condition for all freedoms. The free market system is considered supreme in that it upholds efficiency and freedom. Enoch Powell terms it the 'irresistible market'.[61] It follows that any trends towards state controls of production or welfare should be resisted. Not all free market advocates, it must be interjected, are opposed to all state interventions. Even the classic exponent of free trade, Adam Smith, considered some state education to be necessary. The nineteenth-century supporters of 'laissez-faire' generally supported legislation to protect child labourers even if opposed to factory legislation in general.[62] The claim is that state interference should not be so great as to disturb the competitive system between private interests, should '. . . not distort the market or impede its functioning' and so should not undermine efficiency and individual freedom.[63]

The protagonists of the free market system explicitly state its advantages as freedom and efficiency. This also involves the implicit recognition that both the workings of the system and their definitions of its advantages depend upon a particular view of individual motivation. They regard men and women as primarily motivated by individual, economic self-interest. The laws of supply and demand are held to operate because individuals are so made that they seek to sell (their goods or labour) to the highest bidder and to buy (goods or labour) from the cheapest. It follows that a person's income or wealth reflects his economic worth. Thus man is seen as economic man to such an extent that society should be organised mainly around this facet of his nature. Further, if people are allowed to be economically free, to trade and spend as they choose, then they are masters of their own lives. As Friedman explains, they can be considered individually responsible for their own destinies.[64]

## Poverty in the Free Market

The workings of the capitalist system were largely identified and defined during the eighteenth and nineteenth centuries. Although in the twentieth century the laws of supply and demand are still held to function in Western society, it is clear that state intervention into the spheres of production and welfare has modified market forces. Nationalised industries, even if required to make a profit, may lack competition from similar industries. Extensive social-security, education, housing, health and social-work provisions have meant that many welfare goods are not paid for as a straight economic transaction. The 'cash nexus' is not universal. It follows that the advocates of the free market have to explain social deprivations within economies where private enterprise is largely unchallenged as well as in what can be called welfare economies. Here attention will be given to their explanation of poverty in the free market.

From Adam Smith to the present day, upholders of the market system have studied the large-scale economic and social factors which make up any economy. Yet within this, many have tended to explain poverty in terms of individual failings. Within the private enterprise system, as Friedman said, people can be considered wholly responsible for their actions and conditions. The market forces allocate monetary rewards to those with talent, initiative and effort and those who fall into poverty have only their own moral and physical limitations to blame. Poverty is thus chiefly attributable to individual laziness. Bremner, in his study of attitudes towards the poor, summarises this outlook as follows: 'Indigence was simply the punishment meted out to the improvident by their own lack of industry and efficiency. Far from being a blessed state, poverty was the obvious consequence of sloth and sinfulness.'[65] Alternatively, it could be regarded as the result of physical or mental handicaps which meant that the individuals concerned had marketable skills of little worth. Even so, here too was the implied judgement that even the handicapped could compensate by extra effort.

Such opinions, as Bremner shows, were typically expressed in Victorian times. But they still persist today and individuals may still be held responsible for not availing themselves of the opportunities offered by private enterprise. Page blames the unemployment of some on their dislike of work and their willingness to live off the state.[66] In similar vein, Friedman says that some people choose not to save and must thus be held individually responsible for their '. . . penurious old age'.[67] Enoch Powell forcibly states that private firms are responsible for maximising profits, with the implication that it is not their brief to promote the welfare of their employees.[68] It is the responsibility of individuals to see that they earn enough to stave off poverty. The message is still clear that where the free market system allows demand and supply mechanisms to operate then the opportunities exist to make money. Should they lack the drive or inclination to avail themselves of earning opportunities, the responsibility must rest with themselves as individuals rather than with management or government.

*Poverty in the Welfare State*

The free market no longer exists in its nineteenth-century form. The succeeding century has not abolished private enterprise but it has challenged its supremacy by the creation of public industries and the expansion of central and local government education, housing and social services. The modern successors to Smith, Malthus, Mill, Ricardo and other classical economists are by no means opposed to all these developments. Indeed, nearly all would favour state provision of social security benefits at subsistence levels, and state education for those unable to buy their own. However, in general, far from diminishing poverty they argue that the welfare expansion actually increases those aspects of mankind which are to be blamed for poverty.

Firstly, it is held that easily available welfare benefits reduce the incentive to work. Social security benefits, they continue, have reached the level where people are content with life on the dole. The theme is not original. De Tocqueville over a hundred years before warned:

> There are two incentives to work: the need to live and the desire to improve the conditions of life. Experience has proven that the majority of men can be sufficiently motivated to work only by the first of these incentives. The second is only effective with a small minority .... A law which gives all the poor a right to public aid, whatever the origin of their poverty, weakens or destroys the first stimulant and leaves only the second intact.[69]

Public aid is now established and writers such as Friedman and Boyson fear that de Tocqueville has been proved right. The former believes that any state aid '... reduces the incentives of those helped to help themselves'.[70] The latter, in discussing the modern social security system, claims:

> There is also encouragement for the lower paid with large families to become unemployed or to go sick. Similarly, millions of workers

are encouraged to break the monotony of factory routine by strikes
when meagre strike pay can be augmented by supplementary benefits
to their families and tax rebates for themselves.[71]

The reduction of the desire to work means that some individuals
are not motivated to take themselves from the bottom rank
of income recipients. But, further, their readiness to take from
others places a burden on taxpayers. Boyson believes that money
is taken '. . . from the energetic, successful and thrifty to give
to the idle, the failures and the feckless'.[72] Consequently, the
readiness of taxpayers to work is sapped as they see their
earnings taken from them. As the malaise spreads so the whole
nation is infected. Boyson complains that '. . . the general sense
of responsibility and personal pride declines. National economic
strength and personal moral fibre are both reduced.'[73] Seldon
adds '. . . a society in which we are allowed or encouraged
to get as much as we can from one another does not foster
self-respect, morality or integrity.'[74]

In brief, the advocates of the free market system argue that
large-scale state services both impair the traditional route to
escape poverty—by individual hard work—and also promote
a selfish nation unwilling to create the resources with which
to help each other. Further, the tone of some of the leaders
of this school—but by no means all—is that the poor have
avidly taken advantage of the social services, being content
to enjoy free benefits rather than working for themselves and
the nation. The poor are still to be blamed for their poverty.

Secondly, the welfare state is accused of holding back economic
progress by weakening the basic economic unit of society—the
family. In America, this theme has been aggressively articulated
by Irving Kristol, who is concerned at the effects on the male
spouse of welfare benefits being available to women:

Above all, welfare robs the head of the household of his economic
function, and tends to make of him a 'superfluous man'. Welfare
it must be remembered, *competes* with his (usually low) earning
ability; and the more generous the welfare programme, the worse
he makes out in this competition . . . Is it surprising, then, that—un-
manned and demoralized—he removes himself from family responsibilities that no longer rest on his shoulders?[75]

Kristol's assertion is that, as women can receive as much from welfare as they can from low-income husbands, the family has no need of the latter, who therefore abandon their homes. Social services, accordingly, lead to social disorganisation in the form of family breakdowns. Poverty is caused because the fathers are not encouraged to work in order to support their families, while the male children receive no model of the hard-working male figure on which to shape their future lives.

In Britain, a more sophisticated and persuasive case has been put forward by the psychologist Bremner. She starts with the major points that the growth of statutory services has made families dependent upon the state rather than upon its members. Families now lean on welfare provision for a whole range of things such as housing, income, education and moral support. Bremner believes this dependency impinges upon moral freedom, which she sees as the capacity to judge and act upon alternative courses.[76] Further, she asserts that it harms personal and family growth by making the population immature and childlike.[77] Her reasoning is in common with Seldon, another leading figure of the Institute of Economic Affairs. He also claims that welfare leads to dependency which morally impoverishes the family: 'State welfare encourages the notion that the "state" should provide, not the family or individual: it has thus impoverished us by inciting us to beggar and demean one another.'[78]

How does the dependency and maturity affect economic life? Dependent families, it is claimed, do not possess the qualities of drive and initiative which are necessary both to improve the lot of each family and to increase national resources as a whole. Dependent families lack the motivation and therefore the freedom to invest their economic talents. Further, drawing upon statements by the American Haggstrom, Bremner shows that the dependency of the poor can create the family traits of extreme aggression or apathy. Behaviour of this kind may make family members unsuitable for employment or may even threaten the continuing harmony of the unit. At worst, the family may break up, making one section of it completely dependent upon social security benefits.

The imposition of dependency is growing but, according to Bremner, is also resented. She draws upon a specially commissioned survey to demonstrate that most people prefer that they, rather than the government, should decide how much of their money should be spent on housing, holidays, retirement and medical treatment. She believes, therefore, that most families are opposed to the loss of their economic freedoms.

It will be recalled that the chapter is considering explanations which focus on individuals. The present section has put forward the view that the replacement of the free market by the welfare state system has developed individual and family behaviour which promotes rather than lessens poverty. The third side to the case of the free marketers is not specifically related to individuals but for the sake of completeness will be included here. In general the theme is that the overall impact of extensive state universal services has dire economic consequences. As mentioned before, it is asserted that the costs of the services raise income tax to such a level that the incentive to earn is reduced. If the desire to earn is lowered, then the accumulation of the nation's wealth will decline.

Apart from heavier taxation, it is claimed that the vast grip imposed by the state on welfare services drives away the economic and social contribution which private enterprise could make. For instance, the fall in the number of and quality of private houses to let is almost certainly connected with the expansion of council housing and legal restraints (especially rent control) placed on private landlords. Boyson even complains that 'Housing subsidies and rent controls ... have produced the appalling slums and homelessness of the present day.'[79] Whether this be so or not, there can be little doubt that private landlords now contribute less to the growth of the housing stock.

The restraints placed on private welfare enterprises are regretted by writers such as Boyson, Seldon and Lees for another reason. They believe that private services are more efficient than state ones. For instance, they argue that private pension schemes have to compete with each other. They have to be efficient in order to attract custom. Therefore they waste less money than state pension schemes, which are compulsory. The profits made by the private companies can then be ploughed back into economic life to contribute to a more affluent society. As Seldon expands, 'The market creates more wealth than state direction because it mobilises the resources and talents of every individual, who can use knowledge that is beyond the capacity of officials or planners to organise.'[80]

By contrast, state services are regarded as inefficient and wasteful. By using up but not creating resources they are held to reduce the economic assets of the nation. Consequently, there is less money available for the low-paid and their financial position is made worse not better. As Boyson forcibly sums up his views, 'Where poverty remains it is the fault of politicians whose double sin has been to spread benefits too widely and raise taxes on a scale that hinders the increase in the national income.'[81] The exponents of the 'economic man' explanation thus regard extensive state welfare services as harmful, not beneficial. They imperil the individual and family motivations which cause people to work their way out of poverty, while simultaneously harming national economic powers which could have been used for the benefit of all income groups.

## Solutions

The contemporary supporters of the free market are no more insensitive to the problem of poverty than were the classical economists. They, therefore, do propose solutions which, not surprisingly, reflect the nature of their explanations of poverty.

The modification of poverty is associated by the authors with a return to a private enterprise economy. In regard to welfare matters, two main objectives are articulated. Firstly, a reduction of state involvement in the provision of social services (and consumer goods). Writers such as Friedman and Boyson envisage a massive withdrawal of statutory involvement. Boyson wants housing completely out of local authority and central government control while other '. . . legislation and state interference should be cut back and limited to a requirement that all should insure against ill-health, misfortune and old age.'[82] Friedman calls for the substantial reduction of state education and even for the abolition of legislation which compels people to insure themselves against misfortune.[83] More moderate voices envisage a continuing and significant state contribution but not to the

*Poverty*

extent of a virtual state monopoly over welfare. The second objective is the expansion of private social services ranging from fee-paying schools to health, unemployment and pension schemes run by private-enterprise companies.

Taken in conjunction with a more general return to the free market, the reduction of state social services and the availability of private alternatives, the advocates would see man as becoming 'free' again. Poverty would be countered in the following ways. The opportunity to make money, the removal of high taxation and limitations placed on state benefits would encourage people to work. Fewer would be unemployed, more would take themselves out of the low-income brackets. As families would be less dependent on the state, parents would have to accept responsibilities for their children, and the qualities of initiative, hard work and pride in achievement would be stimulated. Meanwhile, the growth of private welfare schemes would lead to greater efficiency. Individuals would receive better services when sick, old or unemployed (and so would receive more money), while the need to insure themselves with the best private companies would encourage the traits of thrift and foresight. Simultaneously, the efficient enterprises would be ploughing their profits back into the market. As Seldon claims, 'National economic expansion can best be helped by putting welfare by stages into the market where the consumer will rule instead of the politician.'[84] The economic expansion would mean the availability of extra resources to be shared out amongst the population. Thus both individuals and the economy would be better placed to deal with the possibility of poverty.

The construction of multiple private schemes and services would not obviate the need for some state schemes. Some individuals might not join the former and hence it is conceded that a statutory 'safety net' should save them from destitution. However, such state services should be limited to the really needy by the use of means tests. Lees writes: 'A means test is a fact of life that we cannot afford to do without. In the present discussion of reform of social security, the question is not whether to have a means test or not but what form it should take.'[85] Such selective tests would not only keep down the amount of money spent on social services but would further encourage individuals to insure privately against the prospect of having to endure them. The tests thus imply some measure of blame or condemnation upon those who use them. Its justification is that the incentive to work is thereby strengthened still further. Such sentiments have much in common with that of Benjamin Franklin: 'I think the best way of doing good to the poor is not making them easy *in* poverty, but leading or driving them *out* of it.'[86]

Before leaving the solutions proposed by the advocates of the free market, it is worth noting that some have now suggested a scheme to tackle poverty which would actually involve considerable statutory involvement. In another publication by the Institute of Economic Affairs, Christopher, Polanyi, Seldon and Shenfield argue for the introduction of Reverse Income Tax.[87] RIT would mean using the income tax system to make payments to persons whose incomes fell below a particular poverty line.

Whatever the implications for statutory involvement in the above suggestion, two final points can be made about the proposed solutions of the free marketers. Firstly, any relief of poverty is limited to levels which would still retain clear differences between different sections of the population. Thus Christopher, Polanyi, Seldon and Shenfield accept the minimum rates of supplementary benefit as the poverty line whether it is attained by RIT or any other means. If man is primarily motivated by economic considerations, then it follows that considerable differences in rewards and standards of living must continue if he is to be encouraged to work hard enough to reach the higher material reaches. The aim is usually to alleviate the stringencies experienced by those at the very bottom but not to promote greater equality in any significant way. Secondly, a major objective is to recognise the autonomy of individuals by freeing them from the restrictions of the state. If state control of production and welfare is loosened then the individual can choose. As Friedman states, '. . . a major aim of the liberal is to leave the ethical problem for the individual to wrestle with.'[88] If the free individual chooses to achieve and save, that is to his credit. If he chooses to be idle, then his poverty is his responsibility. The free system, according to its advocates, offers him the alternatives.

*Criticisms of Economic Man*

The supporters of the competitive, free market system, particularly
the work of the Institute of Economic Affairs in Britain and
Friedman in the USA, have stimulated much controversy and
criticism. Notably, however, much of the debate has focussed
on the relative merits of universal and selective social services,
their costs, effectiveness and outreach. Little attention can be
given here to that debate. The points to be made in this section
are direct criticisms of the claims that poverty can be explained
either by individual deficiencies within the free market or by
recent state interference with that market. Implicit in the criticisms
is a challenge to the belief that man is primarily an economic
being.

A basic tenet of the advocates of the free market is that
it gives rewards to those willing to work hard, use their initiative
and be thrifty. Being a 'free' system, it allows such individuals
to use their economic talents. However, if consideration is given
to the nineteenth and early part of the twentieth centuries—before
state intervention challenged the primacy of private enterprise—
then the historical evidence does not show such straightforward
procedures in operation. Notably, it was during the heyday
of 'laissez-faire' that widespread poverty first made its impact
on public notice. Charles Booth, who contributed to that impact,
castigated those individuals who did not want to work, but
he also pointed to a more substantial number who wanted
to work but could not find employment and to those who
worked hard but received incomes too small for their needs.[89]
As mentioned in chapter 1, Seebohm Rowntree made similar
observations from his survey carried out at the end of the
nineteenth century. In 1910 an official government report also
emphasised the powerlessness of individuals, no matter how
well motivated, when circumstances were against them:

> The evidence is overwhelming of the evil consequences arriving
> from intermittent employment and irregular earnings. It is obviously
> a matter of considerable difficulty, if not impossibility, to arrange
> the family budget with any regard to thrift, when the incomes
> hardly ever represent a full week's work ....[90]

Highly skilled craftsmen, anxious to exercise their trade, could

also face destitution. Middleton's work examining the 1930s
reveals skilled carpenters, masons and gardeners who wanted
to work hard but were compelled to do nothing.[91] On the
other hand, amongst the rich and powerful in the nineteenth
century were some who appeared lazy, feckless, immoral and
lacking in talents. But market forces did not bring them to
poverty any more than take Booth's hard workers out of it.

No doubt effort, initiative and drive may help some persons
out of poverty, just as laziness and apathy may push others
down. But these virtues or vices cannot account for all affluence
or all social deprivations. The reason is that the theory of
the free market, of the perfect balance between demand and
supply, of the appropriate rewards for effort, is based on a
hypothetical situation. In practice, as Lees himself concedes,
'The market allocation process works imperfectly....'[92] A
number of external factors intervene which constrain the individual's powers to bargain, buy, sell and work.

What are these external factors? Some have already been
listed in the discussion about genetic man. Firstly, the inheritance
of wealth. Atkinson shows how crucial is the part played by
inherited resources.[93] Its possessors have an immediate economic
advantage over others. Further, they will avoid poverty even
if they do not wish to work. Secondly, there is education.
Education and training are not distributed equally to all citizens
and are not even allocated according to ability. Consequently,
some persons are not able to develop their talents so as to
offer them to the market. Further, use of the market both
in regard to obtaining work and purchasing the cheapest and
best goods requires information. As such information is usually
more available to the better-educated, the less well-educated
are at a disadvantage. Thus, regardless of their willingness to
work, their initiative, their thrift, they are at a considerable
handicap when it comes to finding employment and to purchasing
worthwhile goods. Thirdly, there are the large-scale economic
and social trends. In both Victorian and contemporary Britain,
unemployment and low wages were linked with national and
international trade recessions. Against such forces, individual
effort seemed insignificant. Again, both centuries have seen population shifts from the inner cities to the suburbs. As resources
and jobs left certain areas, those residents forced to remain—

because of age or family ties or the lack of money to move—often faced poverty.[94] By the end of the nineteenth century, and increasingly during the twentieth, large-scale organisations were shaping the economy. Extensive, interlocking private firms could decide on output and set their prices and negotiate with trade unions over levels of employment and wages. The collective forces outweighed those of individuals. It is not surprising that Cassen should conclude that individuals do not have freedom in the 'free' market, for many external factors limit or constrain the use they make of their contribution.[95] The socially deprived have the least claim to be entitled 'free'. If lacking in education, they probably have very limited choice of careers. In times of recession they may have no alternative but to be unemployed. If lacking information, they may not be well equipped to purchase the best goods. If lacking money, they will not be able to afford private social services.

The contention being evaluated is that in the private enterprise system the market rewards the willing and able individuals by taking them out of poverty. The conclusion is that, even within economic systems dominated by private enterprise, individuals are not in control. As Josephine Shaw Lowell wrote of those plunged into poverty by the recession of the 1890s, the condition is '. . . as much beyond their power to avert as if they had been natural calamities of fire, flood or storm'.[96] However, this conclusion is not meant to contest the moral value that people *should* work. Nor is it questioned that hard work is often one of the requirements involved in making money. The point is rather that even in a system where state intervention in commerce and welfare is at a minimum, poverty cannot be explained in terms of individual weaknesses and failings. It follows that man cannot be regarded as subject only to the economic forces of demand and supply. Rather there are wider social movements of population, and the political organisation of employers and employees, which also shape his conditions and responses. Further, it will be shown in succeeding chapters that people's behaviour and aspirations are influenced by cultural and social-class values which do not necessarily make economic profit the end of being. Men and women will sometimes take employment even when they can receive more from social security benefits. They work because there is a social expectation that they should do so. They may take employment because it satisfies needs for company and emotional support. They may refuse higher-paid posts in order to undertake those which they feel are more enjoyable or worthwhile. People are not exclusively dominated by the profit motive, and their behaviour must be set in its social as well as its economic context. Poverty cannot be satisfactorily explained by reference to individuals' economic drives within a free market system.

Turning from the free market, it will be recalled that the more recent welfare society was accused of increasing, even creating, poverty by reducing the motivation to work, harming the family, forming inefficient services and draining the economy. How valid are these points?

The heart of the matter concerns whether the extensive modern state social services do make people less willing to labour, more ready to sponge off the state. In one sense the question is impossible to answer. No studies in Britain, to the writer's knowledge, have examined scientifically a group of people subjected first to a lack of welfare services and then subsequently to an extensive state system. However, it is possible to enquire whether the wish to work still exists in modern society. The answer would appear to be a definite affirmative. Attitudes towards employment will be further discussed in a subsequent chapter. Here it suffices to report that extensive research amongst the poor and the unemployed by Goodwin,[97] Daniel[98] and Hill[99] found the desire to work still strong. However, continuing unemployment may make some give up in despair of ever getting a job. Interestingly, even the report by the Institute of Economic Affairs now accepts that Reverse Income Tax would not be a work disincentive.[100] It can be concluded that talk of modern statutory benefits destroying the work motive, initiative and 'moral fibre' has no supporting evidence.

Similarly, the case that modern social services have made families so dependent upon the state that their motivation to function as economic units is impaired, does not stand close scrutiny. Kristol claimed that the availability of welfare benefits to women as well as men encourages the latter to desert, knowing the former will not starve even if impoverished. Yet there is no clear connection between family break-up and welfare availability. Divorce rates are no higher in countries with advanced welfare systems, such as Britain, Sweden and New Zealand, than in those with less reliance on extensive social services. Indeed, the divorce rate in the USA is greater than that in Sweden although the former has far less state involvement in welfare.[101] Of course, separations and desertions can occur without a formal divorce, yet as Fletcher demonstrates, they happened before the rise of the welfare state, while there is no substantial evidence to show that marriage and the family unit is a declining institution.[102]

Turning to the more reasoned explanation forwarded by Bremner, it will be recalled that she asserts that families have become too dependent on the state, that dependency leads to behaviour which aggravates or causes poverty, and that a survey proves that people desire to be more free of state interference. She thus perceives a causal link between the social services and the impoverishment of the family.

Bremner's view that the freedom of families to choose for themselves has been removed by state services appears to assume that most families were free in some previous era. Yet one of the strongest arguments for introducing state social services was precisely that, under the former private-enterprise system, families had no choice but to accept low incomes, no freedom to obtain medical and educational benefits, and no right to help from the personal social services. Thus modern supporters of the welfare state, particularly Townsend and Titmuss, justify extensive social services on the grounds that they promote healthy family life. Certainly, the income maintenance, housing and health services can claim to have alleviated the gross social deprivations which broke up so many families in Victorian times. Although poverty can still be a major factor associated with children being separated from their families,[103] there is no comparison—as Middleton so vividly documents—with the ill-health, destitution and early mortalities which tore families asunder in the era before the welfare state.[104] Further, there is no unequivocal evidence that modern families feel less responsibility for their members. A number of studies of families indicate that greater geographical mobility does make contact more difficult, yet notwithstanding the greater difficulties, kinship ties are still strong and the family remains the greatest and most useful social service in the country.[105] Amongst the very poor, there is case evidence of parents making enormous efforts and sacrifices to maintain their families.[106] In general, families still uphold their economic and other responsibilities. Members are still eager to work in order to support their kin.

Next, it is important to comment on Bremner's use of Haggstrom's work to argue that welfare services lead to dependency which, in turn, promotes extremes of behaviour—ranging from aggression to apathy—that inhibit work, enterprise and initiative. Haggstrom's thesis was rather that the dependency and unhelpful behaviour were related to long-standing poverty, low levels of welfare benefits, and the spirit of condemnation with which they are sometimes administered. The implication is that poverty promotes dependency, not that dependency leads to poverty. Haggstrom's paper is entitled 'The Power of the Poor' and he concludes that the poor must break their dependency by pressing for social reforms. Far from supporting Bremner's position, Haggstrom actually advocates stronger statutory social services.[107]

Lastly, some methodological doubts must be raised concerning the survey employed by Bremner. The opening statement of the questionnaire, which was read out to interviewees, contained loaded sentiments about persons making their 'own decisions' rather than having the government doing so for them. There then followed a list of personal decisions which the interviewees were asked whether they or the government should make. Obviously, the structure of such questions is akin to self-fulfilling prophecies, and the respondents opt to be free from an apparently oppressive state government. Yet if the opening statement had been loaded in the opposite direction, claiming that government help could free people to have better living conditions, etc., then different answers would have been given. But whatever the result of the survey, it does not, in any way, show that state social services lead to family behaviour of a kind which precipitates people into poverty.

Lastly, the advent of the welfare state was considered to contribute to rather than prevent poverty by creating wasteful, inefficient state services which not only offered an inferior service but were a drain on the economy. The debate about the relative merits of statutory and private welfare services is too well rehearsed to need repeating here. The supporters of extensive state services, led by Titmuss and Townsend have made the following powerful points.[108] Firstly, a combination of private welfare for the affluent and public welfare just for low-income persons usually entails low-status and inferior services for the latter and so reinforces their functioning at the bottom of society. Secondly, extensive services (such as health and education) can offer a more evenly spread resource to all the nation. Such services can be paid for out of national expenditure—so avoiding means tests—but with the income tax system recouping money from those able to contribute. Thirdly, state services are more efficient than private ones. Titmuss's comparison of the British National Health Service and the private health companies of the USA is a well-known example of this argument. It must be added that although state services are costly and non-profit-making, they can be regarded as making investments. The educational sector prepares and trains youngsters for positions of employment. Health services contribute to maintaining a fit work-force. And so on. If the qualifications, skills and health of contemporary workers are compared with those of the days before the welfare state, then the contribution of the statutory social services becomes obvious. The creation of workers for industry is not the sole or even the main purpose of the social services. But they do contribute to this end and hence it is not justifiable to dismiss their costs as wasteful or non-productive.

*Usefulness of the Explanation*

Explanations which blame poverty on the natural weaknesses of individuals in the free market or on the individual failings stimulated by welfare services founder when set against the part played by large-scale social and economic forces in creating social conditions and rewards. Consequently, the solutions proposed by the free marketers would not modify poverty. A return to the private-enterprise system of the nineteenth century would not equip the low-income recipient to cope with national economic recessions any more than it did a hundred years ago. A large-scale reduction in statutory social services would not improve work habits or modes of family functioning.

However, the analysis and the evaluation of the economic

man explanation do indicate some aspects worth pursuing. Firstly, the advocates of the free market have strongly criticised the statutory social services and highlighted some of their weaknesses. They have thereby raised the possibility that social services can contribute to as well as modify social deprivation. Secondly, by continually stressing individuality they have acted as a balance to views which only emphasise national or international movements. This tension between the micro and the macro has a long history. Any reader of William Booth's account of Victorian poverty will be aware of it. The General always took pains to state men and women's individual relationship to God and their individual responsibility for their actions. Yet he also blamed poverty on collective forces, on '. . . a society, which by its habits, its customs, and its laws, has greased the slope down which these poor creatures slide to perdition'.[109] It appears that any explanation of social deprivation, while not accepting the individual as a completely independent being, must examine the manner in which social and economic circumstances affect individual behaviour and the manner in which individuals react to or against such circumstances.

If poverty is to be abolished or substantially modified, then obviously some changes will occur in society. The champions of economic laissez-faire—which they identify with individual freedom—provoke thought about the kind of society that is desirable. They argue that under a fully socialised state—as in parts of eastern Europe—people do not possess the freedom to trade, to choose from a wide range of goods, to choose the occupation they desire. They identify these freedoms as essential values in society and would not forfeit them even in order to reduce social deprivation. But the issue is not simply that of freedom versus poverty. A number of authors who are as fully committed to private enterprise as Hayek, Boyson and Friedman now concede that the free market or capitalist system also restrains certain freedoms. One, the former cabinet minister, Peter Walker MP, wrote:

> For many of our fellow country-men their freedom under the law is the freedom to live in one room in an ugly tenement building . . . the freedom to work in noisy, dirty factory conditions which many of us would be unwilling to tolerate.[110]

Similarly, Meade, while supporting the economic freedoms of the free market, also calls for extensive state intervention as the means of contributing to (not causing) a more equal spread of incomes. He has thus, as a supporter of free enterprise, moved to accept man's right not just to choose on the market but also his right to protection against the ill-effects of the market.[111] Men like Walker and Meade are asking whether it is possible to have a society which retains both the private freedom to trade, buy and sell and the individual freedom to escape from slums, deprivation and poverty. Their voices indicate that it is not sufficient just to offer an explanation of social deprivation. For once this leads on to proposals for solutions, when other issues have to be considered. A major one is which freedoms can be retained in a society which is committed to the abolition of poverty? The raising of this issue, which will be discussed towards the end of this book, owes much to the work of the supporters of economic man.

## PROBLEM MAN

The idea that the majority of the problems of society could be located in a small minority of individuals or families has been popular throughout this century. Titmuss commented on a long but discontinuous concern with '. . . a segment of families in the population, supposedly characterised by similar traits, and thought to represent a closed, pathological entity'.[112] The families certainly came to public attention during the Second World War probably, as Hall suggests, because evacuation brought middle-class people into contact with such families.[113] It was during these years that the Pacifist Service Units developed a particular concern and expertise for dealing with problem families. After the war they became the Family Service Units (FSU), a federation of units now operating in over twenty towns, whose social workers have offered an intensive service to such clients.

What are problem families? They have been described as '. . . always on the edge of pauperism and crime, riddled with mental and physical defects, in and out of the courts for child neglect, a menace to the community of which the gravity is out of all proportion to their numbers'.[114] An even more lurid portrait is:

> ... the home, if indeed it can be described as such, has usually the most striking characteristics, nauseating odours assail one's nostrils on entering and the source is usually located in some urine sodden faecal-stained mattress in the upstairs room. There are no floor coverings, no decorations on the walls, except perhaps for the scribblings of the children and bizarre patterns formed by absent plaster. Furniture is of the most primitive, cooking utensils absent, facilities for sleeping hopeless.[115]

Going beyond description, a number of authors, finding it impossible to define problem families, have listed their problems or characteristics. Amongst the most frequently mentioned are a lack of care for their homes, low standards of child care, poor health, an inability to respond to the social services and social-work help, and delinquent or criminal behaviour.[116] In addition, they typically received low incomes and experienced poor housing conditions. Wootton, commenting on the studies, says that poverty is the common characteristic.[117] Hall, at least, is prepared to use the material to make a definition, stating

> ... the phrase appears to denote families with multiple problems whose standards of living, and particularly child care, are markedly low, and who seem to be little influenced by, or even resistant to, measures of general social amelioration.[118]

The picture that emerged from such writings in the 1950s and 1960s was of an almost ineducable minority whose multiplicity of problems and adverse behaviour made them quite distinct from the rest of society. As they also tended to have large families, Wright and Lunn found the situation 'alarming'.[119] The fear was that their habits and example might spread. As far as this chapter is concerned, the significant feature was that problem families were often regarded as the poor and that the explanation offered for their existence was a psychological one stressing the interaction between individuals.

*Psychological Explanations*

Problem families have been regarded, as Wootton points out, as the main element in crime, immorality, unemployment and a host of other social problems.[120] In regard to poverty, the argument has involved three steps. Firstly, poverty is not necessary in the welfare state. Secondly, those who are poor tend to be individuals or families with a multiplicity of problems, that is problem families. Thirdly, the reason for their problems tends to be psychological. These three strands can now be considered in more detail. Taken together they constitute a popular explanation of poverty of the 1950s and 1960s.

Handler comments of post-war Britain that '. . . it was assumed that with the floor provided by the welfare state most people would be able to take advantage of the opportunities offered by society . . .'.[121] Similarly, Seed—an experienced FSU worker— wrote that '. . . the widespread assumption in 1950 was that no one needed any longer to be poor . . .'.[122] Goldring starts his history of the FSU with the statement that poverty '. . . ought not to be possible today'.[123] It followed that where poverty did occur, the blame could not be attached to society or the social services. Rather, it must be due to some individual deficiencies in the persons who remained poor.

If poverty stemmed from the individual failure to take advantage of the welfare state, then it was to be expected that the same persons would be unable to cope in other areas of their lives. Problem families appeared the prime example. Studies, especially those by Stephen, Philp, and Philp and Timms, suggested that problem families could be identified by their loose morals, drunkenness, delinquency, criminality, child neglect, inability to manage money and property, and poverty. It followed that poverty was one of a grouping of problems. The poor were the problem families and any account of their poverty would also explain their other problems.

Why then did the families have such multiple problems? During the 1920s and 1930s their failings were often attributed to genetic inferiority. By the 1950s the answer was sought in psychology. In particular, the work of John Bowlby was influential in asserting that defective behaviour in adults was attributable to unsatisfactory emotional relationships in their childhood. To use his oft-repeated words, he believed it essential that an infant has in his early years '. . . a warm, intimate and continuous relationship with the mother (or mother substitute) in which both find satisfaction and enjoyment'.[124] He argued that '. . . the quality of the parental care which a child receives in his earliest years is of vital importance for his future mental health'.[125] Where mothers were unable to supply such a relationship or where children were removed into institutions, the result was 'maternal deprivation'. The deprived children then developed inadequate personalities, unable to enjoy loving relationships, unable to cope with their own feelings, unable to sustain working habits. Bowlby declared that

> . . . in a society where death rates are low, the rate of employment high and social welfare schemes adequate, it is emotional instability and inability of parents to make effective family relationships which are the outstanding cause of children becoming deprived of a normal home life. . . . the investigator is confronted with a self-perpetuating circle in which children who are deprived of a normal home life grow up into parents unable to provide a normal home life for their children . . . .[126]

Many social workers, and a number of authors, found in Bowlby's thesis an explanation of why the behaviour of 'problem families' differed from the rest of the population. Blackler gave it prominence as one of the most important accounts of 'social failure'.[127] From a history of the Family Service Units, it is clear that this psychological interpretation had considerable influence on those social workers working most closely with the families. For instance, one FSU employee says:

> Nearly every parent came from a home where they were deprived of love and security in early childhood, because of this lack remained insecure, unable to believe in themselves as individuals and that they were worthy of love and being wanted.[128]

Deprived children were seen as growing into deprived adults so unable to cope with life that their problems dominated them, leaving them nothing but squalor, deviance and poverty.

Bowlby's work was supplemented by that of a distinguished psychiatric social worker, Elizabeth Irvine. Her starting-point was to describe the behaviour of problem families. In 1954 she wrote that they were characterised by

> Inability for sustained or planful activity, so that appointments are not kept and arrangements not carried out. Foresight is lacking, so that money which will be needed for necessities tomorrow is squandered today on luxuries, attractive rubbish, or day-dream stimulants (such as 'the pictures'). There is no 'sense of time', no 'sense of money', no 'sense of property', in fact, a failure to grasp three of the most important elements in our culture. There is impulsiveness and lack of control in various spheres, including those of sex and aggression. Often there is a compulsive need for oral satisfaction, whether in the form of sweets, cigarettes or drink. In some instances the usual inhibitions on anal interests have not been developed, children are not toilet-trained and faeces lie about on the floor or are stored away in tin baths or cupboards.[129]

From this evidence, Irvine concluded:

> These characteristics seem to add up to a picture of extreme immaturity; is not most of this behaviour the sort of thing one would expect from a two-year-old, three-year-old or four-year-old left without adult guidance or control?[130]

She went on to explain that, as children, the problem parents had experienced defective relationships within their own family. They had not progressed along normal developmental lines, had not matured. When adults, they still behaved like young children who lack the ability to control their impulses, to plan, to save, to take care of property. Consequently, they could not manage money, housing or employment.

Irvine's application of the concept of emotional immaturity also received support from a number of workers engaged with problem families. Thus Goldring records one social worker supporting 'weekend availability' on the grounds that his clients were like immature children: 'If we believe that families need to be treated with the care we give to children, then we need weekend availability. You don't tell children to come back on

Monday.'[131] It followed that although the families were poor, the mere provision of money would not solve their problems. As one worker put it, '. . . if every family in our care became rich overnight they would still be inadequate and unhappy families and in danger of breaking up . . . .'[132] The explanation for their continuing problems, then, was their individual incapacities to deal with the normal tasks of living. It could not be blamed on external pressures or shortages. Thus, even if given an adequate income, they would waste it, spend it on non-necessities and refuse to save. To cite one of the FSU workers again, unless '. . . the emotional problems were also solved the family could be back in a slum and deep in debt again within months'.[133]

Bowlby and Irvine were not the only authors to explain problem families—and hence their poverty—by use of psychological concepts. Another psychiatrist, Howells, regarded them as mentally sick, and declared:

> These seriously disturbed families, greatly discorded, sick in the extreme, are often termed problem or hard-core families. The key to their understanding lies in understanding their emotional state. Material measures make no difference to them. We have tried environmental manipulation for years. A psychiatric illness needs a psychiatric prescription.[134]

> Our challenge is the sick family, the product of preceding families, sick in the past. They flow by into the future to found more sick families. Let us grasp one as it goes by and see what we can do to change it.[135]

Bowlby and Irvine would probably not concur with the condemnatory tone of Howell's writing. But they would accept the psychological emphasis, the individual explanation, the stress on the 'one' family. Thus it is worth distinguishing this explanation of individual family behaviour resulting from relationships within the one family, from the family patterns to be explored in the next chapter, which are held to derive from cultural factors. The former is derived mainly from psychological insights, the latter from sociological concepts.

Given the maternal deprivation and personal immaturity explanations, what solutions are recommended for the problems

of the problem families? Some consider that nothing can be
done except to sterilise or imprison them.[136] More humanely,
the 1950s saw the growth of the view that psychologically dis-
turbed adults needed individual treatment which would change
their behaviour. The method seen as most appropriate was
casework. As taught during this period, casework involved a
trained social worker employing psychological techniques within
an individual relationship in order to modify, relieve or change
the functioning of a client.[137] Irvine, speaking of casework
for problem families, called it '. . . not only the appropriate
method of treatment, but also the best way of exploring the
psychological condition of the individual members, and the relationships existing between them'.[138] Through casework, social
workers might enable their clients to see the reason for their
deviant behaviour and, it was anticipated, then be able to change
it. Irvine saw the social worker playing

> . . . the part of a warm, permissive and supportive parent, thus
> supplying the basic experiences of the early stage of socialisation,
> which for some reason the client seems to have missed. With great
> patience and tact, the client can sometimes be led through a phase
> corresponding to that in which the child likes to 'do it with mother'
> to one in which he begins to taste the satisfaction of 'doing it
> myself'.[139]

In other words, the social worker was to use casework to
make up for the emotional deprivations suffered by the clients
during childhood. The hope was that they would develop into
mature adults able to cope with life and thus free of serious
problems. It should be added that the financial needs of the
problem families were not ignored. But lack of money was
not regarded as the essential difficulty. As Irvine concluded,

> I would suppose that help of this practical kind would be frequently
> required, but I am sure it cannot be effective except as an integral
> part of a total casework process, that it has to be given in full
> cognisance of what this means in relationship terms.[140]

The casework orientation influenced many social-work agencies
including local-authority children's departments. But its appli-

cation to problem families was most intensively pursued through the Family Service Units. Their workers have scrubbed out homes, offered emotional support and practical advice as well as the therapeutic casework just outlined. Subsequently, there followed some involvement with groups and the community. Yet even here, the idea of treatment was often based on a psychological analysis. Thus a group worker wrote:

> I began to realise that my role in a group of such immature women would be that of mother providing the experience of a secure, caring relationship. I was filling in gaps in my members' childhood experience. Only by regressing and allowing me to close some of these gaps were they able to feel secure enough in the group to expose themselves and eventually to progress towards maturity . . . .[141]

Moreover,

> As far as the FSU is concerned, working with communities means extending the techniques and attitudes of family casework to the larger group of the community.[142]

Although, as will be mentioned, the approach of the FSU has altered of late, the work written at their twenty-fifth anniversary reveals a form of social work mainly drawn from psychological insights. As the author says of the workers, 'All lay stress on an individual relationship with the family.'[143] The poor were frequently identified as problem families. The problems were due to unhappy psychological experiences. The solution was seen as direct treatment of the individual.

The psychological explanation, the apparent need for intensive casework and the deserved reputation of the FSU for integrity, compassion and dedication also contributed to organisational changes within the British social services. Handler documents the reasoning that considered that, since social problems were largely due to malfunctionings within families, then there was a case for a single social-service department to deal with the whole family.[144] Such a department would be able to offer individual treatment of an intensive kind. The organisational implications will be explored in chapter 4. Here it is time to turn to some criticisms of the 'problem man explanation'.

## Multiple Problems and Individual Causation

It was shown that during the early post-war years, a school
of thought held that welfare provisions meant poverty could
be avoided by all. The poverty that did persist was attributed
to a core of families whose adult problems resulted from unhappy
and depriving childhoods. This coupling of multiple problems
and childhood deficiencies can be queried on four main grounds.
Firstly, there is now strong evidence to dispute the view that
childhood deprivations necessarily lead to adults whose functioning is abnormal. That it can happen is not disputed, but the
work of Rutter and others shows that the result is not inevitable.[145] Secondly, the assertions that problem families are characterised by immaturity and that the immaturity leads to serious
problems have not been convincingly demonstrated. It is true
that single case histories may paint a picture of immaturity.
But such cases are notoriously unreliable as a base for generalising
about behaviour. As yet, studies have not included control groups
of persons who are not called problem families, and thus there
are no grounds for asserting that one section of the population
is more mature than another. Thirdly, and in any case, studies
show—as will be mentioned below—that frequently the children
of such families receive affection, kindness and security. However,
generational studies—that is, studies that follow the history of
problem families through more than one generation—demonstrate
that this may not be sufficient to save them from multiple
problems when grown up. Fourthly, the crucial factor in stimulating problems can be environmental pressures rather than internal
deficiencies. Thus Wright and Lunn's generational study observed
that a reason why problem families kept children away from
school was '. . . that they have not the required clothing'.[146]
More substantially, Rutter and Madge's review of the research
concluded that '. . . when social disadvantage and stresses are
widespread these will more often play a part in the genesis
of emotional disturbance'.[147] Most significantly of all, the generational study of problem families, in noting the improvement
of their married children, gave credit to better housing conditions,

good school buildings, changes in education and higher incomes.[148] According to the maternal deprivation and immaturity explanations, the problem families should be unable to take advantage of these opportunities. That their position did improve suggests that their condition was influenced by factors outside of internal family dynamics. Individual causation could not have been completely crucial.

## Multiple Problems and the Poor

The popular problem-family thesis was not just that individual pathology created problems for adults but also that they experienced multiple problems, one of which was poverty. As explained in chapter 1, families frequently suffer from more than one social deprivation such as low income, poor housing and ill-health. But this is not to say that the poor are always those with a multitude of overlapping personal problems. Rutter and Madge point out that the poor may not have such problems while on the other hand problems of delinquency, child behaviour, drunkenness and marital disharmony, can be found amongst the affluent.[149] Rein draws attention to two studies of slum residents in Detroit and New York. The expectation had been that '... those who live in slums had emotional, personal and behavioural problems that inhibited their ability to make the transition into decent physical accommodations'. Instead, it was found that eighty-five per cent had no serious problems of this nature and that their greatest need was for adequate housing and income rather than therapy.[150] It is clear that poverty is not just another personal problem.

The poor cannot be dismissed as the psychologically sick. Nor can the problem of poverty be confined to a core of problem families. Advocates of a connection between poverty and problem families, it will be recalled, claimed that poverty was not necessary in the welfare state. They further believed that only a small minority were so inadequate as to get themselves into poverty—the number being put at less than one per cent of all families.[151] More recent studies, however, as outlined in chapter 1, have established that poverty is extensive in the welfare state with numbers being calculated at between seven and thirteen million. Even the most extreme believers in the concept of problem families would not put them at this figure. Poverty is possible in the welfare state and the numbers are so widespread that any explanation must go beyond a core of problem families.

## The Concept of the Problem Family

So far, criticism has been levelled at the individual and psychological account of problem families and at the claim that the poor are the problem families. Even more fundamentally, the very concept of problem families as a separate, pathological, problem-bound, entity has been attacked. The evidence—and oddly enough it can often be found in the studies meant to justify the concept—suggests that the so-called problem families frequently display the strengths and qualities which are common to most of the population. Thus it is Goldring who writes: 'Perhaps the most striking of all the themes that emerges from a study of FSU families is the basic strength of the relationship between parents and children.'[152] Wright and Lunn's comprehensive generational research was possible only because the families had maintained close links with their married children. They also observed that the ill-treatment of children was 'occasional', not frequent. The same writers also found that nearly half the men and over three-quarters of their male adult children were in full-time employment, despite a high amount of physical disability and job shortages.[153] Outside of their employment and treatment of children, the problem families often display motives, behaviour and hopes in line with society's values. Sainsbury noted in his study that '. . . the moral and ethical standards they admired were frequently identical with those which the social workers were concerned to promote'. Far from being uncaring about their situation '. . . nearly half the families made thoughtful and socially acceptable attempts to meet their problems unaided before referral'.[154] Again, Wright and Lunn hinted at unselfish, altruistic behaviour when the families found room in their overcrowded houses for married offspring or for non-relatives whom they took in '. . . either as a source of income or out of a fellow-feeling for those in need'.[155] It is not being disputed that there exist certain families with a large number of problems. It is not doubted that some of the parents neglect their children, get drunk and waste money. However, it appears that many of these families hold (even if they cannot attain) aspirations similar to the rest of society, while much of their behaviour is such that in general they cannot be separated from the rest of society and regarded as pathological entities whose personal oddities make them quite different from the mainstream population.

If the concept of the problem family as the reservoir of society's problems held true, then it could be expected that similar problems would not be widespread outside their ranks. But the evidence does not support this contention. For instance, overcrowding is said to be a characteristic of problem families, and around 29 per cent of them live in these conditions.[156] Yet although, according to the Census of 1971, in the Gorbals Ward of Glasgow 43.1 per cent or 3,165 persons were in such conditions, to the writer's knowledge these and other problems did not mean they were deemed problem families. Similar points could be made about the occurrence of debts, unemployment, truancy, delinquency, poor health, poor standards of furnishings and so on. These features appear in others as well as those called problem families. The present writer has recorded, by way of illustration, two families known to him in Birmingham. They lived near each other and suffered similar housing deprivations, rent arrears and depression. One family was officially visited as a problem family, the other was not.[157] Not surprisingly, Rutter and Madge end their review of the research by saying: 'Problem families do not constitute a group which is qualitatively different from families in the general population.'[158] The implication is that their problems, including their poverty, have their location in a much wider explanation than that which focusses on the individual inadequacies of an apparent problem minority. But if problem families merge into a larger gathering of the socially deprived, what distinguishes them or gives rise to the concept? The answer seems to be that problem families are those whom agencies call problem families. This definition is explicitly accepted by Philp and Goldring when they limited their studies of problem families to those families on the books of the FSU. Obviously, those families who did not wish to cooperate with the social workers—no matter how extreme their problems—would not be counted. Families unknown to the agencies also could not be included. It can· be realised that the concept is not really of a particular family grouping but concerns the way in which social-work agencies detect certain clients and how and if they decide to work with them.

The concept of problem families as an entity different from the rest of the population, along with the individual psychological explanation for their existence, has now been called into question. It is not surprising, then, if attempts to counter problem families (and poverty) by the use of casework aimed at individual change have produced unpromising results. Rein points to well-researched programmes which used casework on problem families (compared with control groups who were not treated). Little was achieved.[159] It is interesting to observe that a number of FSU workers have now accepted the limitations of the individually orientated approach as *the* solution to poverty. One unit organiser stated that the effect of casework '. . . was minimal because the environment was so bloody awful. The classic one-to-one situation couldn't take account of the environment'.[160] The FSU quarterly journal now contains an emphasis on social policy and changes in the forces external to clients. The individual approach still has an important place but there is appreciation that changes in social deprivation require something more. One worker advocated community work because 'This is more rewarding than casework because that is so often bound up with problems like rent or housing which are not psychological . . . . Many FSU cases should not have happened if other things had been right.'[161] The problem-family analysis started by saying that 'other things' were right and so poverty should be avoided. Significantly, some of the workers most closely involved with problem families now say that many of the problems would not occur if the external matters were in order.

Before leaving problem man, it is as well to make clear what the critique does *not* claim. It does not say that there are no personal problems which require casework help. On the contrary, Sainsbury's research suggested that the social workers' most telling work was '. . . in the area of personal and family feelings'. But, as the same author admits, the individual approach had little effect on material conditions.[162] However, it has not even been said that social work is irrelevant to poverty. The last chapter will attempt to show the connection between them. Finally, it is not asserted that personal problems and poverty are never connected. Individual malfunctioning may occasionally lead to poverty, but the notion which seems more worth exploring is, to quote the American psychiatrist Beiser, that personality abnormalities of the poor tend to come from the impact of poverty on the individual rather than vice versa.[163]

Problem families cannot be accounted for by explanations which focus on individual deficiencies. Problem families cannot be equated with poverty. The question of poverty needs to be cast in a broader framework. This point was grasped by Tawney over half a century ago, in an era when it was common to blame individuals for their poverty. This chapter can do no better than to recall his words. Tawney was speaking of a profitable firm which had put its many hundreds of employees on short time so reducing their wages and placing some in poverty:

> Of the men employed a certain number were thriftless and a certain number spent too much on drink. This was very regrettable. But the primary question for the student of poverty is not, I suggest, why some score individuals incurred more distress than others, but why some thousands of persons were pinched and why some hundreds were half starved while employed by a business which was to its shareholders a gold mine. Improve the character of individuals by all means—if you feel competent to do so, especially of those whose excessive incomes expose them to peculiar temptations. This is a good in itself which needs no justification. But unemployment, short time and low wages fall upon just and unjust alike.[164]

Following Tawney's injunction, the following chapters will turn from individuals and examine explanations which focus on culture, organisations and social structures.

REFERENCES

1 A. Fried and R. Elman (eds) *Charles Booth's London. A Portrait of the Poor at the Turn of the Century Drawn from his 'Life and Labour of the People of London'* Hutchinson (1969) p. 11
2 C. Booth *Life and Labour of the People of London* vol. 9, Macmillan (1897) pp. 53, 70
3 B. S. Rowntree *Poverty: A Study of Town Life* Macmillan (1901); 2nd edn Longmans (1922) repr. Howard Ferrig (1971) p. xix
4 T. Stephens *Problem Families* Pacifist Service Units (1945) p. 67
5 G. Pearson 'Welfare on the Move' Unit Four of Open University *Social Work, Community Work and Society* forthcoming, p. 13
6 Reported in the *Guardian* 3 May 1977
7 J. Meade and A. Parkes (eds) *Biological Aspects of Social Problems* Oliver and Boyd (1965) p. v
8 *ibid.* p. 112
9 R. Herrnstein *IQ in the Meritocracy* Allen Lane (1973) p. 129
10 *ibid.* p. 99
11 *ibid.* p. 143
12 *ibid.* p. 134
13 *ibid.* p. 145
14 *ibid.* p. 140
15 *ibid.* p. 145
16 *ibid.*
17 *ibid.* p. 142
18 See R. Boyson (ed.) *Down With the Poor* Churchill Press (1971)
19 H. Eysenck *The Inequality of Man* Temple Smith (1973) p. 72
20 J. Kogan 'What Is Intelligence?', *Medical World* (Oct. 1973)
21 L. Kamin *The Science and Politics of I.Q.* Wiley (1976). The correspondence was in *The Times* at the end of 1976
22 M. Rutter and N. Madge *Cycles of Disadvantage. A Review of Research* Heinemann (1976) p. 97
23 Cited *ibid.* p. 111
24 J. Seglow, M. Kellmer Pringle and P. Wedge *Growing Up Adopted* National Foundation for Educational Research (1972) chs 8, 9, 10
25 B. Tizard 'In Defence of Nurture' *New Society* vol. 27 no. 588 (10 Jan. 1974)
26 Rutter and Madge *op. cit.* p. 114
27 *ibid.* p. 100
28 *ibid.* p. 115
29 R. Stewart 'How Malnutrition Handicaps Children' *New Society* vol. 31, no. 643 (13 Feb. 1975)
30 See account of the Milwaukee project in N. Block and G. Dworkin (eds) *The IQ Controversy* Quartet Books (1977)
31 C. Jencks *et al. Inequality* Allen Lane (1973)
32 Eysenck *op. cit.* p. 120
33 J. Gibson and M. Young 'Social Mobility and Fertility' in Meade and Parkes *op. cit.* p. 71
34 Eysenck *op. cit.* p. 104
35 Cited in Rutter and Madge *op. cit.* p. 116
36 See Public Schools Commission *First Report* vols I and II, HMSO (1968)
37 Rutter and Madge *op. cit.* p. 116

38 Cited in H. Wilson 'The Socialisation of Children' in R. Holman (ed.) *Socially Deprived Families in Britain* Bedford Square Press (1970) pp. 125–6
39 *ibid.*
40 F. Riessman *The Culturally Deprived Child* Harper (1962) p. 18
41 Jencks *et al. op. cit.* pp. 179–80
42 Rutter and Madge *op. cit.* p. 151
43 Cited in Eysenck *op. cit.* p. 135
44 M. Meacher 'The Coming Class Struggle' *New Statesman* 4 Jan. 1974
45 Eysenck *op. cit.* pp. 140–1
46 Rutter and Madge *op. cit.* pp. 151–2
47 P. Chapman and L. Berg *The Train Back* Allen Lane (1972)
48 A. Atkinson *Wealth, Income and Inequality* Penguin Books (1973)
49 A. Giddens 'The Rich' *New Society* vol. 38, no. 732 (14 Oct. 1976)
50 Rutter and Madge *op. cit.* p. 158
51 *ibid.* pp. 202–3
52 For a fuller discussion, see E. Slater and V. Cowie *The Genetics of Mental Disorder* Oxford University Press (1971)
53 Eysenck *op. cit.* ch. 6
54 J. Thoday 'Genetics and Education' *New Society* vol. 6, no. 147 (22 July 1965)
55 F. Hayek *The Road to Serfdom* Routledge (new edn 1962)
56 M. Friedman *Capitalism and Freedom* University of Chicago Press (Phoenix edn 1963)
57 D. Lees 'Welfare: Choice and the Market' *New Society* vol. 5, no. 140 (3 June 1965)
58 *ibid.*
59 *ibid.*
60 Friedman *op. cit.* p. 5
61 E. Powell 'The Irresistible Market' *New Society* vol. 3, no. 71 (6 Feb. 1964)
62 See A. Coats 'The Classical Economists, Industrialisation and Poverty' in *The Long Debate on Poverty* Institute of Economic Affairs (1972) pp. 151–3
63 Friedman *op. cit.* p. 191
64 *ibid.* p. 1
65 R. Bremner 'Shifting Attitudes' in P. Weinberger (ed.) *Perspectives on Social Welfare* Collier-Macmillan (2nd edn 1974) p. 64
66 R. Page *The Benefits Racket* Stacey (1971)
67 Friedman *op. cit.* p. 188
68 Powell *op. cit.*
69 Cited in Weinberger *op. cit.* p. 238
70 Friedman *op. cit.* p. 192
71 Boyson *op. cit.* p. 2
72 *ibid.* p. 5
73 *ibid.*
74 A. Seldon 'Welfare By Choice' in A. Lochhead (ed.) *A Reader in Social Administration* Constable (1968) p. 264
75 I. Kristol 'Welfare: The Best of Intentions The Worst of Results' in Weinberger *op. cit.* p. 242
76 M. Bremner *Dependency and the Family* Institute of Economic Affairs (1968) p. 11
77 *ibid.* p. 59
78 Seldon *op. cit.* p. 264

79 Boyson *op. cit.* p. 4
80 Seldon *op. cit.* p. 272
81 Boyson *op. cit.* p. 7
82 *ibid.* p. 8
83 Friedman *op. cit.* pp. 35, 87, 91
84 Seldon *op. cit.* p. 272
85 Lees *op. cit.*
86 Cited in Weinberger *op. cit.* p. 64
87 A. Christopher, G. Polanyi, A. Seldon and B. Shenfield *Policy for Poverty* Institute of Economic Affairs (1970)
88 Friedman *op. cit.*
89 Booth in Fried and Elman *op. cit.*
90 *Report of the Registrar-General* cited in N. Middleton *When Family Failed* Gollancz (1971) p. 30
91 *ibid.* p. 183
92 Lees *op. cit.*
93 A. Atkinson *Unequal Shares: Wealth in Britain* Allen Lane (rev. edn 1974)
94 See P. Hall 'City Planning and the Urban Crisis' paper given at Ditchly Conference. Gulbenkian Foundation (1975)
95 R. Cassen 'Welfare: State's Role' *New Society* vol. 5, no. 141 (10 June 1965)
96 Cited in Weinberger *op. cit.* p. 69
97 L. Goodwin *Do The Poor Want to Work?* Brookings Institute (1972)
98 W. Daniel *A National Survey of the Unemployed* PEP broadsheet (1974)
99 M. Hill, R. Harrison and A. Sergeant *Men Out of Work* Cambridge University Press (1973)
100 Christopher *et al. op. cit.* pp. 73–4
101 See the international figures in A. Sillitoe *Britain in Figures* Penguin Books (1971) p. 69
102 R. Fletcher *The Family and Marriage in Britain* Penguin Books (rev. edn 1966)
103 R. Holman *Inequality in Child Care* Child Poverty Action Group (1976)
104 Middleton *op. cit.*
105 e.g. M. Young and P. Willmott *Family and Kinship in East London* Routledge (1957); C. Rosser and C. Harris *The Family and Social Change* Routledge (1965); P. Willmott and M. Young *Family and Class in a London Suburb* Routledge (1960)
106 M. Brown and F. Field *Poverty and Inflation* Child Poverty Action Group (1974)
107 W. Haggstrom 'The Power of the Poor' in F. Riessman, J. Cohen and A. Pearl (eds) *Mental Health of the Poor* Collier-Macmillan (1964)
108 e.g. P. Townsend (ed.) *Social Services for All?* Fabian Society (1968); R. Titmuss *The Gift Relationship* Allen and Unwin (1971)
109 W. Booth *In Darkest England and the Way Out* International Headquarters of Salvation Army (1890) p. 48
110 P. Walker 'The Moral Case for Capitalism' *Sunday Times* 26 May 1974
111 J. Meade *The Intelligent Radical's Guide To Economic Policy* Allen and Unwin (1975) pp. 14–15
112 R. Titmuss, foreword to A. Philp and N. Timms *The Problem of the 'Problem Family'* Family Service Units (1962) p. v
113 P. Hall *The Social Services of Modern England* Routledge (6th edn 1963) p. 159
114 Women's Group on Public Welfare cited *ibid.*

115 Cited by E. Irvine 'The Hard-to-Like Family' *Case Conference* vol. 14, no. 3 (1967)
116 In particular, see A. Philp *Family Failure* Faber (1963); Stephens *Problem Families*, *op. cit.*
117 B. Wootton *Social Science and Social Pathology* Allen and Unwin (1959) p. 56
118 Hall *op. cit.* p. 160
119 C. Wright and J. Lunn 'Sheffield Problem Families: a Follow-up Study of Their Sons and Daughters' *Community Medicine* 26 Nov. and 3 Dec. 1971
120 Wootton *op. cit.* pp. 51–62
121 J. Handler *The Coercive Social Worker* Markham (1973) p. 116
122 P. Seed *The Expansion of Social Work in Britain* Routledge (1973) p. 61
123 P. Goldring *Friend of the Family* David and Charles (1973) p. 13
124 The popular version was J. Bowlby *Child Care and the Growth of Love* Penguin Books (1953)
125 J. Bowlby *Maternal Care and Mental Health* World Health Organization (1951) p. 11
126 Cited by C. Blackler 'Problem Families' in Lochhead *op. cit.* p. 235
127 *ibid.* p. 233
128 Goldring *op. cit.* p. 35
129 E. Irvine 'Research Into Problem Families' *Journal of Psychiatric Social Work* (May 1954)
130 Irvine 'The Hard-to-Like Family' *op. cit.*
131 Goldring *op. cit.* p. 71
132 *ibid.* p. 35
133 *ibid.* p. 21
134 J. Howells *Remember Maria* Butterworths (1974) p. 89. See also J. Howells 'The Psychopathy of a Problem Family' *Medical World* vol. 25 (1956)
135 *ibid.* p. 93
136 Seed has collected some of these harsh opinions; *op. cit.* p. 67
137 Two much-read casework textbooks were H. Perlman *Social Casework: A Problem Solving Process* University of Chicago Press (1951) and F. Hollis *Casework: A Psychosocial Therapy* Random House (1964)
138 Irvine 'Research Into Problem Families' *op. cit.*
139 *ibid.*
140 *ibid.*
141 Goldring *op. cit.* pp. 129–30
142 *ibid.* p. 146
143 *ibid.* p. 36
144 Handler *op. cit.* p. 49
145 M. Rutter *Maternal Deprivation Reassessed* Penguin Books (1972)
146 Wright and Lunn *op. cit.*
147 Rutter and Madge *op. cit.* p. 248
148 Wright and Lunn *op. cit.*
149 Rutter and Madge *op. cit.* pp. 249–51
150 M. Rein, *Social Policy,* Random House (1970) p. 347
151 See Rutter and Madge *op. cit.* p. 251
152 Goldring *op. cit.* p. 81
153 Wright and Lunn *op. cit.*
154 E. Sainsbury *Social Work With Families* Routledge (1975) p. 112
155 Wright and Lunn *op. cit.*

156 *ibid.*
157 R. Holman 'Social Workers and the Inadequates' *New Society* vol. 29, no. 622 (5 Sept. 1974)
158 Rutter and Madge *op. cit.* p. 255
159 Rein *op. cit.* p. 235–6
160 Goldring *op. cit.* p. 148
161 *ibid.* p. 154
162 Sainsbury *op. cit.* p. 98
163 M. Beiser 'Poverty, Social Disintegration and Personality' *Journal of Social Issues* vol. 21, no. 1 (1965)
164 R. Tawney 'Poverty as an Industrial Problem', inaugural lecture Ralan Tata Foundation (1913)

CHAPTER 3

# Cultural Explanations: Family Behaviour and Poverty

The view that social deprivation persists because poor families transmit behaviour which creates poverty has received considerable attention both in the USA and Britain. In the USA, Oscar Lewis's famous culture of poverty theory postulated poor families functioning within a culture quite separate from the main stream of society. The thesis gained wide currency and certainly influenced elements of the American War on Poverty.[1] A related explanation saw a body of families unable to use or be fully incorporated into the prevailing culture although it did not see them as a distinct culture. They have been termed 'culturally deprived', and in Britain a cycle of deprivation thesis was popularised by a minister of state, Sir Keith Joseph MP. In this chapter separate attention will be given to the two explanations. However, they possess strong similarities, particularly in identifying family behaviour as the vehicle which transmits poverty. Consequently, the same criticisms and evaluation can be made of them together.

## THE CULTURE OF POVERTY

The concept of culture has been developed by anthropologists as they have attempted to contrast different tribes, races, nations or societies. It refers to a systematic, integrated pattern of living. More specifically, one anthropologist states that '... the culture of a particular people or other social body is everything that one must learn to behave in ways that are recognisable, predictable, and understandable to those people.'[2] Obviously different peoples possess different cultures. In explaining these variations, anthropologists have examined how people have collectively responded to different environmental and historical conditions. For instance, the Eskimo culture can be viewed as the response, over hundreds of years, both to the arctic environment and to the developing intrusion of Europeans. The form or shape of the responses become the values, the ethical standards, the approved behaviour, the very way of life of the people concerned and is perpetuated from generation to generation.

Different peoples, in different parts of the world with contrasting climates and historical experiences, can be expected, then, to display different cultures. A notable anthropologist himself, Oscar Lewis developed the idea of culture in another way. He argued that, within the very midst of one culture, there could also exist a culture of poverty. It made up a way of life quite distinct from that of surrounding people and, as culture is passed on from generation to generation, constituted the explanation for much social deprivation.

*Oscar Lewis*

The thesis of a culture of poverty was first proposed by Lewis in 1959 and subsequently enlarged as he studied Mexican and Puerto Rican families.[3] He claimed that the poor were so alienated from the rest of their society that they had had to develop ways of coping. The coping mechanisms became so inbred and extensive as to constitute a culture within a culture. This poverty culture, he argued, had distinct characteristics sufficient to make its members quite different from others in the same region or nation.

In all, Lewis claimed that the culture of poverty was made up of '. . . some seventy interrelated social, economic and psychological traits'.[4] However, for convenience, these can be narrowed down to four major groupings. Firstly, the poor are characterised by a lack of participation and integration into the major institutions of the larger society. They do not belong to trade unions, voluntary societies, or political bodies. They make little use of hospitals or departmental stores. Their reluctance is linked with '. . . a critical attitude towards some of the basic institutions of the dominant classes, hatred of the police, mistrust of government and those in high positions, and a cynicism which extends even to the church.'[5] Similarly, they may not share the values of the larger society. Even where there is awareness of the values, the poor do not live by them. Thus even if lip service is paid to the act of marriage, '. . . few will marry'.[6]

Secondly, the culture is marked by 'A minimum of organization beyond the level of the nuclear and extended family'.[7] This is to be expected if the poor do not participate in clubs, trade unions, or movements. However, Lewis does concede that, despite the general disorganisation, there might be sufficient cohesiveness to engender a sense of community.

Thirdly, family and sexual practices are at variance with the outside culture. Thus he notes '. . . the absence of childhood as a specially prolonged and protected stage in the life cycle, early initiation into sex, free unions or consensual marriages, a relatively high incidence of the abandonment of wives and children. . . .'[8]

Fourthly, attitudes of helplessness, dependence and inferiority prevail. Linked to the poor's resignation and fatalism, there is little motivation for work, for advancement, for change. In addition, the poor process '. . . a lack of impulse control, a strong present time orientation with relatively little ability to defer gratification and to plan for the future'.[9]

The behaviour and attitudes of the members make poverty inevitable, according to Lewis. Unmotivated and helpless people do not work their way out of poverty. Those unwilling to postpone pleasures do not save. Change will never come if they are unwilling to organise. Further, the inevitable poverty does not breed resentment because the culture of poverty is a way of accepting poverty. For instance, the resignation and fatalism enables people to live with their plight.

A culture is transmitted to succeeding generations by all the institutions of that culture. Within it, Lewis gave particular attention to the family with its patterns of child-rearing and socialisation as the means of implanting values and forms of behaviour. The parents passed on to their children the attitudes that accepted poverty, not the skills to remove them from it. He wrote

> By the time slum children are aged six or seven they have usually absorbed the basic values and attitudes of their sub-culture and are not psychologically geared to take full advantage of changing conditions or increased opportunities which may occur in their life-time.[10]

The children, and their children, are thus doomed to remain within the culture, a self-perpetuating entity quite cut off from the outside world, quite separate in their values, behaviour and economic resources.

*Support for Lewis*

The culture of poverty thesis has received considerable acclaim. In Britain, Cullingworth accepts that Lewis has established the existence of a '... different social system' and that the poor lack the skills '... for dealing with the majority culture ...'.[11] But in America, support was even more widespread. Sabin, a psychologist, outspokenly declared:

> Oscar Lewis ... has popularized the term and has argued that the culture of poverty may be observed in many parts of the world where similar historical antecedents have resulted in a social organization that contains declassed or degraded persons. He is undoubtedly correct.[12]

Sabin added that the culture of poverty was so distant and separate that it could be spoken of in the same way as social scientists referred to the culture of the Hopi.[13]

The influence of the culture of poverty view, however, cannot be attributed only to Lewis. Writing almost concurrently with him was Riessman, a well-known educationalist, whose starting point had been to question why certain children performed badly at school. He concluded that such children tended to come from the poor who, he stated, were characterised not only by a '... psychology of the deprived ...' but by the possession of '... a culture of their own'.[14] Riessman then described the culture in terms not dissimilar from those of Lewis. The poor were '... alienated, not fully a part of society'. The poor person held the world, not himself, responsible for his misfortunes but did nothing to alter the situation for 'He is not interested in politics ... and generally belongs to few organizations'.[15] Moreover, Riessman agreed that '... it is important to see how the customs are transmitted through the family to the child'.[16]

Riessman was most concerned to show how the culture of poverty failed to equip its members for school. The attitudes and skills instilled by the culture did not correspond with those of schools, which were shaped by the dominant culture. Consequently, the child from such a background '... is not happy at school, does not read well, appears unmotivated, is antagonistic to teacher, possesses no well-formulated career plans'.[17] Not surprisingly, the child gains little from education and on leaving settles down to a life of poverty.

Riessman attributed responsibility to the culture. But he differed from some of his colleagues in also placing some blame upon the educational system. He believed that, although the members of the culture of poverty were negative towards schools and teachers, they were not wholly opposed to education.[18] However, the teachers had failed to appreciate this and had deduced from the children's poor performance on IQ and language tests that nothing could be done to help them. Riessman did believe that teachers could change the children of the poor. He did not draw the boundaries between the two cultures as tightly as did Lewis. Indeed, along with other writers of the period, such as Will and Vatter, and Warren,[19] he appears to be describing a sub-culture which does possess obvious links with the core culture. Notwithstanding these links, the poor are viewed as having values, beliefs and behaviour patterns which mark them off from others, which create poverty and which are passed from family to family.

The influence of the culture of poverty thesis in the USA coincided with a period in which some attention was directed at the problems of black people. Not surprisingly, the thesis was used to explain the persistence of poverty amongst them. Glazer claimed to have identified certain characteristics of their life style, in particular broken homes, irresponsible male behaviour and an acceptance of illegitimacy. Such a disorganised family pattern was both foreign to the values of the dominant society and failed to provide its members with the motive or capacities to avoid poverty.[20] Moynihan continued the theme in an official report, holding quite categorically that the cause of blacks' problems '. . . is the deterioration of the Negro family . . . the family structure of lower class Negroes is highly unstable, and in many urban centers is approaching complete breakdown'.[21] As Valentine put it, Moynihan '. . . paints with bold strokes a lower-class "sub-culture", highlighted by "matriarchy", emasculated males, educational failure, delinquency, crime and drug addiction'.[22] Such patterns of behaviour could not prepare children to succeed in society. They would be trained only to repeat the failure, delinquency, crime and immoralities of those nearest to them. Moynihan thus saw the sub-culture not just as the perpetuator of poverty, but as dangerous in upholding behaviour inimical to the rest of society.

If the poor were seen as dangerous, then members of the culture of poverty were likely to be dismissed as inferior or disreputable. Banfield condemned the pauper because he '. . . prefers near-destitution without work to abundance with it'.[23] Matza produced a paper entitled 'The Disreputable Poor'. He saw the poor as a collectivity who, unlike other Americans, were not ashamed of their poverty and did not want to work. Their traditions were passed on from generation to generation, leaving them permanently at the bottom of the pile. He wrote: 'The core of disreputable poverty consists of dregs—persons spawned in poverty and belonging to families who have been left behind by otherwise mobile ethnic populations.'[24] It should be added that authors such as Glazer, Moynihan and Matza, for all their tone, were not insensitive to the sufferings of the poor. Matza explains that he uses the term 'disreputable' because the dominant society sees the poor in this light. The very features which made their sub-culture distinct were ones which the main culture held in repugnance.

From Lewis to Matza, the authors show differing outlooks

and emphases. Nonetheless, their underlying themes are the same, namely, as Valentine summarises, that the poor '. . . possess a distinct sub-culture, and . . . do not share the dominant larger culture typified by the middle class'.[25] The culture is passed from generation to generation and equips members only with the attitudes and characteristics which accept poverty, not with the motivation and skills to escape. Consequently, lack of money is not regarded as the reason for social deprivation. Banfield selects one characteristic of the culture and says: 'Extreme present-orientedness, not lack of income or wealth, is the principal cause of poverty. . . .'[26] More generally, Halsey sums up:

> The culture of poverty insists in its simplest form that the poor are different not primarily because of low income but because they have been habituated to poverty and have developed a sub-culture of values adapted to these conditions which they pass on to their children.[27]

## CULTURAL DEPRIVATION

If the culture of poverty theory has been strong in the USA, in Britain greater emphasis has been given to a related explanation—cultural deprivation. According to the former, the poor make up a culture or sub-culture quite separate from and outside of the rest of the population. According to the latter, the poor are part of the prevailing culture but their inadequate socialisation experiences when young have meant they are not equipped to benefit from it. In short, they are deprived of those aspects of the culture which allow other members to keep themselves from poverty.

The part played by socialisation experiences is so central to this explanation that its meaning must be defined. Danzinger, in his book on the subject, regards socialisation as '. . . the process whereby the individual becomes a participating member of a society of human adults . . .'.[28] Elsewhere, it is described as the processes that lead to individuals acquiring ways of acting, thinking and feeling with other members of their culture or sub-culture.[29] Socialisation involves the transmission of values, skills, attitudes and patterns of behaviour from generation to generation.

The three major agents of socialisation are considered to be family, school and peers. Of these the family is held to be of crucial importance in that it deals with children in their earliest and most formative years. The child-rearing practices employed by parents are thought to shape their children's personalities. Indeed, it is often assumed that certain ways of adult functioning are related to particular child/parent experiences. If the child-rearing practices are deficient, then the children will not develop into adults who can fit into the prevailing culture with all its opportunities for education and advancement. (Again, a contrast can be made with the culture of poverty thesis in which the children are adequately socialised but into a culture which accepts poverty.) However, Danzinger points out that if deficient socialisation methods lead to social problems, then the pathway to improvement also seems clear: '... if you wish to make any real changes ... change your methods of child training'.[30]

It will be realised that the theory of cultural deprivation connects inadequate family experiences with subsequent social deprivation. It will now be illustrated by reference to a study made in the 1950s, a book published in the 1960s, and a government view put forward in the 1970s.

## The Deprived and the Privileged

In 1953 a psychologist, Spinley, published an influential study. She wanted to discover why different groups of people, perhaps living within a few miles of each other, could turn out so varied in behaviour and circumstances. To do so, she selected two contrasting groups, slum-dwellers in a part of London and a sample of adults who had attended public schools. Spinley called them the deprived and the privileged; today they would probably be termed the very poor and the very affluent. The two groups are considered by Spinley to be so different that at times her tone is similar to Lewis's when he describes separate cultures. But she explicitly states that the poor are part of the larger culture in which '... all the members would be expected to possess certain values and behaviour patterns, while differing on others'.[31]

By use of participant observation, interviews and a postal questionnaire, Spinley accumulated material on both groups' childhood experiences and their present attitudes and behaviour. Amongst the slum-dwellers, she identified 117 typical experiences which she narrowed down to ten major ones—early indulgence by parents, a sudden decline of parental attention following the birth of the next child, a dominant mother and weak father, weak emotional ties, precocious awareness of sex, conflict in the home, violence, lack of privacy, inconsistency of parental treatment, the stimulation of the value of gaining wealth together with the impossibility of achieving it. She then argued that these childhood experiences created or moulded a basic personality type which, she noted, was characterised by insecurity, sexual disturbance, inability to form close relationships, absence of a strong ego, inability to postpone satisfactions, marked narcissism, aggressiveness, a tendency to flee from unpleasant experiences and a rebellious attitude towards authority. Such personality attributes were not sufficient to enable their bearers to use the advantages and opportunities of the prevailing culture. As Spinley put it, they were not equipped to move out of the slum. Insecurity, sexual disturbance and an inability to form close relationships are hardly conducive to the formation of a stable family unit in which the male accepts full responsibility for providing for his children. The inability to postpone satisfactions would not promote the capacity to save money. The aggressiveness and tendency to flee from unpleasant situations would inhibit progress at work, where taking orders and persistence at difficult tasks might be required. The absence of a strong ego and the narcissism might lead the slum-dweller to prefer crime or delinquency.

By contrast, Spinley argued that the public-school group enjoyed a stable home life, parents who wanted them, parents with clearly defined roles, consistent discipline, a boarding school which taught a definite code of behaviour and the likelihood that ambitions could be achieved. These childhood experiences, Spinley inferred, produced a personality characterised by a strict super-ego, an acceptance of authority, satisfactory sexual development and '. . . a basic anxiety overlaid with conscious feelings of security and confidence'.[32] Such personalities were law-abiding, accepted the values of the dominant culture, had enough security to form stable family units along with enough anxiety to drive them to achieve. They were thus equipped to continue the successful lives of their parents. lives which entailed affluence, not slums.

## Children in Distress

In discussing poverty, Halsey points to Clegg and Megson's *Children in Distress* as an example of the '. . . point of view directed towards the more pathological aspects of cultural deprivation'.[33] Drawing upon many years as a distinguished educational administrator, Sir Alec Clegg and his colleague assert that a major cause of poverty is not lack of money but certain aspects of parental behaviour. Amongst the characteristics of such parents are cruelty, immorality, derangement, apathy, quarrelsomeness, '. . . fecklessness and selfishness'.[34] Above all, such parents are 'work-shy'. Devoting a whole chapter to the work-shy, the authors explain that they are referring to '. . . the man who could work but will not and who is prepared to neglect his children and spend on himself the money which the community provides for their maintenance . . .'.[35] They claim that such men exist '. . . in considerable numbers in certain communities'.[36] They provide (from examples given by head teachers) a number of case illustrations such as:

> His mother has long given up the struggle. His father suffers from what is known in this district as 'glass back'. I have known him for $7\frac{1}{2}$ years and he has never done a regular day's work in that time.[37]

People dominated by such traits are seen as different from most other members of society. They are different in that they do not possess the attributes—unselfishness, drive, a willingness to work—which enable the rest of the community to provide acceptable emotional and economic standards for their families.

Clegg and Megson are particularly concerned about the effects of the parents' life styles on their children. Their poverty and squalor can mean ill-health for the children. The parents serve as an inadequate model so that the children follow their example of not caring or trying and '. . . their power to learn is seriously impaired'.[38] The lack of love is reflected in the children's behavioural problems at school and delinquency outside. One teacher is cited as saying,

> These children are almost always grade III physically and mentally. They stand with the dice loaded against them in poor, often squalid homes . . . . There is nearly always heavy catarrh, with deafness and poor vision . . . . They sometimes steal—because they have so little of their own and because that is the example set to them—and already there is this feeling of being outside society with its anti-social implications.[39]

When leaving school, such children can not hope to obtain secure well-paid employment. The behaviour that characterises them will lead to poverty.

## The Cycle of Deprivation

Perhaps the best-known version of the cultural deprivation explanation is that popularised by a former Secretary of State for Social Services in 1972. Sir Keith Joseph asked why social deprivation should persist '. . . in spite of long periods of full employment and relative prosperity and the improvement in community services since the Second World War . . . .'[40] Conceding that the answers were many and complex, Sir Keith selected inadequate child-rearing practices as outstandingly important. His belief was that such practices shaped personality particularly during the initial five years of life:

> These first years are crucial: the roots of much deprivation go back to infancy. A child's growth is rapid and the capacity to develop intellectually and to form and to maintain emotional and social relationships is established so early that it soon becomes increasingly difficult to put things right. The basis of future behaviour patterns is laid when an infant experiences a rewarding relationship

with his mother and through consistent guidance and love gains control over impulse. The process it seems clear is extended through a relationship with the father and with others who form the intimate family circle.[41]

Unfortunately, Sir Keith continued, there were (and are) a core of poor families who do not provide good care, whose treatment of children does '. . . not take account of these known factors about early development'.[42] They are the parents '. . . who either out of ignorance or for some other reason do not give their children the consistent context of love and guidance, understanding and firmness.'[43] The consequence of such inadequate child-rearing is reflected in the development of the children. Sir Keith asserted that when a child is deprived of the love and guidance of adequate parents, '. . . he is deprived of that background most likely to lead to stability and maturity.'[44]

As the result of such upbringings, the children emerge deficient in their bodies, their emotions and their educational capacities. They are deprived of the requirements needed to cope with a demanding and challenging culture. Their childhood has not given them the language and reading skills to do well at school. Their lack of emotional and relationship capacities will be revealed in unstable marriages and an inability to get on with other people. As their parents have not instilled the right attitudes about work and ambition, they will fail to succeed in an occupation. Overall they will just continue in the poverty of the backgrounds from which they came.

Further, and here is a central point of Sir Keith's thesis, such children when they grow into adulthood will be unable to use anything except the same inadequate child-rearing methods on their own children. The succeeding generation will thus also experience poverty. It is this process which Sir Keith called 'the cycle of deprivation'. He also refers to it as 'transmitted deprivation' in which '. . . the problems of one generation appear to reproduce themselves in the next'.[45] The vehicle of transmission is inadequate family practices. Three further quotations from his speech will serve to illustrate his thesis.

[The children] will carry into adolescence and adult life an inability to form trusting and stable relationships—because they have never experienced them; and will become in their turn the parents of the next generation of children who are deprived, emotionally and intellectually.[46]

Parents who were themselves deprived in one or more ways in childhood become in turn the parents of another generation of deprived children.[47]

Do we not know only too certainly that amongst the children of this generation there are some doomed to an uphill struggle against the disadvantages of a deprived family background? Do we not know that many of them will not be able to overcome the disadvantages, and will become in their turn the parents of deprived families?[48]

Social deprivation, then, according to a leading politician, frequently stems from inadequate child-rearing practices which fail to prepare children sufficiently for effective participation in the prevailing culture. The cycle can be seen more clearly in figure 1.

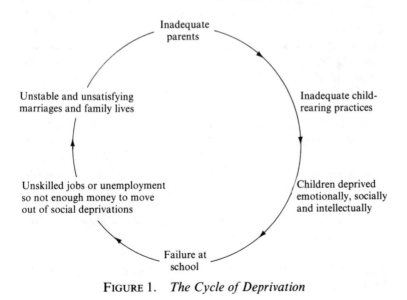

FIGURE 1. *The Cycle of Deprivation*

*Language and Motivation*

The exponents of the cultural deprivation explanation would argue that the inadequate socialisation experiences deprive the recipients of a whole range of necessary skills and attitudes. Of these, two have been awarded a special emphasis—language and motivation.

Keddie observes that 'Recently research has concentrated on attempting to show that the crucial feature of cultural deprivation is linguistic and cognitive deprivation.'[49] The view is that the children of the poor are not provided—by their socialisation experiences—with the language skills taken for granted by most members of the culture. Amongst the proponents of language deficiency, two emphases can be distinguished. One draws upon the work of Bernstein to argue that lower-social-class children in general are equipped only with a restricted code or style of speaking whereas others also possess the elaborated code.[50] The restricted code typically involves short sentences, extensive use of implicit meanings, and much repetition. The elaborated code has longer sentences, explicit meanings and an extensive range of syntactic alternatives. The former is suited to interpersonal communication. The latter, it is argued, is necessary for more sophisticated exchange of information and for educational and business purposes. The other emphasis draws less upon Bernstein's work but still claims that poor parents do not provide adequate language training. As well as the authors already discussed, mention should be made of Hunt. Talking of socially deprived children, he states:

> They lack first of all an opportunity to learn language. The parents of these children ... typically talk less often to their children ... these parents seldom ask questions designed to prompt their children to discern various kinds of relationships among things and people and to use language to describe these relationships and to communicate them. In fact, when their children do ask questions or talk out, parents of the lower class often tell them to 'shut up' with no reason why.[51]

Once such children start school and compete with pupils who have been equipped with the language skills necessary for education, then '. . . no one has to tell the children of the poor that they are failing . . . they tend to drop out of school at the earliest opportunity.'[52] Worse, their occupational advancement is limited, to say the least, for '. . . our advancing technology is reducing—and reducing drastically—the economic opportunities for those with limited linguistic and numerical skills.'[53]

Even if the children did possess language and other skills, they would be unlikely to use them—according to the advocates of the cultural deprivation explanation. 'The children of the poor seldom have an opportunity to learn to take initiative, to be motivated towards future goals and toward status through achievement.'[54] As children, they are not motivated to learn. As adults, they are not motivated to save, to use initiative to achieve or even to work. Consequently, they cannot avail themselves of the economic opportunities of a society which is an oyster to those with the skills and desires to open it.

In many ways, the cultural deprivation view is similar to the problem family explanation put forward in the last chapter. Both regard faulty parenting as the vehicle which fails to equip the new generation for a competitive society. But the problem family concept stresses individual pathology. The cultural deprivation thesis identifies a more common pattern amongst a certain grouping of families. As Halsey puts it,

> . . . the sub-working class family is held to be the major villain of the piece, failing to provide the early training in literacy, numeracy, and acceptance of work and achievement habits which constitute the normal upbringing of the middle class child. . . .[55]

## Breaking Into The Cycle

Both the culture of poverty and cultural deprivation explanations regard social deprivation as a generational cycle. According to the former, the children of the poor are automatically assimilated into a separate culture which accepts poverty as a way of life. According to the latter, the children are not equipped with the tools to succeed in the culture of which they are a part. In either case, solutions are seen in terms of making the poor a fully functioning part of the mainstream culture.

Thus Lewis—after dismissing the possibility of a large-scale revolution to change American society—thought it best '. . . to attempt slowly to raise their [the poor's] level of living and to incorporate them into the middle class'.[56] How can the poor be changed? Three major means of intervention have been proposed.

   Firstly, to change the practices of existing poor parents. Spinley anticipated that widespread use of health visitors would change their behaviour so that '. . . one method of infant rearing will tend to become universal'.[57] The implication is that if slum-dwellers adopt the child-rearing practices of the privileged, then they too will raise children whose personalities are equipped to succeed. In a not dissimilar vein Sir Keith Joseph, in his 1972 speech, called for adult educational programmes to overcome the parental ignorance of the poor along with casework services to meet their emotional needs.[58] Subsequently, his Department published a book in which he wanted '. . . to look at parenthood, which is the key to the intergenerational processes at work within the family'.[59] The publication then suggests a variety of means—domiciliary visiting, parental involvement in play-groups, close links with schools, periods in residential establishments, marriage guidance—by which poor parents could be enabled to understand the child-rearing methods their children need.

   Secondly, to compensate the children for the deficiencies of their parents. In the USA, a strong argument behind the Headstart programme for the under-fives was that it would give poor children the educational and social skills of which their parental background had deprived them. Hunt, an enthusiastic supporter of Headstart, believed that not only would the children profit but that parents could also attend in order to learn how to treat children. With such a programme he believed that '. . . it is conceivable that we could bring a major share of the children of the persistently poor into the mainstream of our society within a generation.'[60] In Britain, thinking and practice developed on the same pattern. In the late 1960s and early 1970s, the government began to accelerate the expansion of nursery education, arguing in a circular of 1973: 'Nursery education is particularly valuable as a means of reducing the educational and social disadvantages suffered by children from homes which are culturally and economically deprived.'[61]

   Although most supporters of the cultural and family explanations advocated intervention before the age of five, some educationalists considered that it was not too late to compensate the school-age child. Clegg and Megson thought that the school could provide the '... affection, stability and security' which the bad home had failed to give. From this base, the children could then develop the skills, the emotions, the positive attitudes towards school and work, which would put them on a par with others.[62] Riessman, while also identifying the school as the agent of change, advocated a different approach. The essential step was for teachers to recognise the culture of poverty, for 'Only by understanding the culture of the under-privileged ... can discrimination be rooted out.'[63] If they studied the children's culture, teachers could shape their lessons accordingly. They could build on the practical orientation of the culture and win obedience by masculine strength rather than love.[64] Riessman's belief was that the children of the poor would then become willing to learn to advance, to move out of poverty.

In case little impact was made on present parents or on improving the educational and social functioning of poor children, a third approach was considered necessary—to prepare the children for their parenthood. Stanton in 1969 argued that 'Any effective modification of child-rearing practices ... can only be achieved through appropriate education of parents, particularly mothers.'[65] To achieve the change, he recommended that schoolgirls from deprived areas be trained, with the aid of visits to day nurseries and nursery schools, to appreciate the value of play and language development. Eventually, they would be able to offer their children better child-rearing practices than they received themselves. Another educationalist, Bullivant, agreed and discussed how schools could teach good parentcraft—cleanliness, baby care and bringing up children. By so doing she claimed that '... schools could help cure the problem of inadequate parents'.[66]

The explanations being discussed are that the poor are culturally different or deficient and that their limitations are mainly transmitted by inadequate family practices. Not surprisingly, therefore, the proposed solutions look to abolish poverty by improving family behaviour. This approach is well summarised by Gladwin writing in a period when the USA was launching projects to counter social deprivation.

The whole conception of the War on Poverty rests upon a definition of poverty as a way of life. The intellectual climate in which it was nurtured was created by studies of the culture of poverty ... [which] provided the basis for programs at the national level designed very explicitly to correct the social, occupational and psychological deficits of people born and raised to a life of poverty.[67]

These explanations held—and still hold—considerable sway amongst social scientists, educationalists, government officials and politicians. It is now appropriate to evaluate their theory and practice.

### EVALUATING THE CULTURAL EXPLANATIONS

The culture of poverty and cultural deprivation theses have now been described by reference to the authors most closely associated with them. The two explanations agree that the poor are qualitatively and distinctly different from the rest of society. According to the former they constitute a separate culture while, according to the latter, they are unable to participate properly in the dominant culture. Further, they agree that poverty is transmitted from generation to generation and that the main agent of conveyance is child-rearing methods.

The theses can be evaluated along the following lines. Firstly, some consideration must be given to the status of the research studies which have initiated and popularised the explanations. Secondly, information can be gathered to determine if and to what extent the poor are different from others. The material will also enable some points to be made about the child-rearing methods employed. Thirdly, generational studies will be consulted to see whether poverty does remain within the same line of families. After considering the two explanations in the light of the findings, some attention can be given to the outcomes of action programmes which have attempted to apply the solutions proposed by the advocates of the cultural approach.

*Criticisms of the Studies*

The studies by Lewis, Riessman, Spinley and others have been awarded much credit and have influenced both thinking and practice. Yet their writings have since come under severe attack for their impreciseness, their dubious methodology and the quality of the material which has been accumulated.

Roach and Gurslin, in a detailed consideration of the concept of the culture of poverty, point out that its authors generally fail to define 'the poor', so that it is not clear whether the poor and the lower working class are the same or two different groupings.[68] The point applies particularly to Riessman who uses interchangeably such terms as 'the lower class', 'lower socio-economic groups' and 'the deprived'.[69] The consequence is that the studies identify traits of the lower working class or working class—such as the inability to postpone gratifications—which are then taken to be characteristics of the poor. These characteristics are then linked with an explanation of the poverty of this minority.

The impreciseness in terminology might have been of less importance if the samples employed in the studies had been drawn in a random, non-biased fashion. Consider Spinley's study of the deprived and the privileged. She chose the former from mothers she knew personally in a slum area, the latter partly by asking universities to give names of students who had attended public schools. Being drawn in different ways the two groups were hardly comparable. They were not matched for age and sex, indeed the former were overwhelmingly female. Further, no consideration was given to those persons born in the slum area and subjected to its child-rearing methods but who had achieved success and moved away. Similarly, no study was made of those public-school children who were not successful enough to get to university. The design of the sample meant that the child-rearing practices of the slum-dwellers *had* to be equated with poverty and those of the public-school group *had* to be equated with success.

Spinley did at least compare two groups. Clegg and Megson presented a number of case studies and then generalised about the poor. Lewis, too—as Valentine shows in detail—based his theory upon a small number of families.[70] Such an approach is notoriously unreliable. It is akin to a psychiatrist having a number of poor people on his case load and thereby concluding that mental illness is the cause of poverty.

In order to be acceptable, research investigations must collect information in ways that are comparable and accurate. Spinley ignored this basic research requirement. Her material on the slum residents was gained by participant observation, by interviewing some of the mothers and through interviews with social workers. Yet information about the privileged was obtained from a postal questionnaire. Further, the questions given to each group were not always in the same form. Spinley argued that although the slum mothers could talk about the way they raised children, the public-school group—who might not be married—would be unable to recall all the methods used upon them. She admitted that the information gained from the public-school sample

... does not parallel closely in form that gained from a field study of a small slum area. That is to say, the statements listed above are not worded in the same manner as are the numbered statements in the 'typical' slum life history, nor is there an exact correspondence in the life areas covered.[71]

If the material about the two groups differed completely in the means of collection and partly in content, then Spinley was hardly justified in making any comparisons between the nature of and the causes of their behaviour. But Spinley does fully explain her methodology. Lewis does not say what questions he used, how he coded and categorised the replies and by what criteria he used some while excluding other materials. Similarly, Clegg and Megson do not discuss why some case histories are cited as examples of the behaviour of the poor while presumably others are rejected. These criticisms could be continued in regard to other writers. Thus in Keddie's edited volume, some scorn is poured on studies of language in which a formal interviewing situation reduces a child to '... defensive, monosyllabic behaviour' which is then used as material to demonstrate the lack of linguistic capacity of the poor.[72] Along with the impreciseness of the concepts and the limited nature of the samples, the doubts about the accuracy and reliability of some of the material serve to throw doubt on the very studies which have underpinned the cultural explanations. As Allen concludes, in his careful sifting of the studies, the status of the research is such that broad conclusions about cultural explanations '. . . should be viewed with extreme caution bordering on skepticism'.[73]

*How Different Are The Poor?*

The central theme of the culture of poverty explanation is that the poor are quite different from the non-poor. Their attitudes, values and behaviour are so distinct as to constitute a separate way of life, a way which inevitably leads to an acceptance of poverty. The cultural deprivation thesis also envisages the poor as falling so far behind the rest of the population in their motivations and skills that they make up a self-perpetuating residue doomed to poverty. Are the poor so different?

One way of testing the theses is by examining the characteristics of the poor against the non-poor. The differences which the authors claimed to exist can be clustered into four main areas: firstly, attitudes towards work; secondly, motivation regarding education, participation in organised activities and aspirations for advancement; thirdly, values as reflected in sexual behaviour, postponing gratifications and the treatment of children; fourthly, the possession of social skills, particularly language. Drawing upon studies which, in the main, employ reliable samples and methodologies, the existence of any differences will now be examined.

Do the poor want to *work*? The cultural explanations tend to regard the poor as different from the rest of society in that they prefer not to work or, at least, are not very enthusiastic about it. Being adverse to occupational advancement, they are prone to low incomes and poverty. In the USA, a number of investigations into work habits have occurred and they provide reliable data with which to test these assertions. Goodwin has published the results of two studies. In one he used a sample of over 4,000 adults to measure the attitudes, goals, beliefs and intentions towards work of various income groups. He found that far from rejecting work, the poorest persons identified their personal self-esteem with work as strongly as any other groups. Further, they expressed as much willingness to take job training as a means to advancement. Whatever the reason for their poverty, it was not a lack of desire to work their way out of it.[74] Further, in a related study, Goodwin interviewed 210 middle-class families, 220 mothers receiving welfare payments and 267 mothers who were in long-term receipt of public support. He compared their attitudes and behaviour in regard to the work ethic, acceptance of semi-legal activities such as gambling and fiddling, and acceptance of government handouts. He concluded that although higher income groups believed that the poor did not want to work, in fact, the latter were '. . . similar to the non-poor in basic work ethic and rejection of illegal sources of income'.[75]

Goodwin's findings receive support from the results of the New Jersey–Pennsylvania Negative Income Tax Experiment in which families were given a guaranteed minimum income whether they worked or not. It was expected—from the culture of poverty viewpoint—that the poor would opt not to work if they were ensured of an adequate income. Wright recorded the effects using a total sample of 1357. She found, in general, that the desire to work was so strongly entrenched that the poor chose to do so even if offered an income for not working. Wright concluded: 'Contrary to predictions derived from economic theory and culture of poverty speculations, the preceding analysis failed to uncover any discentive effects on work behaviour.'[76] She did not deny that a minority of the poor possessed unusual behaviour patterns but she added: '. . . even the poor who exhibit a variety of allegedly detrimental or "pathological" personality traits . . . still showed no discentives as a result of NIT.'[77]

The general tenor of these conclusions is confirmed by other American surveys. Davidson and Gaitz from a sample of 1,441 found no significant differences between the poor and non-poor regarding work attitudes.[78] Rein points to the 1968 *Manpower Report of the President* which discovered that unsupported mothers frequently chose to take employment even when it involved no financial gain.[79]

Studies of attitudes to work and the results of guaranteed incomes have not been made on the same scale in Britain as in the USA. However, important investigations do tie in closely with the American findings. Hill tends to discredit the idea of a significant pool of the 'work-shy'. Accepting that some may decide to remain unemployed, he points out that '. . . large numbers do remain in work, despite the fact that it is highly unremunerative'.[80] He explains that amongst all groups in society there are strong psychological and social pressures in favour of employment.

The widespread existence of the will to work is also stressed in a small but intensive study of the unemployed by Marsden and Duff. The men had often been treated badly by employers and employment, yet the authors observed, 'What remains striking, however, is the persistence of the will to work.'[81] The authors also found work to be of central importance, not just as a source of income but as a means of status, identity and company. They added:

> We found that so strong are the pressures and informal sanctions supporting work in our society that some of the workless cling to the desire to work, to a much greater extent than our society has a right to expect in view of what they had experienced through work and unemployment.[82]

To sum up, few of the exponents of the cultural explanations drew their views from reputable research. When investigations which compare the work attitudes of the poor with the non-poor are brought into the debate, then considerable doubt is cast on the assertion that the two are quite distinct. No doubt, some of the poor are apathetic and do not wish to work. However, these attitudes are not widespread enough to be equated with poverty. Many of the poor work when there is no financial incentive to do so. Others are unemployed against their will. In general, the poor share the common cultural orientation towards work—they place value on working, feel they should work and accept that status is associated with occupation.

Apart from motivation towards work, the poor were also held to be marked out by their lack of *motivation* towards other activities. The cultural exponents believe that poverty is perpetuated because the poor are characterised by a lack of desire for the education which brings personal advancement or the political action which might change their collective position. However, research investigations do not entirely support these generalisations. Sears and Maccoby report that the socially deprived are as much as or even more concerned than the middle class that their children should do well at elementary school.[83] Similarly, Frank Riessman's own work revealed lower-class parents regretting their own lack of education and wanting it for their children.[84] British studies come to the same conclusion.[85] Again, Len Reissman found few differences between the poor and others in their aspirations and in the sacrifices they would make to achieve them.[86]

Just as studies do indicate a willingness to benefit from education, so they also reveal that numbers of poor persons do participate in collective, organised activities. Valentine cites research which shows community organisation even amongst shanty town dwellers.[87] In ironic vein, he also challenges Lewis's claims by pointing to examples in Lewis's own writings of organised activities and of the poor discussing political parties and trade unions.[88] Heffernan concedes that few poor persons are actively involved in the running of political parties but argues that few individuals of any social grouping are so engaged. He draws upon indicators of talking about politics, campaigning, voting and holding office to deduce that numbers of the poor are interested in and concerned about political organisation.[89]

The conclusion is that the poor do appear to start with motivations and aspirations common to the rest of society. However, orientations can change. It seems that their hopes about education may decrease by the time their children reach secondary education. The continuance of motivation is related to opportunity. Thus Rein, discussing a huge response by the young unemployed to jobs created by the American Poverty Programme, commented: 'The experience of the early projects suggests that apathy is not so crucial as was thought. As soon as the projects offered an opportunity that seemed genuine, there was more response than could be handled.'[90] Again, Jacobs—in a study which will be discussed in chapter 6—shows that it is not unknown for the socially deprived to organise political action.[91] But if the opportunities do not exist, if change is deemed impossible, then apathy and lack of interest can replace motivation.

Attitudes towards work and education involve value judgements. It will be recalled that, in addition to these two areas, there were a number of other *values* which, the cultural exponents claimed, distinguished the poor from the non-poor. For instance, Lewis, Glazer and Moynihan argued that the poor had different sexual and moral values. Lewis, Spinley and Joseph also believed that the poor had less regard for their children than did members of other groups in society. Again, Lewis followed by Spinley and Clegg and Megson stated that the poor placed no value on saving or postponing immediate gratifications in order to reach a long-term goal. To the culture of poverty theorists, the value differences are the basic ground for claiming that the poor do possess a separate culture. To the cultural deprivationists they are evidence that the poor do not possess the attitudes and orientations which would enable them to profit from their culture. What are the research findings?

In the USA, Rainwater's review and research concludes that there is little evidence that the poor hold unorthodox views on sexual morality.[92] Bogue's study of 315 women dependent upon welfare benefits also casts serious doubts on the views that their sexual practices are seriously different from other women.[93] In Britain, Schofield's research did not find that sexual intercourse or pregnancy before marriage was more likely amongst the lowest income group.[94] Of course, the sexual standards and behaviour patterns of society may be changing but the existing data signifies that the practices of the poor move with them rather than constituting a different system.

Turning to beliefs about saving and postponing gratification, Miller and his colleagues conclude that there is little difference between different social groupings in the value placed upon thrift.[95] No doubt the poor do not experience the conditions which allow or encourage savings as a permanent feature of life. Nonetheless, the research suggests that they are at one with the rest of the population in accepting the desirability of such a practice.

Nor can it be said that the poor have less regard for their children. Reference has already been made to the wishes of such parents that their children will succeed at school. Further, there is evidence that poor parents often make considerable sacrifices for their children. In a study of sixty low-income families, Brown and Field found that half the parents but only six children had gone without a proper meal over a certain period. Their action constituted '. . . just one example of the way poor parents, like all parents, go without in order to do "their best" for their children'.[96] Three points must be added to the general conclusion that the poor value their offspring as much as other parents. Firstly, it is not denied that some inter-class differences exist in child-rearing practices. However, the differences are not extensive and the fact, as the Newsons show, that lower-class practices gradually move towards middle-class ones is an argument in favour of one culture which affects all its parts rather than of two separated cultures.[97] Secondly, individual poor parents may hold their children in low esteem and treat them cruelly but this does not prove that the poor in general behave in similar manner. Thirdly, poor parents may not always be able to raise their children in accordance with their own values. The present writer's own research and review of other studies reveals that often parents who abandon or part with their children do so against their own will. Usually, the beliefs and wishes they hold towards children are those of the population at large.[98]

The implication of research is that the poor do not hold values which are drastically or significantly different from higher income groups. This conclusion is underlined in a study by Sainsbury of a group of long-term socially deprived families:

> The interviews showed the presence of a higher regard for values—particularly in relationships—than the social workers often realised; in many families there was also an apparent acceptance that however great the stress and unpredictability of life within the family, order and structure are desirable.[99]

> . . . the moral and ethical standards they [the families] admired were frequently identical with those which the social workers were concerned to promote.[100]

Lewis, Spinley, Joseph and the other writers already discussed saw the poor as different not only in values but also in skills. In particular, they were deemed lacking in *language skills*. The culture of poverty writers considered that the poor possessed a language substantially distinct from that of the mainstream culture. Those who stressed the cultural deprivation thesis regarded them as extremely deficient or backward in the language of their culture. Their views have been attacked by a number of writers whose research and criticisms can now be briefly summarised.

Pearl argues cogently that the poor are not limited to the restricted code. He points out that through the popular press, radio, television, as well as their schooling, 'The very poor come into as much contact with the standard code as the very rich.'[101] They therefore acquire understanding of that code. This does not mean that their language is identical with that of other sections of the population. From existing evidence, he concedes that 'It differs in style, tempo, syntax and vocabulary from the affluent.'[102] But this does not make it a separate language and does not make it an inferior one which cannot be used for intelligent conversations, learning and business.

Support for Pearl's case can actually be found in the work of Frank Riessman—himself a supporter of the cultural deprivation thesis. He did not find the poor lacking in conversational abilities and he draws upon the work of Martin Deutsch to show that the socially deprived are frequently articulate '. . . in unstructured situations . . . .'[103]

Perhaps the best-known critic of the language deprivation theory has been Labov whose research has concentrated on black children from American ghettos. Labov does not dispute that the poor use non-standard English. Their children lack precision in spelling and practice in handling abstract symbols. However, this does not mean that they are inferior or backward in language. Labov demonstrates experimentally that the poor can conceptualise, use vivid language and can reason quickly. He states forcibly:

The concept of verbal deprivation has no basis in social reality: in fact, Negro children in the urban ghettos receive a great deal of verbal stimulation, hear more well-formed sentences than middle-class children, and participate fully in a highly verbal culture.[104]

Further, Labov argues strongly that in itself the language of the poor does not have to be a barrier to learning. He gives examples to show them reasoning and working verbally on problems. He concludes that it is '... a myth that lower-class children are non-verbal ...' and '... a myth that middle-class language is in itself better suited for dealing with abstract, logically complex and hypothetical questions'.[105]

Labov's findings accord with those of Torrey. She also concedes that the grammar of poor children is not as correct as that of others. She then demonstrates that far from being a restricted code, their language is capable of richness, artistry and subtlety. Further, she discounts Bernstein's assumption that '... dialects of lower socio-economic classes are intrinsically less adequate for educational purposes than middle class dialects.[106] And she concludes, 'From the above evidence it seems unlikely that the failure of many urban children to progress in reading is primarily due to structural differences between their dialect and school English.'[107]

Research in Britain on the language of the poor does not match that in America, although Rosen has attempted to dispel the idea that the lower social class can be distinguished by its lack of the elaborated code.[108] However, investigations which involve interviews with the poor often comment on their capacities to think, converse and sustain arguments. Thus Sainsbury records of his interviews: '... concentration was usually considerable: interruptions were not tolerated ... the respondents themselves brought any straying thoughts back to the subject in hand.'[109] Similarly, those who have shared work relationships or friendships with low-income families will, like the present writer, have observed conversations which are articulate, thoughtful and knowledgeable. Keddie, in attempting to apply the work of Labov and Torrey to Britain, concludes that variations in the use of language do occur between different social groupings but that the differences are not substantial. It is '... a dialectical variation of Standard English rather than a different kind of speech from that required for formal and logical thinking'.[110]

The studies of language are complex but, to summarise, the following points can be made. Firstly, the speech of the poor often (but not always) does show variations from that of more affluent persons. Accent, emphasis, style and dialect are likely to characterise one group rather than another. The poor are more likely to misspell or mispronounce words and to use faulty grammar. Secondly, the variations are not sufficient to prove that the poor have a different language. They have access to the constructions, the codes, the meanings of the language of the dominant culture. Thirdly, the speech used by the poor cannot be considered 'inferior'. It has descriptive powers, a richness of words, and allows logical thought and argument. Fourthly, the variations in speech used by the poor may be interpreted by the non-poor to denote inferiority or inability. Thus the work of Eeels and Havighurst recorded that '. . . deprived children use a great many words with a fair amount of precision, but these are not the words used in the schools'.[111] Middle-class persons may assume that the children are linguistically inadequate but this is not to say they are. The role played by external agencies will be raised again later in this chapter.

So far, the differences between the poor and the non-poor have been explored by reference to specific attitudes or skills. La Barre attempted to examine their behaviour in general by *a two-year study of poor families*. As part of a much larger investigation, she drew out thirty-two poor couples with a young child or children. All resided in the same locality, two-thirds had incomes below the official poverty line and most experienced overcrowded conditions.

Far from displaying character weaknesses, La Barre detected many strengths in the poor families. She recorded that most were '. . . hardworking, self-supporting and self-respecting. Most of the families were, by several pertinent indices, stable and well-organised'.[112] She emphasised the stability and responsibility of the husbands. They had few educational qualifications and were employed in low-paid occupations such as mechanics and caretakers. They were committed to working and preferred to remain in secure posts rather than risk seeking better-paid but less secure ones. The researcher observed that they had a

faithful, daily industriousness in work that is often dull, exhausting, and unrewarding in itself, under the debilitating and corroding humiliation and frustration of being always—or nearly always—low man on the totem pole, with little hope of promotion whatever one's abilities.[113]

Not only were the fathers good employees, they also tended to help in home-making tasks, so contributing to a general level of family stability. La Barre noted that there was an absence of symptoms of disorganisation and the parents achieved '. . . some measure of orderliness and cleanliness without the money or appliances that middle-class housewives take for granted'.[114]

Of course, a minority of families were disorganised, did display the behaviour which comes to public notice and is taken to be typical of the poor. But this is no more representative than are the bizarre and unstable practices of some affluent families. La Barre's main point is that many of the poor do not display the cultural characteristics attributed to them by the cultural explanations. Even without these features they still remain in poverty.

How different are the poor? This section has examined the evidence about attitudes to work, motivation, values and language skills. Some of the poor are not different at all. Their attitudes, values and practices are akin to the non-poor and they are distinguished mainly by their poverty and social deprivations. Other poor persons may show some variations but the differences are of degree rather than kind. The research findings do not support the contention that the poor are participants in a separate culture nor that they are confined to a minority who are far behind the attitudes and morals of the rest of society.

*Transmission Through Families*

Both the culture of poverty and the cultural deprivation explanations draw attention to the transmission of poverty from one generation to the next. Whether culture in general or child-rearing practices in particular are regarded as the agent of transmission, the outcome is the same. Poverty is almost inevitably handed on from parents to children. To cite Sir Keith Joseph again, 'Parents who were themselves deprived in one or more ways in childhood become in turn the parents of another generation of deprived children.'[115]

Certainly, the idea that the same line of families are always poor has much popular support. When publicising his views,

Sir Keith received public support from one Director of Social Services who said that, of 20,000 households in his city, nearly all the social problems came from 800 families, most of whom had been known to the welfare services for five generations.[116] Yet, when a researcher investigated the claim, the informant could not supply any evidence with which to uphold his charge.[117] Attention must concentrate less on popular statements, more on the findings of research.

Mention has already been made of Wright and Lunn's intergenerational study of families. Their investigation covered not just poor families but problem families, i.e. the core whose inadequate child-rearing and other behaviour patterns have been particularly noted. The researchers point out that a third of the children of problem parents also became problem families. More important, is the corollary that two-thirds did not. Moreover, the new generation had fewer rent arrears, less contact with welfare agencies and improved work records.[118] The trend of this British study is confirmed by an American study of low-income families. Handler and Hollingsworth found that of a sample dependent upon welfare benefits only a third had parents who had been similarly placed (and many of these only for a brief period). They concluded that the stereotype of 'second generation' claimants was inaccurate.[119]

In Britain, following the public statements made by Sir Keith Joseph, some research resources have been devoted to investigating the cycle of deprivation. In one sponsored study, Paterson (in her pilot sample) selected families believed to have had long-standing familial contacts with the social services. In short, the group was not a random sample of the poor but one biased towards showing a generational pattern. Even so, of the twenty-three families whose histories were pursued only one had been known to welfare agencies for five generations and only seven for four generations. What of the siblings of the parents in the twenty-three families? These totalled 149, and, as far as could be ascertained, sixty-six had no deprivations, indeed some were reported as 'prosperous'. In general, Paterson was impressed by the '... interruption of the transmission mechanism and the apparent non-recurrence of the cycle of deprivation.'[120] Her provisional conclusion was that '... difficulties found in one generation did not necessarily reappear in the next generation and the transmission did not appear to be an inevitable regular feature.'[121]

The three investigations just summarised suggest that poverty is not simply handed down from one family to another. This point is confirmed in a major review of research relevant to the cycle of deprivation specifically commissioned by the Department of Health and Social Security. Within it, Rutter and Madge report that—on the one hand—children from the same poor families and subjected to similar child-rearing practices may, as adults, experience very different economic circumstances.[122] On the other hand, some persons fall into poverty without having parents who were poor. It must be added that Rutter and Madge did find some evidence of continuities of poverty. However, they considered it more important to report that 'At least half of the children born into a disadvantaged home do not repeat the pattern of disadvantage in the next generation. Over half of all forms of disadvantage arise anew each generation.'[123]

In order to clarify the research on generational transmission, it is important to specify what is not being said. The investigations do not prove that child-rearing practices are never repeated in some families. For instance, violence towards children is sometimes—but not inevitably—repeated in succeeding generations.[124] Again, it is not denied that there are some cycles of deprivation, that some lines of families do continue in poverty. However, the significant finding is that the children of many other poor families do escape while those of some non-poor families do become poor. These findings are at variance with the culture of poverty and cultural deprivation theses which regarded the effect of culture or inadequate child-socialisation methods as so strong that poverty was the inevitable lot of the next generation. The conclusion must be that other formative influences are also at work.

### Cultural Explanations of Poverty

In order to evaluate the culture of poverty thesis, Rossi and Blum made an extensive review of the relevant research up to 1966. Initially they criticised the weak research methodology of the investigations that has led to the formulation of the theory. Turning to other studies, they then found no support for the claim that poverty is passed from generation to generation by cultural processes. They further concluded that

There is little firm evidence for the existence of a 'culture of poverty' which marks off the very poor as distinctively different from S.E.S. [socio-economic status] levels immediately above them. The poor appear to be quantitatively rather than qualitatively different.[125]

This chapter has attempted to show that investigations made since 1966 serve to confirm Rossi and Blum's contentions. The poor are not characterised by a refusal to participate in organised activities; by a disinclination to work; by a lack of aspiration for education and progress; by a rejection of the sexual mores of the main society; by an acceptance of inferior ways of rearing and treating children. The culture of poverty thesis is not a satisfactory explanation of poverty in western society.

What of the cultural deprivation explanation? Its basic tenets are that a minority of parents employ inadequate child-rearing methods which lead to children and then adults whose personalities, inclinations and skills are so underdeveloped that they cannot benefit from the wider culture of which they are a part. In turn, the child-rearing methods they inherit produce yet another generation of the poor and so on. As a complete explanation of poverty, it too must be rejected. At times the poor opt to work even when it is financially more profitable to draw social security. Some of the unemployed poor are desperate for employment. Again, numbers in poverty care deeply for their children while others possess adequate language skills. The poor and non-poor cannot be neatly divided into the culturally deprived and others. Further, child-rearing practices cannot be the sole means of the transmission of poverty, for sometimes the children of the poor escape while others fall into poverty. Despite the rejection of the cultural deprivation view, it must be conceded that *some* of the poor do display attitudes and behaviour which appear to reinforce their condition, that *some* cycles of deprivation can be identified and that the child-rearing methods of *some* poor parents do not seem in the best interests of their children. These cases, of course, are the ones which have given rise to the theory that *all* the poor behave in these fashions. The data available, then, can appear perplexing, not to say conflicting. Some clarification may be found if three points are taken into consideration.

Firstly, the different or deviant behaviour exhibited by some of the poor may occur, not because they are the minority subjected in the distant past to inadequate child-rearing methods, but because they have been subjected to recent prolonged and adverse experiences. For instance, students of the unemployed mention that men who endure long periods out of work may react (contrary to their previous inclination) by losing the will to work. Again, there is evidence that parents whose educational aspirations for their children were high at primary school have lost them at the secondary stage when it is obvious that their children do not fit into the educational system.[126] Heffernan points out that where the poor are less likely to become involved in political action, it is not because they are ignorant about politics or not wishing for action, but because experience has shown them to be powerless to effect change.[127] Thus the behaviour of a minority may not reflect different beliefs or values but may be a reaction against their failure to attain those values. As the anthropologist Harris stated, '... people may be encultured to behave in one way but be obliged by situational or functional factors beyond their control to behave in another way.'[128]

Secondly, the child-rearing practices which have been so strongly condemned by some writers may also be a reaction to circumstances. It is odd that writers, such as Spinley, in identifying a lack of parental attention, allowing children little privacy, inconsistency of discipline and weak emotional ties as characteristic child-rearing methods of the poor, did not ask whether the parents wanted to use these approaches. If they had possessed the resources of the privileged group—ample space, time, domestic gadgets and sufficient money—they might well have raised their off-spring along other lines. As already mentioned, the present author has examined the relationship between social deprivation and parents who part with their children. Faced with material anxieties, accommodation difficulties and other distressing problems, some parents could not cope properly with their children and even placed them with other people.

However, generally such actions were at odds with their own beliefs and values concerning good parenthood.[129] Similarly—and the matter will be taken up in chapter 5—other child-rearing practices employed by some poor parents may be in contradiction to their own wishes. If this is so, then any cycle of deprivation may start with poverty stimulating unacceptable child-rearing methods rather than vice versa.

Thirdly, consideration must be given to the part played by social agencies in exaggerating or formulating the apparent deficiencies of the poor. Consider language. Clearly some researchers are able to communicate with and evoke articulated responses from the poor. Others find them non-communicative and inarticulate. As Labov declared, '. . . the social situation is the most powerful determinant of verbal behaviour . . .'[130] It seems clear that where children from poverty backgrounds have been placed in formal test situations with which they are unfamiliar, then the social situation tends to work against them. Anxious and uncomfortable, they may give monosyllabic answers and not reveal their verbal capacities. In turn, the officials of the agency applying the test may assume that such children are backward in verbal ability, that they can not benefit from schooling and that their home backgrounds are the cause of their failures. Although there is evidence that such children can use the same codes as more affluent children, they may never be offered educational (and occupational) opportunities as the result of these early test results.[131]

Even if tests are not used, Labov argues that variations in dialect or grammar may still assume 'symbolic importance' in that they are construed to mean that children from poverty backgrounds lack the verbal skills necessary for educational advancement. The teachers do not expect and do not encourage academic development. Consequently, the children actually do fall behind in language and other capacities. The agency has therefore identified the child as culturally deficient, hindered his progress and, to cap it all, usually blames the parents for what happens.[132] Whether Labov's analysis is precisely correct or not, the data put forward by him—and others—is sufficiently weighty to ensure that this book must examine the interaction between welfare agencies and the poor.

Although cultural deprivation cannot be taken as the final

explanation of poverty, there is no doubt that at times some
of the poor display behaviour which appears to support it.
However, the above considerations show that the behaviour
may well stem, not from transmitted family patterns, but from
responses to more immediate forces. As in the previous chapter,
attention is again directed at the influence of external factors.
These forces appear to operate in two main directions. As
just explained, they can cause people to act at variance with
their own wishes and values. Further, they can define the direction
of social deprivation, that is they make certain persons or
groupings more vulnerable to poverty. For instance, Wright
found that unemployment did not necessarily descend upon
the lazy or those alleged to be culturally deprived. Instead,
it tended to fall upon those already marked out by certain
'. . . basic economic and social variables . . .' such as '. . . family
structure, composition and size, education and welfare status
. . . factors over which they generally have little or no control'.[133]
In similar fashion, Handler and Hollingsworth explain that society
is so shaped that women who find themselves as single-parent
families are more likely than most other persons to experience
poverty whether they are culturally deprived or not.[134]

Given the capacity of adverse external forces to affect human
behaviour, it is hardly surprising if attempts to solve poverty
by persuading parents to improve their methods of socialisation
or by compensating children for their home experiences have
had little effect. Hunt, himself a supporter of these solutions
advocated by the cultural theorists, admitted that '. . . clinical
psychologists and psychiatrists have tried to change child rearing
practices of lower-class parents by counselling them individually
or in groups. Little or nothing, so far as I can ascertain,
has come of it.'[135] Even more significantly, Bronfenbrenner
undertook, for the US National Academy of Sciences, a review
of all the 'early intervention programmes' designed to compensate
children. His conclusion, which he also reported to the DHSS
in Britain, was that in general they had little lasting effect.[136]
Frequently, the approaches made little impact on parents or
children. But even where they did, the results did not suggest
they would enable the families to be removed from poverty.
Interestingly, Bronfenbrenner also deduced that adverse child-
socialisation methods and child performance depended less on

cultural deprivation and more on outside circumstances. He argued that the 'solutions' he had investigated would have little effect unless there was a transformation of the conditions of life for poor families in order to enable them to provide adequately for their children.[137]

The cultural explanations have been evaluated and found wanting. The research samples which gave rise to the theories were not adequate and led the exponents to overlook the poor who did not exhibit the characteristics of cultural deprivation or the culture of poverty. Nonetheless, they have contributed much. In the USA, Lewis and his successors helped to make poverty a public as well as an academic issue. In Britain, Sir Keith Joseph also attempted to harness public concern and, by forcibly expounding his thesis, stimulated debate and research. One result of the latter is that attention has been directed at the interaction between the patterns of living of the poor and the circumstances and influences which surround them. One such external factor is the welfare system, and the next chapter will look at the relationship between poverty and social service agencies.

#### REFERENCES

1 E. James *America Against Poverty* Routledge (1970) ch. 6
2 C. Valentine *Culture and Poverty* University of Chicago Press (1968) p. 3
3 O. Lewis *Five Families* Basic Books (1959)
4 O. Lewis *La Vida* Panther Books (1968) p. 49
5 *ibid.* p. 51
6 *ibid.*
7 *ibid.* p. 52
8 *ibid.* p. 53
9 *ibid.*
10 *ibid.* p. 50
11 J. B. Cullingworth *Problems of An Urban Society* vol. 3, Allen and Unwin (1973) p. 58
12 T. Sabin 'The Culture of Poverty, Social Identity and Cognitive Outcomes' in V. Allen (ed.) *Psychological Factors in Poverty* Markham (1970) p. 30
13 *ibid.* p. 36
14 F. Riessman *The Culturally Deprived Child* Harper and Row (1962) p. 3
15 *ibid.* p. 27
16 *ibid.* p. 26

17 *ibid.* p. 112
18 *ibid.* p. 2
19 R. Will and H. Vatter *Poverty in Affluence* Harcourt, Brace (1965); R. Warren *Multi-Problem Families* State Charities Aid Association (1960)
20 N. Glazer and D. Moynihan *Beyond the Melting Pot* Harvard University Press (1963)
21 D. Moynihan *The Negro Family* US Dept of Labor (1965) p. 5
22 Valentine *op. cit.* p. 30
23 E. Banfield *The Unheavenly City* Little, Brown (1970) p. 122
24 D. Matza 'The Disreputable Poor' in N. Smelser and S. Lipset (eds) *Social Structure and Mobility in Economic Development* Aldine (1966) p. 317; also in R. Bendix and S. Lipset (eds) *Class, Status and Power* Free Press (2nd edn 1966)
25 Valentine *op. cit.* p. 141
26 Banfield *op. cit.* p. 125
27 A. H. Halsey *Educational Priority* vol. I, HMSO (1972) p. 16
28 K. Danzinger *Socialization*, Penguin (1971) p. 17
29 V. Allen (ed.) *op. cit.* p. 67
30 Danzinger *op. cit.* p. 15
31 B. Spinley *The Deprived and the Privileged* Routledge (1953) p. 15
32 *ibid.* pp. 108–9
33 Halsey *op. cit.* p. 17
34 A. Clegg and B. Megson *Children in Distress* Penguin Books (1968) p. 22
35 *ibid.* p. 29
36 *ibid.* p. 30
37 *ibid.* p. 22
38 *ibid.* p. 28
39 *Op. cit.*, p. 37
40 Sir K. Joseph, Speech to Pre-School Playgroups Association, 29 June 1972, para. 15; sections are reproduced in E. Butterworth and R. Holman (eds) *Social Welfare in Modern Britain* Fontana (1975) pp. 387–93
41 *ibid.* para 43
42 *ibid.*
43 *ibid.* para. 41
44 *ibid.* para. 16
45 *ibid.* para. 17
46 *ibid.* para. 41
47 *ibid.* para. 61
48 *ibid.* para. 18
49 N. Keddie (ed.) *Tinker, Tailor, the Myth of Cultural Deprivation* Penguin Books (1973) p. 9
50 B. Bernstein 'A Socio-Linguistic Approach to Social Learning' in J. Gould (ed.) *Penguin Survey of the Social Sciences* Penguin Books (1965). Bernstein has modified his earlier thesis and would not necessarily ally himself with a cultural explanation of poverty; see B. Bernstein *Class, Codes and Control* Routledge (1971)
51 J. McV. Hunt 'Poverty Versus Equality of Opportunity' in Allen *op. cit.* p. 54
52 *ibid.* p. 53
53 *ibid.*
54 *ibid.* p. 54
55 Halsey *op. cit.* p. 17

56 Lewis *La Vida, op. cit.* p. 59
57 Spinley *op. cit.* p. 139
58 Joseph *op. cit.* paras 46–7
59 DHSS *The Family in Society, Preparation for Parenthood* HMSO (1974) p. 7
60 Hunt *op. cit.* p. 60
61 Cited in M. Young (ed.) *Poverty Report 1974* Temple Smith (1974) p. 169
62 Clegg and Megson *op. cit.* p. 101
63 Riessman *op. cit.* p. 24
64 *ibid.*
65 M. Stanton cited in the *Guardian* 13 Oct. 1969
66 B. Bullivant 'Vicious Cycle' in the *Guardian* 3 April 1973
67 T. Gladwin *Poverty USA* Little, Brown (1967) p. 26
68 J. Roach and O. Gurslin 'An Evaluation of the Concept "Culture of Poverty"' *Social Forces* vol. 45, no. 3 (1967)
69 Riessman *op. cit.* pp. 3–4
70 Valentine *op. cit.* ch. 5
71 Spinley *op. cit.* p. 94
72 Keddie *op. cit.* p. 27
73 Allen *op. cit.* p. 373
74 L. Goodwin *Do The Poor Want To Work?* Brookings Institute (1972)
75 L. Goodwin 'How Suburban Families View the Work Orientations of the Welfare Poor' *Social Problems* vol. 19, no. 3 (1972)
76 S. Wright 'Work Response To Income Maintenance' *Social Forces* vol. 53, no. 4 (1975)
77 *ibid.*
78 C. Davidson and C. Gaitz 'Are The Poor Different?' *Social Problems* vol. 22, no. 2 (1974)
79 M. Rein *Social Policy* Random House (1970) p. 254
80 M. Hill 'Are The Work-Shy A Myth?' *New Society* vol. 16, no. 409 (30 July 1970); M. Hill, R. Harrison and A. Sergeant *Men Out of Work* Cambridge University Press (1973)
81 D. Marsden and E. Duff *Workless* Penguin Books (1975) p. 259
82 *ibid.* p. 264
83 R. Sears, E. Maccoby and H. Levin *Patterns of Child Rearing* Row Peterson (1957)
84 Riessman *op. cit.* pp. 10–11
85 R. Davie, N. Butler and H. Goldstein *From Birth to Seven* Longman (1972) ch. 4
86 L. Reissman, *Inequality in American Society* Scott, Foresman (1973) p. 67
87 Valentine *op. cit.* pp. 55–6
88 *ibid.*
89 W. Heffernan *Political Behaviour of the Poor* Institute for Research on Poverty, University of Wisconsin (n.d.) pp. 3–4
90 Rein *op. cit.* p. 156
91 S. Jacobs *The Right to a Decent House* Routledge (1976) p. 106
92 L. Rainwater 'The Problem of Lower Class Culture and Poverty-War Strategy' in D. Moynihan (ed.) *On Understanding Poverty* Basic Books (1968)
93 D. Bogue 'A Long-Term Solution to the A.F.D.C. Problem in Prevention of Unwanted Pregnancy' *Social Service Review* (Dec. 1975)
94 M. Schofield *The Sexual Behaviour of Young Adults* Allen Lane (1973) pp. 139, 168
95 S. Miller *et al.* 'Poverty and Self-Indulgence' in L. Ferman (ed.) *Poverty*

*in America* University of Michigan Press, Ann Arbor (1968)

96 M. Brown and F. Field *Poor Families and Inflation* Child Poverty Action Group (1974) p. 12

97 See J. and E. Newson *Four Years Old in an Urban Community* Allen and Unwin (1968)

98 See R. Holman *Inequality in Child Care* Child Poverty Action Group (1976)

99 E. Sainsbury *Social Work with Families* Routledge (1975) p. 6

100 *ibid.* p. 112

101 A. Pearl 'The Poverty of Psychology—An Indictment' in Allen *op. cit.* p. 351

102 *ibid.*

103 Riessman *op. cit.* pp. 76–7

104 W. Labov 'The Logic of Nonstandard English' in Keddie *op. cit.* p. 21

105 *ibid.* p. 42

106 J. Torrey 'Illiteracy in the Ghetto' in Keddie *op. cit.* p. 70

107 *ibid.*

108 H. Rosen *Language and Class* Falling Wall Press (1973)

109 Sainsbury *op. cit.* pp. 5–6

110 Keddie *op. cit.* p. 13

111 Cited in Riessman *op. cit.* p. 74

112 M. La Barre 'The Strengths of the Self-Supporting Poor' *Social Casework* vol. 49, no. 8 (1968)

113 *ibid.*

114 *ibid.*

115 Joseph *op. cit.* para. 61

116 Reported in *The Times*, 21 Oct. 1974

117 See A. Paterson *The Inter-Generational Cycle of Deprivation* University of Edinburgh Press (1975) p. 3

118 C. Wright and J. Lunn 'Sheffield Problem Families: a Follow-up Study of their Sons and Daughters' *Community Medicine* (26 Nov. and 3 Dec. 1971)

119 J. Handler and E. Hollingsworth *The Deserving Poor* Markham (1971) pp. 56–68

120 Paterson *op. cit.* p. 21

121 *ibid.* p. 17

122 M. Rutter and N. Madge *Cycles of Disadvantage* Heinemann (1976) pp. 24–30

123 *ibid.* p. 304

124 *ibid.* p. 236

125 Cited in L. Reissman *op. cit.* p. 50. See also P. Rossi and D. Blum 'Class, Status and Poverty' in D. Moynihan (ed.) *On Understanding Poverty* Basic Books (1968)

126 See J. Bynner 'Deprived Parents' *New Society* vol. 27, no. 594 (21 Feb. 1974)

127 Heffernan *op. cit.*

128 M. Harris *Culture, Man and Nature* Crowell (1971) p. 140

129 Holman *op. cit.*

130 Labov *op. cit.* p. 33

131 See W. Robinson 'The Elaborated Code in Working Class Language' *Language and Speech* vol. 8 (1965)

132 Labov *op. cit.* pp. 52–3

133 Wright *op. cit.*

134 Handler and Hollingsworth *op. cit.* p. 68
135 Hunt *op. cit.* p. 57
136 U. Bronfenbrenner 'Children, Families and Social Policy' in DHSS *op. cit.*
137 Reported in J. Tizard, P. Moss and J. Perry *All Our Children* Temple Smith (1976) pp. 202–3

# CHAPTER 4

# The Deficient Agency

Writing in the mid-1960s, Professor Martin Rein observed: 'The growing criticism of professional and organizational rigidities of social welfare services may well be one of the important bench marks of the 1960s.'[1] Social service agencies had long been accustomed to attacks from those who wanted welfare spending reduced. The decade of the 1960s was marked by criticisms from another source, from those who wanted to improve the services in order to reduce social deprivations of various kinds. The attention of many writers and researchers was turned away from the inadequacies of the deprived and towards the inadequacies of social welfare agencies.

Consider education. The previous chapter has already mentioned that in the USA Riessman had charged schools with not adapting to the cultural deprivations of pupils and thus failing to counter the processes which doomed them to poverty. Subsequent students focussed even more squarely on the schools. Cicourel and Kitsuse condemned the view that educational failure was due to the personal deficiencies of children and stated that

> Organizational personnel almost never questioned the inadequacies, defects, or failures of the 'system' ... the efficiency of the tests used to identify ability, the courses designed to develop it, and the teachers assigned to evaluate the degree of development.[2]

They and other researchers, therefore, examined the part the agencies played in causing educational failure and allied social deprivations. Outside of education, similar investigations were made of the personal social services and other social welfare organisations. The faults of the agencies were seen, by a number

146

of writers, as the cause of poverty.

The starting point of the deficient agency explanation is the belief that society already possesses a framework of welfare services which are capable of combating social deprivation. McCashin, after reviewing the literature, writes: 'According to this model an adequate basic framework of services already exists and much can be done in the way of alleviating poverty if these services and benefits were properly delivered.'[3] The services *should* counter deprivation for their main purpose is regarded as helping those who are in need. Meyer explains:

> The primary function of institutionalized human services, of course, is the improvement of the quality through provision of adequate financial resources, housing, recreation, health care, transportation, access to the advantages of the city . . . .'[4]

It follows that if social deprivations do exist, then the agencies are not properly fulfilling their tasks. Further, it is concluded that social deprivations can be resolved by identifying and remedying the faults within agencies. This deficient agency explanation can be expanded and explained in more detail in three directions. Firstly, by examining the view that welfare services fail because of technical inefficiencies within certain agencies. Secondly, there is the view that the inefficiency arises from a lack of coordination or cooperation between various services. Thirdly, that there is a key service, central to combating social deprivation, and that this service is not functioning properly.

## TECHNICALLY INEFFICIENT SERVICES

The social services, it is argued, exist to reach those in need, especially the most severely deprived. However, much evidence has been accumulated to show that the services often fall far short of their laudable objectives. For instance, the income maintenance services should relieve poverty, but large numbers of persons do not obtain the benefits which are their due. The Child Poverty Action Group draws upon official statistics to reveal that over a quarter of the families entitled to supplementary benefit, family income supplement and rate rebates do not receive them. Indeed, for 1975 if the outstanding sums from these benefits are added to that not claimed for rent rebates and allowances and free school meals, then nearly £600 million was not claimed.[5]

Not only do some services fail to reach the most deprived but they may actually favour the least needy. Studies of voluntary American social work agencies in the 1960s were among the first to identify the 'disengagement from the poor'. The lower the social class of the applicant, the less the chance that the agency would offer them substantial help.[6] In short, the agencies preferred higher-class clients. In Britain, such a pronounced bias would not be found within social work agencies but questions have been raised about the more general services of health and education. In 1968, Titmuss wrote:

> We have learnt from fifteen years' experience that the higher income groups know how to make better use of the [health] service; they tend to receive more specialist attention; occupy more of the beds in better equipped and staffed hospitals; receive more elective surgery; have better maternity care, and are more likely to get psychiatric help and psychotherapy than low income groups—particularly the unskilled.[7]

His assertion stimulated a lively debate about who gained most from the National Health Service. The debate cannot be repeated here but it is worth noticing that Phyllis Wilmott draws upon official data to show that the poor,

> . . . although they suffer more ill health (and die younger) what they do not get is either the best or the most appropriate service. There is an increasing body of evidence that shows that they use preventive services less often, that they accept lower standards of care, and that they often demand care for serious health conditions at a later stage of ill health.[8]

This book has already pointed to class bias within the educational services. It suffices here to mention that in terms of state expenditure, the children of unskilled manual workers receive less from nursery education and education after sixteen years of age than those of professional workers although the former numerically outweigh the latter.[9] Parker in her study of the British social services pays especial attention to the distribution of the benefits of the income maintenance, health, education, housing and personal social services. In almost every case, she demonstrates that the belief that the services mainly serve the poor is little more than a myth.[10] Far from the health services improving the health of the poor relative to other workers, far from the educational services equipping them to rise out of poverty, far from income services saving them from social deprivation, there are grounds for concluding with Rein that

> Welfare services act as mechanisms for the distribution of advantages rather than for the reduction of inequalities. Consequently, the most deprived tend to be overlooked and welfare services increasingly serve the more affluent middle classes.[11]

If social agencies are not performing their duties properly and thus not achieving their apparent objectives, what are the reasons? A major explanation is that they have not developed sufficient technical expertise in what is called the delivery of services. The low take-up rate of welfare benefits is sometimes attributed to the agencies' lack of skill in advertising their goods or in composing forms which can be readily understood by the ordinary person. Studies of social security offices have concluded that claimants may not only be bewildered by bureaucratic complexities but, if they surmount these, may suffer from official errors and mistakes.[12] Of course, disgruntled claimants can appeal to a Supplementary Appeal Tribunal but a government enquiry admitted that even the appeals process worked inefficiently. Criticisms were made of the lack of expertise of the tribunals' chairmen, the baffling forms and the forbidding procedures. It was felt that the whole apparatus of the system needed overhauling.[13] In regard to health and educational services, it is argued that the means of reception and communication do not make working-class patients or pupils feel welcome or valued, with the result that they are discouraged from making full use of the agencies. Within the personal social services, too, attention has been drawn to off-putting practices. In studying the former children's departments, Hall makes an important point when he shows that untrained receptionists could wrongly advise callers and so prevent them from obtaining a needed service.[14]

A related reason put forward to account for agency inefficiency is that, over time, agencies begin to concentrate on the internal life of their organisation rather than on the needs of clients or consumers. This is not to imply any deliberate, malevolent plan on the part of the administrators of services. Rather, as organisations grow, greater attention is given to smooth running, to career prospects and to the continuance of an agency upon which thousands of employees may have become dependent. In these circumstances, as became clear in Stevenson's study, agencies may become unwilling to make changes which, although beneficial to clients, might upset staff morale or functions.[15] For instance, services which command income maintenance benefits, educational grants or clothing allowances may fail to publicise them, not because they are unaware of the need but in order to save further demands on busy staff. Zimmerman in an analysis of the intake processes of social work agencies in the USA has identified what must be an extreme form of agencies using clients to perpetuate their own existence. He found that social workers chose clients in order to get the kind of documentary evidence which could be used to convince outsiders, especially resource-givers, that the agency was performing a useful role whether or not the clients were actually helped.[16]

The theme that agency practice can get so twisted as to allow the interests of employees to predominate is also used to explain why those in less need may receive better treatment than those in greatest need. Agencies tend to be manned by middle-class professionals and officials who, the argument runs, respond more readily to articulate, appreciative clients, that is to those nearest to their own social-class position. Of course, these are probably not the most socially deprived clients. Accordingly, Cloward and Epstein attribute the disengagement of American social workers (they do not make their point about British social workers) from the poor to the formers' desire to exercise sophisticated casework techniques which happen to work with articulate, middle-class clients rather than the most socially disadvantaged ones.[17] Similarly, the greater use made of certain health facilities by more affluent persons is explained by the encouragement given by medical staff who relate more comfortably to patients from their own kind of background.

Services may not be properly delivered because of a lack of technical expertise, because the needs of the organisation begin to dominate or because professional or class interests gain priority. Whatever the case, blame is attributed not to the clients but to the failures of a certain agency or the workers within it. The result is that the services do not achieve the objectives of combating social deprivation.

*Solutions*

If poverty is due to the technical failings of the social services, then solutions will be found by improvements within the present framework of these agencies. Indeed, much of what is called 'social administration' has been devoted to studies suggesting ways of maximising the output of welfare organisations. It is true to say that more attention has been accorded to discussions of how to improve delivery mechanisms than to the actual question of whether the explanation of poverty really does rest in the malfunctioning of the social services. Some of the solutions, both those implemented or those just proposed, will now be mentioned.

It was shown that the personal social services sometimes fail to reach the most deprived clients. A solution has been sought in terms of facilitating *access* to the services. Kahn proposes the establishment of separate access centres to inform prospective clients of the services which could meet their needs. He argues that a known access service would deal with their bewilderment in the face of our complex and confusing welfare network. He believes that it would prevent the poor from missing out on services which are designed to redistribute resources in their favour.[18] Already in Ireland, the Community Information Centres operate to link people and agencies, it being taken that '. . . services are of a high standard but people need to know of them'.[19] Once inside the right agencies, consumers may still have to find a way past 'gatekeepers'. Hence suggestions have been made to train receptionists, to use social workers as receptionists, or to have officials always on hand to advise at the point of entry. Such improvements, it is assumed, would result in more persons receiving a service, particularly those who may be excluded at present.

Ways of *increasing the take-up* of income maintenance services, especially supplementary benefit, now occupy a sizeable literature. Reforms advocated include more publicity, more comprehensive yet simplified application forms, and more welcoming attitudes by counter staff. In order that the system operate more justly, the Bell Report urges that Appeal Tribunals should have legally qualified regional chairmen, while a new form of second-tier appeal should be created.[20] Such changes, it is hoped, would give those eligible for benefits both the knowledge and the confidence to apply.

Moving on from improving the access and take-up machinery, some consideration has been given to *countering those organisational tendencies which relegate client interests* to a secondary position. Initially, some emphasis was placed on training administrators and professionals with the expectation that their mode of functioning would change. Subsequently, the case has been put for more effective management techniques. New, improved techniques should enable managers to identify their primary objectives—with service to the needy clients being accorded some priority. The 1960s and 70s witnessed vast organisational reforms of the functions and boundaries of local authorities which were accompanied by a renewed interest in the skills of management. One of the most widely discussed was the concept of and introduction of corporate management.[21] To be sure, corporate management was not designed specifically to relieve poverty. Nonetheless, it was anticipated that a unified, corporate approach within local authorities would lead to a more just distribution and a more efficient use of resources which would thereby benefit the users of services.[22]

Access, improved delivery mechanisms, new styles of management have been suggested as the remedy to inefficient services. In some cases, the suggestions have been implemented, in others not. Agencies are not always as ready to improve their techniques as is sometimes assumed. Stevenson concluded from her study that 'There is no doubt that any organisation tends to protect the status quo and to be resistant to change. Government bureaucracies show this tendency to a marked degree . . .'.[23] If discussion does not lead to agency reform, then perhaps example will.

Accordingly, in the USA, the concept of the demonstration project was developed as a means of change. Demonstration projects occur outside of established agencies in the hope that the former's revelation of what can be done will provoke the latter into making internal improvements in order to have the same successes. As Rein deftly explains, the belief is that 'Once tested, the experimental programmes would spread to all other institutions which serve the poor.'[24] The concept was popularised in the USA prior to the government's official War on Poverty. In Philadelphia, for instance, the Ford Foundation supported a vocational high school run by indigenous black leaders with the expectation that existing state schools would learn from and copy their more effective techniques for reaching deprived children.

A comparable approach was conceived by the British Community Development Project. These joint Home Office/local authority schemes established, from 1970, teams in twelve areas of social deprivation with the general brief to '... find ways of meeting more effectively the needs of individuals, families and communities ... suffering from many forms of social deprivation.'[25] The explanations of poverty on which action has been based have changed over time and even vary between the twelve teams. Yet, at its inception, the Community Development Project did lean heavily on a technically inefficient agency explanation. It held that '... although the social services cater reasonably well for the majority, they are much less efficient for a minority ....'[26] Consequently, a major objective was to improve deficient agencies. Thus one document states that the strategy '... will be aimed at building up the capacity of the statutory services to respond with greater understanding ...'.[27] More pointedly, another said, 'The need, in short, is to find ways of helping people to use the social services constructively ....'[28] The objectives as a whole were summarised as '... to identify needs; to promote greater co-ordination and accessibility of services at the field level; to foster community involvement and to build a communication bridge between the people and local services'.[29]

How were the existing agencies to be changed? Amongst other activities, the CDPs were to adopt what amounted to the demonstration approach. 'First, some familiar activities need to be conducted in new ways, in order to make services accessible and comprehensible to those who will not otherwise see them as relevant to their needs.'[30] In other words, it was believed that if the local CDPs could mount effective welfare rights projects, educational outreach, etc., then their example would be followed by the established statutory services. If they could directly prevail upon the local agencies immediately to adopt improvements, then it was anticipated that services in other local authorities would follow their lead.

Demonstration projects attempt to change the internal workings of welfare organisations by example from outside. More recently, a few local authorities have appointed community workers to encourage improvements from within. This use of the community worker has been noted by Bryant.

> One of the more noticeable recent trends in the local authority sector has been the increase in community work appointments which are linked with some form of service development.[31]

He then explains what is expected of them,

> The service development worker is something of a hybrid between the grassroots community worker and the managerial social planner, with the emphasis normally being placed on technical and communication skills rather than on the political activities of the community organiser.[32]

Such workers, Bryant shows, may attempt to improve committee functioning, to establish better communications within an agency or to improve liaison with other bodies. The approach stresses the importance of maximising the efficiency of present agencies as a means of combating social deprivation. Its existence also shows that the belief that social deprivation is related to the technical failings of certain agencies still holds strong in some quarters.

### UNCOORDINATED SERVICES

During the 1960s, a number of social commentators were concluding that the social services were failing to serve the poor, not so much because of deficiencies within each agency but because of a lack of coordination between a multitude of different agencies. The debate was to reach fruition in the Seebohm Report, the *Report of the Committee on Local Authority and Allied Personal Social Services* (1968). It is not sufficiently recognised that a similar and earlier debate occurred in the USA and that it served to shape aspects of the War on Poverty which followed the Economic Opportunity Act of 1964.

The American analysis of poverty drew upon a variety of explanations.[33] Amongst the most influential was that which attributed blame to the fragmentation of the social services. It should be noted that not only were many voluntary organisations more directly involved in the relief of poverty than they are in Britain, but also that the statutory services could be divided between city, state and federal administrations. The disadvantages ensuing from such a framework were seen as follows. As a number of agencies had similar functions, it was believed that *duplication* of services occurred. This was particularly likely when a number of different officials or social workers attempted to tackle a client's problem from a slightly different perspective. Cases were cited of persons receiving handouts from both voluntary and statutory sources for what was essentially the same problem. Consequently, it was concluded that officials wasted time duplicating each other's visits while resources were not being used as efficiently as possible. On the other hand, clients sometimes required interventions from agencies with very different functions in order to solve their problem. For instance, a low-income family with difficulties in caring for sick children might simultaneously want help from the housing, social work and medical services. However, the *fragmentation* of services into a multitude of specialised agencies could mean that it was impossible to obtain aid from all of them at the same time. Hence, effective intervention was not possible. A related difficulty was that of *discontinuity*. Clients' needs change and, as they change, the clients may require to move from one form of treatment to another. For instance, an unemployed youth might require to be taught to read and write, then to be supplied with a vocational skill, and finally to be offered the services of a job-finding agency. However, in any one area, each service would be the responsibility of different agencies who might not be available when the last form of help was completed. Thus discontinuity of services could mean that the treatment scheme was never completed. Lastly, it was argued that the duplication, fragmentation and discontinuity added up to *confusion* for clients. Faced with a bewildering multitude of agencies, they were unsure which was appropriate for their needs. Inhibited, they might never find the right one. Moreover, it also seemed that the multiplicity allowed agencies repeatedly to refer the most difficult or deprived clients somewhere else, so that those in greatest need remained in limbo. To sum up, Rein points out that the analysis concluded that '. . . resources were already at hand but that they were dispersed, fragmented and poorly coordinated by a system of government and a system of administration that almost inspired the disorder of pluralism as an ideal.'[34]

In Britain, the analysis of agency failure followed, in many respects, the American road. It will be recalled that, in post-war Britain, the social services were divided according to function, at both central- and local-government levels. The latter contained not only children's, welfare, and sometimes mental welfare departments but also had health, education and housing departments with certain social work functions for those in greatest need. Central government soon identified lack of unity as a problem and in 1950 issued a circular encouraging the setting up of coordinating committees between the departments. If coordinating committees were intended to sort out policy and issue differences, case conferences were meant to discuss the actual families who were being seen by a number of different agencies.[35] The results were not satisfactory. Various publications made the claim that the agencies were not effectively helping the most deprived. A particularly influential study was by Donnison, who highlighted the inability of services to deal with more than one major need at a time as the crucial problem. He wrote:

> . . . some families cannot be fitted for a normal life in the community by grants of material aid or by the work of services that are each concerned only with one aspect of their troubles. They must in a sense be 'converted' to a new way of life. The only means

yet discovered for doing this is the personal influence of someone prepared to help them in every way that is needed.[36]

The problem, as conceived by Donnison, was not a lack of efficient coordinating committees but was situated in the very diversity of the social services themselves. The government's response to this and a growing volume of criticism was to set up the Seebohm Committee which eventually reported in 1968.

The Seebohm Committee was not specifically instructed to discuss social deprivation. Its brief was to consider the reorganisation of the personal social services, yet, of course, it found it had to relate these services to the social needs they were supposed to meet. The committee agreed that many people were not having their needs properly attended to and accepted responsibility to devise ways of helping them.[37] The Report acknowledged that the social services were not receiving sufficient resources and then proceeded to make much of an agency or institutional diagnosis of why social needs were not met. The fragmentation of the social services into diverse sections, it was agreed, meant that some clients—such as the socially inadequate, unmarried mothers and 'problem families'—did not fit neatly into one department and could thus be ignored as the responsibility of none.[38] Further, such fragmentation presented difficulties of coordination, especially when it was desired to treat families as a whole and not as a mixture of separate needs.[39] It went on: 'Thus coordination between the various social agencies working in an area is becoming more difficult and is, for this reason, more likely to be deficient, with the result that families and individuals receive less than adequate service and scarce resources are used inefficiently.'[40] Moreover, the fragmentation created public confusion and so made access to the services more problematic.[41] In essence, the committee saw the multiplicity and lack of coordination of the social services as a major fault and an obstacle to meeting the needs of the socially deprived. The Seebohm Report did not initiate the emphasis on the analysis of welfare organisations. Nonetheless, the importance it placed on the deficiencies of the social services meant that the debate about social deprivation became fixed on the machinery of welfare for a number of years.

*Solutions*

As a result of the above analyses, the solution to social problems in the 1960s in both the USA and Britain was seen in terms of the reorganisation and reform of the social services. However, the two countries developed change along very different paths. In the USA, one of the original ideas of the War on Poverty was to improve the efficiency of existing services. As Sundquist explains, 'At the beginning, the war on poverty was not a battery of governmental programs but a co-ordinating concept.'[42] Already the government, under President Kennedy, had a host of actual or pending services and programmes to join the well established ones. The need, therefore, was to unify them, '. . . to consolidate and co-ordinate the effort'.[43] At central level, the Office of Economic Opportunity (OEO), created by the Act of 1964, was intended to coordinate programmes in health, retraining, education, legal aid, etc., in order to meet the needs left out by gaps in the services. At the local level, Community Action Agencies would coordinate voluntary, private and statutory efforts in an effort to improve access to them.* However, as is well documented, the American poverty programme developed in unexpected directions. OEOs director, Sargent Shriver, particularly favoured his agency founding specific, operating programmes. He was not content to coordinate. A number of Community Action Agencies became centres for radical activity with much emphasis on the participation of the poor. Not surprisingly, these developments promoted much political contention. Following the election of the Republicans to office, the period 1969–71 saw a redefining of the role of the poverty programme. OEO had its sphere of operations drastically clipped. At the local level, Community Action Agencies were now expected to make coordination a major activity, with a stress on cooperation, not conflict.[44]

The reforms initiated by the popularly called War on Poverty in the USA, were intended to overcome the organisational weakness

---

* It should be noted that the term 'community action' tends to be used differently in the USA and Britain. In the former, it tends to refer to almost any activity within a community. In Britain, as the final chapter will explain, it refers to a specific form of 'grassroots' intervention.

which resulted in duplication, fragmentation, discontinuity and confusion. Notably, the legislation did not alter the framework of established statutory agencies. In Britain, as has been shown, a similar analysis of the problems was made but the proposed solution was a major recasting of the welfare framework. The Seebohm Report believed that the failures to meet social needs warranted a rationalisation of the personal social services. The government agreed with this recommendation—although it ignored many of its other suggestions—and the Local Authority Social Services Act of 1970 united in England and Wales* the previous children's, mental welfare and welfare departments, along with certain social work functions of the health and education departments, into one Social Service Department. In addition, the report also advocated close cooperation between the new Departments and the Supplementary Benefits Commission with offices being located near each other and with facilities for referring clients.[45] The committee had faith that '. . . organisational change and changes in the distribution of responsibilities will be an important means to this end' (of solving certain social problems).[46] It believed that a unified Social Service Department would rectify the failings of inadequate coordination. The new system would allow needs to be met in a family context, would attract more resources, would use resources more efficiently, would attend to needs which were being overlooked and would make services more accessible and comprehensible.[47]

## FAILURE OF A KEY SERVICE

So far the deficient agency explanation has looked at the view that all or nearly all welfare bodies have serious technical internal faults and the view that focuses on the lack of coordination between the agencies. Another aspect of the explanation concentrates on the deficiencies of a single, key agency. The belief is that there is one major service which is vital to solving the problem of social deprivation if it functions properly. In

---

* In Scotland, the 1968 Social Work (Scotland) Act led to a somewhat different form of reorganisation which included probation within the new Social Work Departments and involved changes in the juvenile court system.

the USA in the 1960s, the two services of education and manpower training were regarded as key elements. In Britain, too, particular weight has been accorded to education while, more recently, the contribution of manpower training has aroused interest as well. The explanation is short and to the point. There is a key service, it is not working properly, and so it is not countering poverty.

*Education*

In the last chapter, mention was made of education as a main socialising agent. Some proponents of the cultural explanation, it was continued, regarded school as one means of changing the behaviour of the poor. While accepting this, other writers put schools into an even more important position. It is the educational institutions which train (or fail to train) young minds, which decide who will study what, which allocate students to schools, which determine who will be encouraged and who will receive the most educational resources. In short, schools say which pupils will be equipped for different kinds of job, which ones will have high or low incomes. Halsey puts it this way:

> Education has always stood necessarily in close relation to class, status and power. In the past half century it has become part of the economic foundations of industrial society, a major avenue of social mobility and one of the principal agencies of social distribution.[48]

Given the key role of education in shaping human life, it is then claimed that schools could be used as the major instrument in countering social deprivation. If the resources of schools were deliberately directed towards the deprived, then the deprived should be equipped to move out of poverty. Such a faith in the potential of schools as an instrument of social change was obviously present in the American War on Poverty. Indeed, its educational ideas '... approached the belief that poverty can be completely abolished through educational reform.'[49] And

America was not the only country: 'The faith in education as an instrument of social engineering, capable of ameliorating social conditions and inequality, was strong in the mid-sixties on both sides of the Atlantic . . .'[50] Halsey put the matter personally and bluntly: 'Some people, and I am one, want to use education as an instrument in pursuit of an egalitarian society.'[51]

The potential of education as this instrument has not been fulfilled. Far from abolishing poverty, the educational institutions appear to play a part in creating or reinforcing it. In chapters 1 and 5 data is presented to show that children from social class v, generally the poorest section of the population, tend to under-achieve at school and to gain fewer educational benefits. During the 1950s and 1960s this data was gathered and used to criticise the failure of schools to promote the abilities of socially deprived pupils. It was pointed out that the educational achievements of children from poor homes had not gained to the same extent as other children's and that educational resources had been disproportionately allocated to the latter.[52,53] Parker, looking back on the development of education, concluded: 'It seems that educational services are markedly inegalitarian in their effects if not their intentions.'[54]

Why were schools inegalitarian in their outcomes? Why did they not fulfil their apparent potential to counter poverty? In the previous chapter, there was discussion of the view that schools do not take account of the cultural handicaps of the poor. Whilst not discounting this outlook, the 'failing school' explanation covered much more. Schools were regarded as perpetuating the disadvantages of deprived pupils because of four main deficiencies which can now be briefly discussed. These were: firstly, faulty or biased selection mechanisms; secondly, inefficient teaching methods; thirdly, unsuitable curricula content; fourthly, an unjust distribution of educational resources.

In the past, children in Britain have been selected for different levels of schools, or of classes within schools, on the basis of ability tests, including IQ tests, or teachers' recommendations. Those allocated to higher schools or classes then received, it was claimed, more intensive teaching which brought greater academic success. However, the validity of these selection mechanisms was very much in question. They discriminated, it was said, against poor children and thus prevented all but a few obtaining the educational success which could improve their position in life.

The teaching methods employed by many teachers were also considered faulty in that they failed to reach and stimulate socially deprived children. In the early 1960s, a group of head-teachers reported that the '. . . basic cause of failure with below average pupils was thought to be a failure to communicate with them'.[55] But not only were teachers failing to communicate. It was postulated that teachers and schools conveyed middle-class values and that consequently staff failed to appreciate the efforts and talents of children from other backgrounds. The famous study by Rosenthal and Jacobson is often cited to show that teachers' expectations of children are so influential as actually to determine the judgements made about the pupils whatever their capacities. Generally this means that teachers expect middle-class children to do well and those from socially deprived backgrounds to do badly.[56] The study has been criticised, but Marsden concludes from more recent research,

> Even teachers who teach children from different backgrounds in mixed ability groups have been shown systematically to underestimate the abilities of working-class and poorer children, with all the consequences entailed in such a self-fulfilling prophecy.[57]

The criticism of the inability of some teachers to communicate with certain pupils was extended to include their parents. The Plowden Report, *Children and Their Primary Schools*, stressed the point that children respond to the interest their parents take in schooling.[58] It continued that teachers had often failed to involve the parents of poor children in school activities, with the result that the latter had received even less encouragement.

A further fault was located in the content of schools' curricula. The subjects and topics employed to win children's attention, it was argued, were frequently outside the interest of working-class children. Midwinter, from inner-ring Liverpool, described, amusingly but sadly, how every set of school readers contained

... that neutered quartet ... daddy, mummy, brother, sister, all
impeccably mannered ... [who] pursue their tedious round of days
in the country, visits to the seaside, journeys to the farm and
tours of the shops, from the secure base of their nineteen-thirties
suburb.[59]

From his analysis, he concluded that often '... the curriculum
is irrelevant to the community, the children and both their
needs'.[60] Not only did the curriculum fail to interest the children
while at school, it failed to introduce them to the skills which
were of use when they left. Thus, subsequently, Eversley, in
discussing inner London, said that school-leavers found job vacancies for skilled chefs, bilingual shorthand typists and qualified office
staff. But, unprepared for these posts,

... the unskilled school child is condemned to work in the transport
industries, in the most junior clerical occupations, and in semi-skilled
jobs in distribution, which offer neither currently high incomes nor
future promotion prospects.[61]

He concluded: '... the London labour market is crying out
for people with particular skills ... Yet the education system
is slow to adapt itself.'[62]

Lastly, the educational system was regarded as deficient in
not locating its best schools and teachers in the areas of greatest
need. The Plowden Report stressed that the districts where
the poor were concentrated frequently possessed the oldest, most
overcrowded, least well-equipped schools. They had the most
difficulty in attracting and holding teachers.[63] Consequently,
the schools were unable substantially to raise their children's
performance. In turn, the children's educational achievements
were not sufficient to take them out of poverty.

## Educational Solutions

The critics of British schools made differing judgements on
the extent to which schools can influence society. Some saw
them as the vehicle through which society could be made equal,

others as a way of improving the chances of a limited number of the socially deprived. But both regarded schools as key institutions whose deficiencies meant that educational benefits were not being received by poor children. It followed, in their reasoning, that a major means of intervening on behalf of the poor was to mend these deficiencies.

A policy of school reform was not advocated just by academics, social commentators and the press. It gained support from the Plowden Report, published in 1967. Although, at times, the Report expressed qualifications, it saw changes in the schools, as Robinson puts it, as a means of solving '. . . the intractable problems of the inner city'.[64] Indeed, the committee believed that the greatest need of socially deprived areas was for good primary schools. The report gained approval from the government, which then attempted to implement, in part, its recommendations for an expansion of nursery education, the allocation of extra educational resources to some primary schools, and the establishment of Educational Priority Areas. But the demand for remedying the deficiencies of schools was not confined to Plowden's proposals. Suggestions and implementation have occurred along four main directions.

Firstly, a widespread campaign was launched against the selection techniques which discriminated unfairly against children from socially deprived environments. Some attempts were made to devise tests which were not biased according to class. More fundamentally, educational authorities have gradually abolished official tests at eleven years as the basis for determining which children go to grammar, secondary modern or technical schools. Instead, most children can now go to local comprehensive schools. The intention was that the schools would take children of all abilities, that the pupils would not feel the sense of stigma and failure associated with failing the selection tests, and that their potential would be drawn out by the extensive resources of the schools. It should be added that some local authorities retained grammar schools and that selection tests may still be retained to determine which class or stream children enter within the comprehensives.

Secondly, consideration has been given to the means by which teachers communicate with and the attitudes they display towards pupils. Teacher-training courses have attempted to make teachers more aware of the impact of class differences on their own judgements. Clegg called for a less formal classroom atmosphere, '... which welcomes individual differences and gives security to those who show them ...', and so enables working-class children to participate fully in the learning process.[65] And just as children are drawn in, so should be their parents. The Educational Priority Areas made one of their main objectives '... to increase the involvement of parents in their children's education ...', and developed schemes whereby parents were visited in their own homes as well as invited to school activities.[66] The intention has been to take the initiative in breaking down the barriers between teachers and the parents of socially deprived children.

Thirdly, a number of suggestions have been made—and some implemented—to make the curriculum more relevant to working-class children in general and socially deprived ones in particular. Colin and Mog Ball advocate a curriculum shift towards pupil involvement in local community activities. By helping the disabled, learning about social security, engaging in neighbourhood groups, they would both have their interests stimulated and would also become acquainted with the world they have to handle after leaving school.[67] Midwinter likewise wanted schools in deprived areas to develop a community curriculum so that children could discuss such themes as television or space travel, subjects which appeal to them and motivate them to work. Subsequently, some of his imaginative ideas were put into effect.

Midwinter's proposals are not necessarily limited to getting children past the existing kind of examinations. Beyond this, he envisages a curriculum which provides a social education for pupils so that '... as citizens, they would be better equipped to cope with the social issues presented to them'.[68] Clegg and Megson, while encouraging teachers to '... base their teaching on their pupils' first hand experience ...', regard the obtaining of CSE or 'o'-level successes as the major objective of curriculum reform. Undoubtedly, some schools have responded to these exhortations while some have attempted to supply marketable skills or, at least, to build into the curriculum visits to workplaces in order to prepare pupils for life after school.

Fourthly, there is the effort to improve educational deficiencies by expanding facilities. In 1965, Halsey declared: 'Educational expansion is another attractive strategy for the egalitarian. It permits reduction of injustice by reducing, or at least deferring, selection and by offering more education to everyone.'[69] The strategy of expansion has been pursued in the promotion of more nursery schools, the raising of the school-leaving age and the building of more institutions of higher education. Since Plowden, there has been a call to channel expansion into socially deprived areas, a policy of 'positive discrimination'. As mentioned, the establishment of five Educational Priority Areas did win extra expertise and resources for their inhabitants while other schools received extra allowances for teachers and equipment. A full account of the work can be found in Halsey's report.[70]

The aim of educational intervention is to improve the functioning of socially deprived children. It is held that the schools are the key distributor of motivation, skill and qualifications. If these advantages can be directed towards the children then, it is hoped, they would possess the capacities to take themselves out of poverty.

### Job Training and Finding

For some, not education but job training is seen as the key service. The attempt to counter poverty, therefore, must concentrate on services which can provide skills and give access to employment. In the USA, the War on Poverty highlighted 'manpower training'. In its early days, particular stress was placed on equipping youngsters. The Neighborhood Youth Corps and the Job Corps Conservation Centers organised schemes to give part-time and summer jobs to youngsters to enable them to afford to stay on at or return to school so as to improve their qualifications. Eventually, programmes were developed for training or retraining adults in order to fit the poor for employment. The New Careers Project was devised to provide the unemployed with upwardly mobile jobs as professional aids, day-care workers and other semi-professional occupations. The present writer was able to visit several such centres in the USA during 1972. Interestingly, when the Republican administration won office in the late 1960s

and began to alter the direction and powers of the poverty
programme, it did not abolish manpower training. Instead,
it shifted direct responsibility to the Department of Labor. Indeed,
during 1969–71, the government backed schemes not only to
train the unemployed but also to remove certain job barriers
such as racial discrimination and closed shops. Even day-care
programmes were backed on the grounds that they might release
mothers to take jobs.[71]

The prominence awarded to job training and finding in the
American poverty programme, probably reflects the fact that,
until then, such services had not been comprehensively developed
by statutory bodies. Once poverty became a public issue, the
deficiencies in the services were identified as a cause and so
manpower training schemes became a key element in the new
programmes. In Britain, such major new schemes were not
considered necessary, for extensive job services had already been
built into the welfare state. Labour exchanges (subsequently
called employment exchanges and job centres) were founded
in 1909 in the hope of bringing employers and employees into
contact. The Youth Employment Service soon followed. In addition, the government has also run Government Training Centres
while Industrial Training Boards have attempted to promote
training within industries.

The existence of a framework of services, however, does not
mean they are efficient. During the 1970s, especially as unemployment increased and poverty persisted, both the shortcomings
and the central importance of employment services began to
be debated. Their inability to find jobs sufficient to take youths
out of a life of poverty was noted. Gillet argued that the
youth employment services '. . . fit the inner city school least
well'.[72] It was felt that they did not communicate well with
the kind of children who were inhibited by officials, while the
interviews they did arrange were with the large 'career structured'
employers rather than jobs near to the homes of the youngsters.
Similarly, it was stated that the employment services were not
as successful in attracting jobs as some commercial agencies.
Even more fundamentally, it was pointed out—with reference
to a total of only fifty-four Government Training Centres in
1971—that the vacancies for skilled workers would never be

filled if the unemployed were not fitted with skills.

Suggestions for improvements have not been lacking. Baxter, for example, after estimating the degree of job changing amongst unskilled youngsters, recommends an improved flow of job and person information between the various social services, and more opportunities for youngsters to improve their qualifications after they have left school.[73] In response, the government has made efforts to up-date the employment services. Further, some new initiatives have been taken in regard to youth. The government's Work Experience Programme provides for unemployed youngsters to be taken on by firms for a limited period in order to gain experience. Similarly, job creation schemes have 'made' a number of jobs for up to one year for some who would otherwise have been unemployed. These projects, now coordinated by the Manpower Services Commission, rest on the belief that work experience will give the youngsters skills and confidence while employers will become aware of their potential. In short, it is hoped that improvements to the key service of job training and finding can result in the kind of jobs able to take the poor out of poverty.

## LIMITATIONS OF THE AGENCY EXPLANATION

The analysis of technical inefficiencies, lack of coordination and weakness of a key service does much to reveal the deficiencies of the social services. However, it will now be argued that these points do not constitute a satisfactory explanation of social deprivation. The reasons will be given under four main headings.

### Efficient Services do not Abolish Poverty

The basis of the agency explanation is the belief that if welfare organisations functioned properly then they would achieve their objectives of meeting social needs in general and dealing with social deprivation in particular. Consequently, emphasis is placed on improving access to services, increasing take-up rates, rectifying administrative faults and introducing sophisticated managerial techniques. If correct, the reforms should lead to more efficient services which then substantially reduce poverty. To a degree, this proposition is being tested. Welfare rights bodies can take much credit for increasing take-up rates. Pressure groups like the Child Poverty Action Group have even succeeded in having new categories made eligible for higher benefits. For instance, the group successfully campaigned to alter the Supplementary Benefits Commission's 'wage-stop' rule which had reduced the rates for claimants previously receiving a low wage.[74] All who desire to alleviate human distress will welcome such successes. But these improvements do not lessen the overall extent of social deprivation. For, as explained in chapter 1, even the receipt of full supplementary-benefit entitlement and other income maintenance services does not necessarily take the persons out of poverty. The improvements raise incomes marginally upwards towards a level which is itself inadequate. Within the present framework, even a technically perfect administration of the social security system would not be sufficient. Turning to the personal social services, attempts to facilitate access and to build in a more welcoming reception are wholly creditable. But—and this will be a theme of the final chapter—these services are not equipped in terms of powers or resources to make a dent in social deprivation. It follows that institutional improvements of the present agencies will in themselves have only a marginal effect on the abolition of poverty.

Similarly, improved managerial and professional performances may raise the administrative excellence of agencies without actually altering social deprivation. Three reasons serve to explain why. Firstly, according to Benington, it is possible for such changes to improve the lot of professionals rather than clients. He studied, at first hand, a city with a reputation for progressive management and which gave priority to moving to a system of corporate management. The new system, no doubt, improved communications, allowed objectives to be set and programmes to be monitored. But, in so doing, the dominant value became, not serving the poor, but 'professional excellence'. Oddly enough, welfare institutions can be subjected to extensive improvements which do not significantly alter the services offered to consumers.[75]

Secondly and, in the present writer's view, more importantly, the improvements do not necessarily change the priorities awarded by services when allocating resources. An illuminating analysis of the effects of local government reorganisation and the introduction of new management techniques has been published by the leader of a local political party. He concedes that corporate management does promote exchanges of opinions, does allow face-to-face communication. Nonetheless, he points out, councillors and officials still speak for certain departments, still represent the vested interests which they did of old. In the new situation, the poor have gained no further voice against the affluent. He comments that in a period of economic restraint, it has not become policy to allow services and benefits to the poor to expand while holding back the claims of others.[76]

Thirdly, and it is a related point, managerial sophistication does not involve a new direction in political decision-making. Benington argues that often administrators and managers are very efficient: 'The machinery of the Welfare State and of local government works sufficiently well in serving the needs of certain areas and certain sections of the population . . .'.[77] The central question then becomes, not how can techniques be improved, but why do some areas or sections of the population gain while others do not? At some stage a political decision has been made. As a housing example, Benington cites a post-war decision of a city to invest in its city centre and to postpone for twenty years a redevelopment plan for one district. The district, neglected, deteriorated physically and became labelled a problem area which was seen as undeserving of help. The decision to neglect the area was not due to managerial inefficiency but to certain political values and powers. Improvements in management, though welcome, cannot be expected to reverse the nature of political decisions.

Nothing in this chapter should be construed as an argument against the desirability of making technical improvements to welfare organisations. Obviously, in many cases the criticisms made of the deficiencies of agencies are valid and should be acted upon. The point being made is that faults within the agencies should not be regarded as the cause of poverty. As has been shown, efficient agencies may promote greater take-up of benefits, may encourage more people to come to them, yet without countering social deprivation. Similarly, an overhaul of the mechanisms of management and administration does not necessarily profit the poor.

## Rationalisation of Services May Not Improve Effectiveness

A second element in the agency deficiency thesis was that lack of coordination between various social services was the cause of their failure. Fragmentation of services, the argument ran, led to duplication, discontinuities and confusion resulting in an inefficient use of resources and hence an inadequate response to social need. Solutions were seen in terms of greater coordination or a unification of agencies. The expectation was that fragmentation would be overcome while, in Britain, the more powerful, united Social Service Department would win more resources which, through efficient administration, would lead to social needs of all kinds being met.

The limitations of this analysis have been revealed in the outcomes of the reforms based upon it. In both the USA and Britain, coordination and unification became major planks in the developments of the social services. In the former, despite the organisational reforms of the poverty programme, duplication, even competition, has continued between voluntary and statutory bodies, between local, state and federal services. The inability of the Office of Economic Opportunity to inspire coordination has provoked a number of American writers to look with envy at the new system across the Atlantic, where legislation compelled the personal social services to come together. Yet, curiously, in Britain the new Social Services Departments have suffered public criticism for their lack of coordination. In particular, a number of official enquiries into cases of client neglect have spotted a lack of continuity and efficiency.[78] Large units do not necessarily overcome the problems of fragmentation. Rationalisation of services does not necessarily mean that consumers receive a better service.

That it is desirable to reduce overlap, discontinuity and confusion is not to be denied. Despite the growing volume of criticism, the present writer believes that eventually the new Social Service Departments will overcome some of the deficiencies of the former agencies. The condemnation arising from a few enquiries may lead the public to overlook improvements which are being made. However, a more fundamental criticism is that improved coordination, even if it is achieved, can be of little benefit if the resources which the services distribute are not sufficient to meet the needs of clients. The crucial role played by resources has been recognised by those who advocated agency reorganisation as a major step towards helping the poor. On the one hand, it was contended that existing resources were sufficient but that coordination was needed to maximise their use. On the other hand, it was argued that a unified department—such as the new Social Services Department or a central coordinating agency —would be large and powerful enough to win enormous additional resources. Both views proved to be fallacious.

The poverty programme within the USA was expected to counter poverty by a more efficient use of existing services. But its leaders soon perceived that coordination meant trying to make do with inadequate not adequate resources. Sundquist shows that the director of OEO, Shriver, and his top colleagues realised that coordination was no more than a technical aid, of little use to the poor in itself. As mentioned, they then attempted to contend for a redistribution of the nation's resources but found themselves accused of subverting their agency's original aims.[79] They had realised that poverty cannot be attributed simply to agency deficiencies but they were too weak politically to sustain the poverty programme in new directions. The original staff resigned or were dismissed.

The American trail was followed in Britain by the government's Community Development Project. As mentioned, the project contained some faith in its capacity to coordinate existing services in order to improve their efficiency. Given this premise, it is not surprising that the government allocated it a minute budget. Indeed, the combined budget of the CDP and the urban programme from 1968–76 was less than £80 million.[80] Subsequently, reports from the various areas where the CDPs were operating began to reveal that it had but limited success in promoting coordination and that existing resources were, after all, too small to make even a dent in poverty. It was in this context that the CDP finally rejected the official view that poverty is due to the deficiencies of agencies and that it could be combated by technical improvements or better coordination.

To be fair, some upholders of the agency explanation have recognised that social deprivation would not be fundamentally altered unless more resources were allocated to those in greatest need. In Britain, the Seebohm Committee explicitly stated not only that 'An effective family service cannot be provided without additional resources', but that their proposed super department would be able to attract them.[81] Paradoxically, the committee also said it hoped that reorganisation would commence even if resources were not forthcoming.[82] The government agreed with the last point, and its bill to introduce reform contained a sentence saying that additional expenditure would not be necessary. The new Social Services Departments did commence during a period of rising expenditure, in real terms, on the social services. But, as Brown makes clear, it never approached the levels necessary to meet known social need. She cites the low availability of domiciliary services to the elderly and handicapped poor, the lack of qualified social workers and the chronic shortage of trained residential staff as examples of the resources the new departments failed to win. Writing in 1972, she continues: '... growth was remarkably slow and appallingly slight for a government that could reasonably have been expected to pay special attention to some of the most underprivileged groups within society.' She adds that even with the increased expenditure, it was '... impossible for the local authorities even to meet the criticisms of inadequate services for which the government itself had produced repeated evidence.'[83] Matters grew even more serious with the economic cutbacks of the mid-1970s. The new departments were not strong enough to resist severe reductions in their growth rates. Consequently, personal services to the elderly, the handicapped and children—and these include many socially deprived persons—have suffered.[84] The coordination produced by a united social services system was not sufficient to gain the resources needed by the poor. It is doubtful whether a lack of coordination should be regarded as a major cause of poverty.

Similar trends have been observed in America. Rein draws attention to one of the best administered parts of the poverty programme in New Haven. The services were well coordinated and did not appear to suffer from duplication or fragmentation.

Clients were not confused, since far more were attracted than could be helped. The experience pointed to '... the crucial importance of resources', for the agency simply could not obtain enough to meet need.[85] The overall impact on the poor of New Haven, therefore, appeared to be small. The same might be said about the poverty programme as a whole. Despite the early promises, the OEO won an average expenditure of less than forty dollars per poor person per year.[86] Although services were improved, the overall effect was slight in terms of attacking poverty. Indeed, James, after studying in the USA, reports that relative social deprivation even grew worse.[87] Reviewing the developments within the poverty programme, Rein concludes:

> The fundamental problem is evidently not the manner in which institutions function but their inability to function at all. The employment services do not have the jobs to offer, the schools cannot pay enough good teachers, the housing authorities cannot build decent cheap houses in attractive neighbourhoods. The services themselves are as impoverished as those who use them .... Anything more must depend on a large-scale re-distribution of resources.[88]

Rationalisation of the social services, whether through a new central office or new social service departments, may or may not reduce the deficiencies of fragmentation, duplication, discontinuity and confusion. If the services lack the essential resources and powers which can counter social deprivation, then their improvements avail little. Thus a service may become efficient in that it overcomes these internal faults, but ineffective in that it helps only a few of those in need or helps them only marginally. Beyond the analysis of a lack of coordination rests a further, political question—what determines whether agencies will be given adequate resources to coordinate?

## There Is No Key Service

If the absence of coordination does not explain poverty, what of the account that focuses on the failing of a key service? Earlier, education was identified as a key service whose potential to counter poverty was not being utilised because of internal deficiencies. Accordingly, important reforms have been made to schools in Britain and the USA. With what results?

Intervention by educational means frequently has the advantage of being accompanied by evaluation. In the USA, the War on Poverty stimulated many imaginative schemes aiming to improve the progress of deprived children. Yet, as Halsey concludes from a review of the findings, '. . . the early optimistic expectations have not been realised'.[89] A study by Hawkridge of a thousand projects found only twenty-one where there was convincing evidence of success.[90] The present writer, during a study term in the USA, decided that generally the improvements in curriculum content and in teaching methods did lead to a few gains in terms of educational achievement but that even these failed to continue after their immediate impact. This is not to say that none were successful—some schemes certainly roused the motivations of parents and pupils—but rather that no widespread effect was made.

Turning to Britain, the whole of secondary education has undergone change, with the introduction of comprehensive schooling being regarded as a counter to the disadvantage of selection. Assessments of the effects of comprehensive education are conflicting but two points emerge. Streaming from the age of eleven years can still occur, but within the comprehensive school instead of between different schools. Thus, early selection bias can still operate against socially deprived children.[91] Further, although comprehensive schools may raise standards overall, the gaps between children from socially deprived backgrounds and others do not seem to close.[92] To complete the picture it should be added that in some areas comprehensives have been established along with grammar schools, and hence selective mechanisms are still used to choose children for the latter.

If comprehensive schools have been introduced to change state secondary education, Educational Priority Areas have been devised to set a new pattern for primary education. As already explained, they have intervened in areas of high need by using a variety of techniques including new approaches at pre-school and primary-school stages, experimental teaching methods, radical curriculum changes and intensive attempts to involve parents and the community at large in the schools. Some successes have been recorded. The numeracy attainments of some disadvantaged children were raised although the duration for which this will be held is uncertain. The effects of some pre-school efforts (but not all) were carried over into primary school, but not to the extent of putting the children on par with others. The impression is gained that the new curricula enriched children's lives even if results are impossible to quantify.[93] Many of the schemes were, however, frankly disappointing. For instance, the giving of extra allowances to teachers in the schools had no discernible outcome on education.[94] In general, the educational interventions could not be said to have markedly or consistently brought the achievements of children from deprived areas up to or near to those from other areas.

Improvements to schools certainly do not appear the means of reducing social deprivation. Halsey, the National Director of the EPAs, who had had much faith in educational reform, finally concluded from the action/research experiment that not only were there limits to an educational approach to poverty but that 'These limits cannot be removed by any kind of EPA policy.'[95] In America, Jencks, after reviewing the evidence, made the point even more strongly: 'We cannot blame economic inequality on differences between schools, since differences between schools seem to have very little effect on any measurable attribute of those who attend them.'[96] Further, some authors now conclude that not only will educational improvements in themselves fail to eradicate poverty but they will have little effect on the educational performance of the children of the poor. Thus Coates and Silburn bluntly assert: 'Education in itself will not solve the problem of poverty. ... More contentiously, it seems to us that educational provision alone cannot solve even the problem of educational poverty.'[97]

The reason for the lack of educational success relates to the criticism being offered of the key agency explanation. Schools are not *the* key agency with the supreme power to transform human functioning on their own. On the contrary, school performance appears constrained by factors outside the educational establishments. This can be shown in three directions. Firstly, research suggests that environmental conditions—housing standards, amenities and family characteristics—strongly influence educational performance whatever the quality of the schools.

Thus the extensive work of Davie, Butler and Goldstein confirms
the earlier work of Douglas that lower-working-class children
in unsatisfactory housing were at a severe educational disadvantage when compared with middle-class children in satisfactory
housing.[98] Marsden wryly points out that even in the 1970s,
after all the reforms, the proportion of a local authority's children
going on to sixth form and university '. . . can still be predicted
from the occupational composition of the area, regardless of
the school system'.[99] The much respected Coleman Report in
the USA went so far as to say:

> Taking all these results together, one implication stands above all:
> that schools bring little influence to bear upon a child's achievement
> that is independent of his background and general social context,
> and that this very lack of independent effect means that the inequali-
> ties imposed upon children by their home, neighborhood, and
> peer environment are carried along to become the inequalities with
> which they confront adult life at the end of school.[100]

More recently Boudon has come to a similar conclusion.[101]
The implication is not that schools can compensate for these
social forces but that the social conditions themselves would
also have to be changed.

Secondly, it is not just that school achievement is strongly
bounded by outside forces. Jencks and his colleagues in their
profound study certainly came to that general conclusion. But
they added that even in those particular cases where schools
did overcome obstacles, the benefits they imparted might still
not be enough to alter a child's life chances: '. . . even when
a school exerts an unusual influence on children, the resulting
changes are not likely to persist into adulthood. It takes a
huge change in elementary school test scores, for example, to
alter adult income by a significant amount.'[102] Educational attainment alone is not, after all, the determining factor in removing
social deprivation. Schools are not the key agency.

Thirdly, school achievements cannot be isolated from other
developments which may be occurring simultaneously in other
parts of society. For instance, schools have succeeded in increasing
the number of school-leavers with passes in academic certificates
in the 1970s. But this does not mean that fewer school-leavers

are unemployed or that those from poor backgrounds are obtaining better jobs. On the contrary, unemployment among the young has become a more serious problem even for those with some qualifications.[103] Educational success can only be implemented into job success if the employment market allows it. No matter how much emphasis is put on one agency, other changes seem to occur in order to maintain poverty. Vaizey concluded that there is '. . . a social mechanism which constantly throws out at the bottom, as it were, a predetermined proportion of poorly paid people.'[104] Changes to a single agency seem not to affect the overall workings of this social mechanism.

The above conclusions should not be used in order to dismiss the value of education or to underplay the need for improvements to educational agencies. Education should not be evaluated solely in terms of certain attainments, and it could be forcibly argued that children from poverty backgrounds are entitled to what society considers the best form of education. Further, it is not held by the present writer that schools have no effect on the educational achievements of children—as would be obvious if all schools closed down! Notably, Halsey remains confident that EPAS are '. . . a viable road to a higher standard of educational living'.[105] Instead, it has been shown that educational achievement depends on a whole variety of factors and circumstances, of which schools are but one. Further, schools have extremely limited effects on whether pupils subsequently move out of—or into—poverty. It follows that education cannot be considered the key service. A concentration on improving schools will not prove to be the solution to social deprivation.

Apart from education, job and manpower training has also been regarded as the key service. This explanation of, and solution to, poverty played a prominent part in the American War on Poverty. But the results were disappointing. Even where the agencies were able to impart skills that led to jobs, certain limitations, as Rein explains, quickly became obvious. Firstly, those who did find employment often did so in marginal occupations paying low wages. Secondly, there was the suspicion that the successful were simply replacing other workers who lacked the advantage of recent training. Thirdly, a creaming-off process occurred so that the agencies trained the most promising recruits but left out the most severely deprived.[106] It seemed that even the improved manpower agencies could not cope.

Further, the agencies, although able to train prospective employees, had little power over employment practices and conditions. The possession of skill is not the only factor involved in obtaining a job. Applicants may need good health and transport. They may require employers who do not discriminate against colour or background. It is too much to expect training agencies to achieve changes of this nature.

Most fundamentally of all, the schemes had little say over the availability of jobs. In the early days of the poverty programme in New York, the training schemes of Mobilization for Youth enabled only one in four of 1,700 youngsters to obtain jobs.[107] Later in the programme, efforts were made to create jobs but with little success. Rein cynically points out that during the 1967 riots in Detroit, 56,000 people were unemployed and 70,000 under-employed. Yet all the training and job creation schemes in the city accounted for only 7,000 persons.[108] The National Advisory Commission on Civil Disorders advised the government to find a million new jobs but it did not respond. Little wonder that Mangum, a specialist in manpower studies, concedes in an evaluation of the poverty programme that job training had little point in a situation where employment opportunities were not expanding.[109] Even if training succeeded in giving a large number of people a certain skill for a particular job, in such a situation employers simply raised the qualifications required for that post. Training without fulfilment led to much disillusionment.

In Britain, too, training agencies have been of limited use in a period of high unemployment. In London, within a recent seven-year period, twenty-two per cent of the total number of jobs in manufacturing industry have disappeared.[110] Similar declines have occurred in other large cities with major cuts in the rail and docks industries. Consequently, many workers may now reside where the jobs do not. Yet they may be too old or too poor to move elsewhere. The lack of jobs cannot be blamed on inefficient training agencies. Rather they reflect large-scale economic changes in the structure of industry.[111] Against these economic trends, job creation schemes—which do not last more than a year—can have little effect.

If people are to be taken out of poverty via well-paid employment, then no single agency can achieve the transformation. Indeed the social services as a whole cannot be held responsible. As Mangum makes clear, the manipulation of the economic growth rate has more influence on job structure than welfare agencies.[112] Rein sums up: '. . . manpower policy must go hand in hand with economic, educational, welfare, and housing policies in efforts to solve the social and economic problems of the big cities and of the sub-employed.'[113] Poverty cannot be solved by improvements to or expansion of manpower agencies. For poverty cannot be attributed simply to the deficiencies of these services—or to any other key agencies. Explanations and solutions must be sought in more complex and comprehensive analysis.

## The Position of the Non-poor

A further limitation of the inefficient agency explanation is that it gives little attention to the non-poor. Social deprivation, it was accepted, is relative in nature, it concerns unacceptable gaps between the bottom section and the rest of society. Any explanation, therefore, should discuss why the affluent are able to maintain their position. True, the account does describe how certain agency failings may mean that the less needy profit from services. But this does not explain why relative poverty continues, even increases, during periods of social service improvements and expansion. For instance, during the 1970s, supplementary benefit rates have periodically been raised and the administration of the social security system improved. But the gap between claimants and others remains. Why? Again, a new benefit, Family Income Supplement, was introduced to help working parents, and continuing efforts have been applied to increase its take-up rate. But, as Parker points out, even the improved FIS is not sufficient to take the low-paid out of poverty.[114] Why?

To look at the matter another way. Solutions by way of reforms to welfare agencies make little, if any, impact on the non-poor. The latter, particularly the affluent, retain their advantages via higher returns from income and investment which are not touched by the coordination of the social services. Titmuss and his successors have also established that they gain proportionately far more than the poor through tax avoidance, tax evasion, occupational pensions and so-called fringe benefits. Indeed, Moonman claims that these sources represent an increasing important element of incomes in real terms, an element which is not reduced by technical reforms of the social services.[115] Michael Meacher, when Under-Secretary of State at the DHSS, himself pointed out that the government, during a period of economic difficulty, had chosen to cut expenditure on the social services rather than reduce benefits—such as tax relief for life insurance and home buying—which maintain the position of the non-poor.[116] The agency explanation does not consider why or how such priorities are set.

The inability of welfare reforms to close the gap between the poor and the non-poor was summed up in an evaluation of the American War on Poverty. Ferman stated that it '. . . was an attempt to supplement existing programmes rather than to alter fundamentally the status and economic position of the poor in our society.'[117] Consequently, the relative distance between the poor and the non-poor was untouched. A comprehensive explanation of social deprivation must consider why society was not prepared to make a more fundamental alteration.

## Dubious Assumptions

The limitations of the agency explanation of poverty are related to two assumptions of dubious validity. Firstly, it assumes that agencies exist only to benefit clients and that, therefore, any agency reforms must better the lot of the socially deprived. The arguments in this critique, however, lend strength to Rein's warning that '. . . we cannot assume, without reservation that they [welfare agencies] all represent humanitarian and equalitarian aims.'[118] On the contrary—and this will be expanded in chapter 5—welfare agencies can have a definite role in upholding social deprivation, a role which technical improvements or better coordination will not remove. Further, some programmes of agency improvement may serve merely to delay more fundamental changes in society. The emphasis on manpower training may mask the need to tackle the problem of low wages. Demonstration projects are often justified in terms of showing agency success in order to attract similar but expanded schemes for the benefit of a larger population. But Rein argues that

> Demonstrations are also a way to dodge action or postpone major change—relatively little money is spent, relatively few people are affected, the real problem is hardly touched. Public criticism concerning needed improvements is blunted, at least for a time. And if public interest has drifted when the demonstration finishes, the whole idea of squarely facing major needs can be allowed to die quietly.[119]

Agency improvement does not necessarily reduce social deprivation. There is more to poverty than that.

Secondly, the explanation assumes that if need can be identified and publicised, then reform will automatically follow. If senior professionals, officials and politicians can be shown the facts, it is believed, then they will act together '. . . for a rational solution to an agreed problem'.[120] It is not doubted that some reforms are necessary, but simply to identify the case does not ensure action. Even where demonstration projects in the USA were successful, large-scale action did not follow.[121] In Britain, the CDP teams in Coventry and Southwark built up an impressive case for change and developed extensive communications to put their analysis over to local and central government, but '. . . neither team found these approaches effective in bringing about even relatively simple and inexpensive changes of practice'.[122] The probable reason was that the proposed reforms, although beneficial for the poor, would have adversely affected other groups. Again, the proposal to shift extensive resources from an affluent ward to a deprived one may be opposed on the grounds of not wishing to arouse the political hostility of the latter. The needs of the poor are *not* the determining factor. Changes to help the deprived may well provoke opposition if they lessen the gap between them and the non-poor. Reform, therefore, is not simply a matter of finding the right technical tools to implement a plan with which all rational people must concur. Interestingly, the experience of the CDPs led to exactly this conclusion; their lack of progress '. . . underlined the crucial political interests at stake . . . it was not merely a question of technical adjustment.'[123] In short, necessary changes do not follow because there are conflicts of interest. Any explanation of, and any proposed solutions to, poverty will have to take these differing interests into consideration.

<h2>Summing Up</h2>

The discussion of the limitations of the agency deficiency view should not be interpreted as an attack on the social services. This chapter does warn that not all agency reforms help the poor. On the other hand, it must be conceded that if appropriate improvements were not made, then the distress of the socially deprived might deepen. Indeed, in the final chapter it will be agreed that extensive changes within the social services could be a part of the overall attack on poverty.

The criticisms are thus not that the social services should not be improved. They are that agency deficiencies do not account for social deprivation. The explanation fails to explain *why* deficiencies exist or *how* profound reforms to benefit the poor can be made. It fails to take into consideration external forces which are outside of the social services but which influence the distribution of resources. It ignores conflicts between different sections of society, some of whom may benefit from others being in poverty.

It follows that a mere improvement of techniques, better coordination of welfare agencies and reforms of a key service cannot of themselves solve the condition of poverty. Rein has made important studies of the social services, as the many references to him in this chapter bear witness. He goes as far as to say: 'If society wants to reduce poverty, dependency and unemployment, then the social services have almost nothing to contribute.'[124] This conclusion is too sweeping but it does underline the futility of seeing the social services as the main determinants of human development. Nonetheless, this is not to say that they can be completely isolated from social deprivation. The next chapter will attempt to discuss why poverty exists and what is the relationship between its continuance and the social services.

REFERENCES

1 M. Rein *Social Policy* Random House (1970) p. 57
2 Cited *ibid.* p. 72
3 T. McCashin *A Strategy for Welfare Rights* National Committee on Pilot Schemes to Combat Poverty (1976) p. 4
4 C. Meyer *Social Work Practice* Collier Macmillan (1970) p. 101
5 Child Poverty Action Group *Social Security and Tax Abuse* fact sheet 1 (1976)
6 R. Cloward and I. Epstein 'Private Social Welfare's Disengagement from the Poor' in M. Zald (ed.) *Social Welfare Institutions* Wiley (1965)
7 Cited in M. Young (ed.) *Poverty Report 1974* Temple Smith (1974) p. 198
8 P. Willmott 'Health and Welfare' *ibid.* p. 198
9 See *Times Educational Supplement* table 1, p. 20 (31 Oct, 1975)
10 J. Parker *Social Policy and Citizenship* Macmillan (1975)
11 Rein *op. cit.* p. 59
12 See N. Bond *Knowledge of Rights and Extent of Unmet Need amongst Recipients of Supplementary Benefit* Coventry Community Development Project (1972)
13 DHSS, chairman K. Bell *Research Study on Supplementary Benefit Appeal Tribunals* HMSO (1975)
14 A. Hall *The Point of Entry* Allen and Unwin (1974)
15 O. Stevenson *Claimant or Client?* Allen and Unwin (1973)
16 Cited in G. Smith 'You and Research' *Social Work Today* vol. 5, no. 10 (22 Aug. 1974)
17 Cloward and Epstein. *op. cit.* pp. 630–2
18 A. Kahn 'Perspectives on Access to Social Services' *Social Work* vol. 26, no. 3 (1969)
19 McCashin *op. cit.* p. 5
20 DHSS *op. cit.* pp. 19–25
21 See J. Skitt (ed.) *Practical Corporate Planning in Local Government* Intertext (1975)
22 A. Alexander 'The Corporate Reproach' *Community Care* no. 150 (23 Feb 1977)
23 Stevenson *op. cit.* p. 202
24 Rein *op. cit.* p. 160
25 Home Office *Community Development* (n.d.) p. 1
26 Home Office press notice, 16 July 1969
27 Home Office *C.D.P. Objectives and Strategy* (n.d.) p. 6
28 Home Office *Community Development, op. cit.* p. 1
29 National Community Development Project (NCDP) *Inter Project Report* (1974) p. 1
30 Home Office *C.D.P. Objectives, op. cit.* p. 4
31 R. Bryant 'Crossing the Boundaries of Social Work' *Community Care* no. 130 (29 Sept. 1976)
32 *ibid.*
33 See E. James *America Against Poverty* Routledge (1970)
34 Rein *op. cit.* p. 337
35 See *Report of the Committee on Local Authority and Allied Personal Social Services* (Seebohm Report) HMSO, Cmnd. 3703 (1968) ch. 4
36 D. Donnison *The Neglected Child and the Social Services* Manchester University Press (1954) p. 116

37 Seebohm Report, paras 74–5
38 *ibid.* paras 76–7
39 *ibid.* paras 79–80
40 *ibid.* para 82
41 *ibid.* para 83
42 J. Sundquist 'Co-ordinating the War on Poverty' in L. Ferman (ed.) 'Evaluating the War on Poverty' *Annals of the American Academy of Political and Social Science* vol. 385 (1969)
43 *ibid.*
44 R. Holman 'The American Poverty Programme, 1969–71' *Journal of Social Policy* vol. 3, pt 1 (1974)
45 Seebohm Report paras 683–5
46 *ibid.* para. 110
47 *ibid.*
48 A. Halsey 'Education and Equality' *New Society* vol. 5, no. 142 (17 June 1965)
49 A. Halsey (ed.) *Educational Priority. E.P.A. Problems and Policies* vol. 1, HMSO (1972) p. 5
50 C. Griffin-Beale 'The Need to Discriminate' *Guardian* 18 Jan. 1977
51 Halsey 'Education and Equality', *op. cit.*
52 F. Field (ed.) *Education and the Urban Crisis* Routledge (1977) p. 6
53 See H. Glennester 'Education and Inequality' in P. Townsend and N. Bosanquet (eds) *Labour and Inequality* Fabian Society (1972); and J. Gretton 'Education and Equality' *Times Educational Supplement* (31 Oct. 1975)
54 Parker *op. cit.* p. 100
55 Department of Education and Science *Report on Education* no. 17, HMSO (1964)
56 R. Rosenthal and L. Jacobson 'Teacher Expectations for the Disadvantaged' *Scientific American* vol. 218, no. 4 (April 1968)
57 D. Marsden 'How Far on the Road to Educational Equality' *Poverty* no. 30 (1974)
58 Central Advisory Council for Education *Children and Their Primary Schools* (Plowden Report) vols. I and II, HMSO (1967)
59 E. Midwinter *Priority* Penguin Books (1972) pp. 15, 115
60 *ibid.* p. 13
61 D. Eversley in Field (ed.) *op. cit.* p. 29
62 *ibid.*
63 Field (ed.) *op. cit.* p. 67
64 P. Robinson *Education and Poverty* Methuen (1968) p. 51
65 A. Clegg and B. Megson *Children in Distress* Penguin Books (1968) p. 101
66 Halsey (ed.) *op. cit.*
67 C. and M. Ball *Education for Change. Community Action and the School* Penguin Books (1973)
68 E. Midwinter *Patterns of Community Education* Ward Lock (1973) p. 67
69 Halsey *op. cit.*
70 Halsey (ed.) *op. cit.*
71 Holman *op. cit.*
72 In Field (ed.) *op. cit.* p. 99
73 J. Baxter 'The Chronic Job Changer' *Social and Economic Administration* vol. 9, no. 3 (1975)
74 See *New Society* vol. 27, no. 598 (21 March 1974) pp. 710–11
75 J. Benington 'Strategies for Change at the Local Level' in D. Jones and M. Mayo (eds) *Community Work One* Routledge (1974)

76 Alexander *op. cit.*
77 J. Benington 'Are These the Roots of Social Distress?' *Municipal Review* (July 1973)
78 See *Report of the Committee of Inquiry Into the Care and Supervision in Relation to Maria Colwell* HMSO (1974); and Norfolk County Council *Review Body to Inquire into the Death of Steven Meurs* (1976)
79 Sundquist *op. cit.*
80 Field (ed.) *op. cit.* p. 17
81 Seebohm Report paras 24, 147–51
82 *ibid.* para 24
83 M. Brown 'Inequality and the Personal Social Services' in Townsend and Bosanquet *op. cit.* pp. 75–6
84 See P. Willmott 'Gains and Losses in Health and Welfare' in P. Willmott (ed) *Sharing Inflation?* Temple Smith (1976)
85 Rein *op. cit.* p. 341
86 *ibid.* p. 339
87 James *op. cit.* p. 110
88 Rein *op. cit.* p. 160
89 Halsey (ed) *op. cit.* p. 21
90 Cited in Halsey *op. cit.* p. 20
91 P. Medlicott 'Streaming and the Comprehensive School' *New Society* vol. 30, no. 632 (14 Nov. 1974)
92 See, for an assessment, J. Ross *A Critical Appraisal of Comprehensive Education* National Foundation for Educational Research (1972)
93 For an account of the results see Halsey (ed.) *op. cit.*; for a critical assessment see Robinson *op. cit.*
94 Halsey (ed.) *op. cit.* p. 194
95 *ibid.*
96 C. Jencks *Inequality* Penguin Books (1973) p. 8
97 Cited in Halsey (ed.) *op. cit.* p. 5
98 R. Davie, N. Butler and H. Goldstein *From Birth to 7* Longman (1972); J. W. B. Douglas *The Home and The School*, Macgibbon and Kee (1964)
99 Marsden *op. cit.*
100 J. Coleman *et al. Equality of Educational Opportunity* US Government Printing Office (1966) p. 325
101 R. Boudon *Education, Opportunity and Social Inequality* Wiley (1974)
102 Jencks *op. cit.* pp. 255–6
103 S. Duncan and M. Young 'Education on the Defensive' in Willmott (ed.) *op. cit.* p. 127
104 J. Vaizey in Field (ed.) *op. cit.* p. 32
105 Halsey (ed.) *op. cit.* p. 198
106 Rein *op. cit.* ch. 19
107 *ibid.* p. 238
108 *ibid.* p. 343
109 G. Mangum 'The Why, How and Whence of Manpower Programmes' in Ferman (ed.) *op. cit.*
110 G. Lomas *The Inner City* London Council of Social Service (1974) p. 2
111 See NCDP *op. cit.*; and N. Moore *Jobs in Jeopardy* NCDP (1974)
112 Mangum *op. cit.*
113 Rein *op. cit.* p. 410
114 Parker *op. cit.* p. 64
115 J. Moonman *The Effectiveness of Fringe Benefits* Gower Press (1973)
116 Reported in *Community Care* no. 80 (8 Oct. 1975)

117 Ferman (ed.) *op. cit.*
118 Rein *op. cit.* p. 71
119 *ibid.* p. 140
120 NCDP *op. cit.* p. 24
121 Rein *op. cit.* pp. 159–60
122 NCDP *op. cit.* p. 32
123 *ibid.*
124 Rein *op. cit.* p. 346

# CHAPTER 5

# Poverty and Society

The final explanation of social deprivation upon which this book will dwell is related to the very structure or make-up of society. Its contention is that poverty cannot be fully understood by isolating the failings of individuals, groups and agencies from the rest of the population. Indeed, it focuses on the non-poor as much as the poor. Yet neither does it regard poverty simply as the result of a capitalist system in which one class of oppressors deliberately impoverishes the other class of workers. However, it does hold that society is structured into distinguishable strata and that this system of stratification is an essential component for understanding social deprivation. In brief, the explanation is that poverty exists in order to support or uphold these social divisions; in turn, certain social mechanisms have developed in order to perpetuate poverty; finally, this poverty promotes responses amongst its victims which serve only to reinforce its existence.

## A Stratified Society

Few people would deny that in Victorian times the population of Britain was a structured one. The difference between, on the one hand, landowners, capitalists and professionals and, on the other hand, wage earners, farm labourers, servants and the unemployed was clear to all. Today, a common belief is that Britain is no longer divided into identifiable groups or categories. It has been argued that progressive taxation, universal education and extensive social mobility have provoked the decline of the middle classes and created a classless society.[1] The popular political slogan 'we are all middle class now' likewise implies the abolition of social differences. Heraud points out that stratification or structure (both terms will be used) can be said to exist when marked and consistent differences in income, occupation, prestige etc. lead to a series of strata consisting of hierarchies or layers distinct from each other.[2] This section will argue that such consistencies can be found in social class, élites, the distribution of resources and the lack of social mobility. It will follow that Britain can be regarded as a stratified society.

## Social Class

The name of Karl Marx will always be associated with social class. He claimed: 'Society as a whole is more and more splitting up into two great and hostile camps directly facing each other— bourgeousie and proletariat'.[3] Yet Marx did not originate the concept of class, nor was he the first to relate it to income, wealth and power. Nonetheless, he has been the major influence which has stimulated the employment of class analysis as a tool through which to study society. It is worth mentioning that many subsequent scholars, while accepting the value of a class analysis, have not agreed that class warfare is an inevitable or desirable outcome.

But what is social class and does it still exist? Westergaard and Resler, in a massive study of the subject, state that class is '. . . a set of closely related inequalities of economic condition, power and opportunity'.[4] They distinguish three major dimensions, namely, a small minority of property owners, directors, professionals and top officials; an intermediate group, the middle class', of managers, supervisors and other white collar workers; and the mass of ordinary wage earners, who sell their labour to the employment market.[5] Cole, in his classic study, explains that social classes are '. . . aggregations of persons around a number of central nuclei . . .'. He points out that classes merge into each other, so that the class identity of people on the fringes is difficult to determine while that of people at the centre is quite obvious. He further clarifies the position by discussing the criteria which seem to define class membership and airs the arguments for a three fold (upper, middle and working class), five fold or even more extensive division of society.[6]

As indicated, a few authors believe that classes have now merged together to such an extent that any discussions of class differences are becoming superfluous. In particular, there is a view that the rising living standards of manual and semi-skilled workers have given them conditions, incomes, life styles and aspirations identical to the middle class. The thesis of—to use the academic term—the embourgeoisement of the working class has been heavily attacked from a number of quarters, not least by Goldthorpe and Lockwood. They established that the economic advance of the working class had been exaggerated while, in terms of promotion prospects, job security, fringe benefits, etc. a divide still stands between the middle and working class.[7] Runciman allowed that some members of the working class had adopted practices previously restricted to the affluent—such as holidays abroad or the possession of a car. But generally differences in the possession of material goods and the kind of life styles confirmed the existence of separate social classes.[8] Westergaard, too, has been a trenchant critic of the embourgeoisement view and has shown that, in terms of hours worked, awkward shifts, lack of promotion prospects, few increments, inferior pay and pensions and greater vulnerability to unemployment, clear boundaries still exist between different classes.[9] Zweig tackled the question in another way by discovering whether people actually placed themselves in different classes. He found that in general they did regard themselves as members of a class and that they used occupation, education, income, breeding and consumption patterns as the basis for their choice.[10] He added the additional and interesting observation that, although most people knew their class, fewer were class conscious in the Marxist sense of wanting to use it as a major vehicle for social change.[11] The evidence that class lines are still a prominent feature of our society is thus strong. Bottomore, in reviewing the material, concluded that social class is the single strongest influence on social and political attitudes. He states: 'The division of society into classes or strata, which are ranged in a hierarchy of wealth, prestige and power is a prominent and almost universal feature of social structure . . .'.[12]

Class exists, but not necessarily as the two major categories identified by Marx. Contrary to his predictions that the boundaries of the two economic classes would harden, there has been a proliferation of office workers, supervisors, social workers and other semi-professionals who do not fit easily into these divisions. Accordingly, various attempts have been made to devise schemes which can incorporate the structural nature of modern Britain. As mentioned, Westergaard and Resler favour the three fold division. At the top, they write of a small group of '... perhaps 5 to at most 10 per cent of the working population'. 'The core of this group is those who own and those who control capital on a large scale.' It also includes top managers, high state officials and members of the entrenched professions.[13] They continue: 'They have wealth: and the near-total security in life, the latitude of choice, the ease in everyday management and manipulation of people and things around them, which all go with wealth'.[14] The incumbents of this class, if employed, are not wholly dependent on selling their labour for often they can set their own pay within broad limits. If members of high status professions, they can control both their conditions of work and the recruitment of their colleagues. This class also includes—or its members are close to—those who administer state power.[15]

Next, Westergaard and Resler identify an intermediate or middle class. Such people as managers of junior grade, executive and technical staff, members of lower tier professions such as teachers and social workers, have the advantages of prospects of promotion, regular salary increments and job security. In these respects, they have some overlap with the minority at the top. On the other hand, they are dependent on selling their skills, have little control over the size of their incomes, and, apart from mortgaged dwellings, have much less wealth and property.[16]

At the bottom, according to Westergaard and Resler, is the broad mass of ordinary wage earners, wholly dependent upon the sale of their labour. Comprising some three quarters or more of the working population, their income turns on the number of hours worked, especially the availability of overtime. Unlike the other classes, earnings are likely to decline after the age of thirty. Prospects of promotion are few and hours of work are long in comparison with other classes. Few members own capital. Above all, members are vulnerable to job insecurity during times of economic recession.[17] The poor—whether working or unemployed—would be numbered in this class.

The three fold division made by Westergaard and Resler does lump together into the bottom group a host of different kinds of skills and workers. Not surprisingly, many social scientists favour a five fold (or six fold if class III is divided between non-manual and manual) socio-economic classification, first published by the Registrar-General in 1911. The system has stood the test of time and its merits have been discussed by Askham.[18] The actual classes, some occupations within them, and the percentage of the population aged fifteen and over in each class in 1971 are as follows:[19]

| | | |
|---|---|---|
| I | Professional (doctors, judges, higher civil servants) | 3.6% |
| II | Intermediate (managers, farmers, administrators) | 17.8% |
| III | Skilled | |
| | a. non-manual (clerks, sales representatives) | 21.1% |
| | b. manual (bricklayers, cooks, plasterers) | 28.4% |
| IV | Partly Skilled (barmen, bus conductors) | 20.9% |
| V | Unskilled (office cleaners, labourers) | 8.2% |

If the classifications do represent actual categories, then it can be expected that data will reveal significant differences between them in styles of living, behaviour patterns, possession of goods, etc. That this does happen can be briefly illustrated with regard to housing, education and employment.

In chapter 1, it was shown that housing deprivation still exists in Britain. It can now be added that the lower the social class the greater the chances of such deprivation. Thus social class V was, and is, especially vulnerable to overcrowding and a lack of basic amenities.[20] Members of social class I are most likely to own their own house and to have plenty of space. By contrast, lower social classes have a greater expectation of the disadvantages of council or privately rented property.[21]

As has been stressed several times already, educational privileges are less available to lower social groups. Their children are less likely to start school before five years of age. In 1972, only three per cent of the children from social class v proceeded to grammar, independent or direct grant schools compared with the national average of 21 per cent.[22] Moreover, according to tests carried out in 1965 on seven year olds, children from the lowest class were less likely to achieve satisfactory educational progress.[23]

Turning to unemployment, social class v are much more likely to be out of work. In 1971, amongst economically active males who were unemployed, 11.8 per cent came from social class v, 5.2 per cent from iv, 4.2 per cent from iii (manual), 3.0 per cent from iii (non-manual), 2.2 per cent from ii, and only 1.4 per cent from i.[24] Even when at work, conditions in terms of income, holidays, perks, tenure and redundancy schemes were the more inferior for those in lower classes.[25]

If further evidence is required, attention can be drawn to chapter 1 where the relationship between social class and health and between class and socially deprived areas was discussed. Enough has been produced to allow two main conclusions. Firstly, as the government publication puts it, '... people in social classes i and ii can be said, on average, to possess different characteristics from people in other social classes, and particularly from those in social class v'.[26] Not only do the differences exist but they persist. The Marxist scholars, Westergaard and Resler, conclude: 'Class inequality is tenacious. Disparities in material conditions and security remain acute against a background of rising levels of average welfare.'[27] Interestingly, the dispassionate government document *Social Trends* makes the same point. After establishing many differences between the classes, it ends with '... such differences do not seem to be much less important than in earlier decades'.[28] Secondly, social class v is especially distinct because of its greater vulnerability to all manner of deprivations. As Askham points out in her study, it stands out by virtue of its lack of possessions, status and power.[29] Overall, to quote *Social Trends* again, '... social class differences still exist in all areas of concern in Great Britain'.[30] In terms of class, Britain remains a stratified society.

*Distribution of Resources*

Class distinctions are reflected in differing possession of resources. In order to stress the structured shape of society, it is worthwhile expanding this point in regard to income and wealth and with reference to access to the political power which can influence the distribution of resources.

During the 1950s, it was widely assumed that a marked levelling off of incomes had occurred as the result of income tax, wage increases won by trade unions and the growth of the social services. Titmuss challenged this view, partly by pointing out that the definitions of 'income' had excluded certain benefits—cars and tax free loans made by employers, expense accounts, etc.— which profited only a small section of the population.[31] Atkinson subsequently made calculations, drawing upon government estimates and the earlier work of Nicholson, to conclude that between 1949 and 1967 the percentage share of income (before tax) received by the top one per cent of the population had indeed dropped from 11.2 per cent to 7.4 per cent. However, the share received by the bottom 30 per cent also fell from 12.7 to 10.4 per cent.[32] Any redistribution profited those in the middle positions. It should be added that even these figures excluded capital gains which, if counted, revealed that in 1959 the top one per cent received 14.1 per cent of income, the top 5 per cent received 26.6 per cent and the bottom 30 per cent only 11.7 per cent.[33] More recently, the Royal Commission on the Distribution of Income and Wealth has confirmed the general direction of these estimates. For 1972–73, the share of total income (before tax) accruing to the top 10 per cent was 26.9 per cent (23.6 per cent after tax), to the top 11–80 per cent it was 67.3 per cent (69.7 per cent) and to the remaining 81–100 per cent it was 5.8 per cent (6.8 per cent).[34]

Turning to wealth, the Royal Commission presented an even more stark picture. In 1973, more than a quarter of all personal wealth was owned by one per cent of the population and two thirds by the top 10 per cent. Large as is the proportion owned by the one per cent, it has declined somewhat from the position estimated by Lydall and Tipping in 1954.[35] However, the beneficiaries do not seem to have been the lowest sections of the community. Atkinson explains,

The evidence regarding changes in the distribution of wealth may be summarised by saying that they suggest some decline in inequality, but that there are reasons for believing that this reflects in part the rearrangement of wealth *within* families rather than the redistribution *between* rich and poor families.[36]

From the now considerable evidence, a number of conclusions can be drawn. Firstly, both income and wealth remain unevenly distributed with a minority holding resources far out of proportion to its numbers. Secondly, although equality has advanced in the sense that the top one per cent has lost some ground, this has not markedly benefited those at the bottom. Of course, to repeat a point made in chapter 1, this is not to say that in absolute terms standards of living have not risen for all the population. But in relative terms great inequalities abound. Thirdly, the concentration of earned and unearned income in the hands of the top minority is shown to be so great that it serves to repudiate the view that there is now no scope for redistribution from the rich to the poor—should such action be considered desirable. Roy Jenkins is an example of an MP who has argued that the decline of class differences means that the poor could only be helped by taking money from the skilled working class.[37] Yet, as Westergaard and Resler make clear, the variations in resource allocation between classes are so great that if the income from private property (mostly accruing to the top minority) was divided amongst married couples they would all receive, at 1971 prices, an extra £9 per week.[38]

Income and wealth are unevenly distributed though the permanence of this position may be less certain if the lower members of society have access to the means of political power which can alter the balance of resources. But studies now suggest that the make-up of political parties also reflects the distribution of wealth and income. The Labour Party is recognised as the representative of working class interests yet the proportion of Labour members of parliament who were actually from the working class fell dramatically from the inter-war years to 1970.[39] Rose further demonstrates a marked decline in the working class composition of its cabinets which fell from 67 per cent in 1929 to 9 per cent in 1967.[40]

In local government, too, the lower social classes are under-represented. Newton and Morris found that since 1925 the Birmingham council has had no member from a social class v background.[41] A survey of London councillors found managers and professionals over-represented to the cost of manual workers.[42] Even the trade unions may not be influential on behalf of the poorest members of society. It is a familiar criticism, to cite Runciman, that trade unions 'started by trying to coerce the Establishment and ended up by joining it'.[43] Whether this be so or not, there is no doubt that social class v members are largely outside trade union influence either because they are in non-unionised occupations or because they are unemployed.

It can be concluded that Britain's stratified nature is revealed in the differing access which groups have to income and wealth. The shape of these groups tends to coincide with social classes. Further, the lower social classes not only lack material possessions in comparison with others but also lack the means of change through political representation.

*Elites*

Social classes are not the only form in which society structures itself. A great deal of recent sociological research has focused on categories much smaller than classes, namely élites.[44] David Boyd defines élites as groups which possess the following eight characteristics: high occupational position, minority form, high status, a distinctive life style, group consciousness and cohesion, exclusiveness but openness, functional capability and responsibility, moral responsibility and power.[45] In short, élites possess power far outweighing their numbers. Of the characteristics, Boyd regards occupation as the key feature. In his research, he identifies six occupations which contain the other characteristics and so qualify to be called élites—they are the higher positions in the civil service, the foreign service, the judiciary, the armed services, the Church of England and clearing banks. Other writers have added the occupations of politicians, directors of large firms, administrators of large organisations such as the BBC, and so on.[46]

The next question is how are élites recruited, where do they come from? It can be answered in three ways. Firstly, élites are drawn mainly from social classes I and II. Obviously, they are not identical with classes but there is a close relationship. Thus Kelsall found that of higher civil servants only three per cent were recruited from those whose fathers were semi-skilled or unskilled manual workers.[47] Amongst members of parliament in 1970, only 31 per cent of Labour and 1.5 per cent of Conservatives were classified as 'workers'.[48] Secondly, they are drawn from the public schools. The Public Schools Commission indicates that over 70 per cent of recruits to the Foreign Office and the judiciary are drawn from this very small part of the population.[49] Around three quarters of Conservative and a quarter of Labour members of parliament are also from the public schools.[50] An examination of the evidence shows that the public schools

> ... have produced most of the top men in British business; and also majorities and near-majorities of those 'distinguished public figures' who are selected to join royal commissions, other government committees of inquiry and such bodies as the BBC's Board, the Arts Council and the British Council.[51]

Thirdly, élites are drawn from Oxbridge graduates. Halsey and Crewe's survey for the Fulton Report found that 64 per cent of the administrative class of the civil service were so educated.[52] They stated: 'The concentration of Oxford and Cambridge graduates is remarkable in the context of the shrinking population of Oxford and Cambridge graduates in the national student population'. Moreover, the higher the grade the greater their predominance. As Sampson crisply put it, 'Permanent secretaries are still very Oxbridge and the Oxbridge vernacular is still the *lingua franca* of Whitehall'.[53] Similarly, Boyd found that in 1970 60.4 per cent of the directors of clearing banks, 77.5 per cent of higher clergy and 84.6 per cent of the higher judiciary had approached their positions via Oxbridge.[54]

It is sometimes argued that although élites exist they are increasingly open to all members of society whatever their background. Contemporary research, on the contrary, reveals that the hold of Oxford and Cambridge and the public schools is as strong or nearly as strong as ever. Boyd, writing in the 1970s, shows that public school influence on the armed forces and clearing banks was actually increasing, while it was unchanged in the other élite occupations.[55] The Oxbridge hold on the Foreign Office, the army and the clearing banks likewise increased, while that on the judiciary, the RAF and the civil service remained virtually unchanged.[56] In politics, the numbers of public school and Oxbridge figures in the Labour Party, particularly in its cabinets, showed no signs of decline until the 1970s.[57] A study of the 1977 cabinet showed that a third had been to Oxbridge and a quarter had a combined public school/Oxbridge background.[58] Nonetheless, the cabinets, shadow cabinets and parliamentary membership of both major parties remained predominantly in the hands of persons drawn from these educational institutions. Hall's conclusion still stands that '. . . over a generation or more, despite all efforts to broaden the recruitment base of some significant professions and occupations, the situation does not as yet differ substantially from that which appertained before the war.'[59]

Few political theorists would now contend that élites are the ruling class. Obviously, society contains many competing interests, including those of organised labour, which influence national life. But élites, by virtue of their positions, possess outstanding powers to mould decision making and affect its execution. Indeed, Bottomore argues that they are becoming more, not less, influential.[60] These élites remain largely the preserve of members drawn from a very narrow social background, a finding which again emphasises the stratified character of society.

## Mobility

The contention is sometimes made that Britain is a socially mobile country, that children from the lowest social classes can move to the top, while others drop down to a class befitting their capacities. Even if such mobility exists, it is not evidence that Britain is not a stratified society. On the contrary, it could be an argument that distinct levels or classes do exist and that people move from one to another. However, the contention is a doubtful one.

Social mobility is usually assessed by identifying whether children move into different occupational types from their fathers'. A difficulty arises because the actual occupational structure of Britain has changed with an increase in the percentage of clerical jobs and a shift from manufacturing to service industries.[61] Thus it can be expected that many children will have different occupations from their fathers although this may not entail their gaining a higher position in society when compared with the corresponding changes being made by other sections of the population.

Despite the difficulties of measurement, a number of important studies have been made. Some mention of them was made in chapter 2 when considering biological explanations. Here attention will be drawn to the findings of some major studies. The best known work in Britain has been that of Glass and his colleagues, published in 1954.[62] Within a classification of eight bands of jobs, less than a third of the men in their sample were at the same job level as their fathers. However, the changes were likely to have been to that of an occupation very near to that of their fathers. There was, the researchers said, '... a rather higher stability over time' than might have been expected.[63] If perfect mobility had existed then some 12 per cent of the sons of unskilled workers would have taken similar jobs. In fact, over double that proportion did so. Again some 3 per cent of the sons of men in the top professional and business posts would have succeeded to similar jobs if parental and social pulls played no part. Instead, nearly 40 per cent did so.[64] Subsequently, Boyd's research confirmed a similar trend regarding movement into élite occupations. He wrote, 'the findings indicate a stable relationship where proportionality has not changed through time' so that in no élite was inter-generational mobility having any marked effect.[65] In short, there was little evidence of substantial numbers of recruits from the larger but lower social classes moving into élite positions. Interestingly, research in the USA has produced comparable findings which establish the fact of social mobility but on a very restricted scale.[66]

Social mobility can also be explored by examining whether individuals change their own level of job over their lifetime (instead of comparing with their father's occupation). Government statistics for the period 1953–63 showed that, of persons who moved to different jobs, only one in five changed job levels (with jobs classified into six grades). Moreover, only one in twelve crossed the divide between manual and non-manual posts.[67]

In 1975, a survey was made of nearly 5,000 men in Scotland. To date, the published material concentrates on movement to and from what the authors call 'the lieutenant class', that is, those professional, managerial and administrative personnel who are in important positions but are not members of an élite. Considerable mobility was expected as the survey covered a period in which the number of lieutenant jobs in Scotland had increased rapidly so necessitating the finding of recruits. The results showed that considerable numbers of recruits—around three quarters—did come from outside the lieutenant class. But this finding did not mean that extensive mobility was the rule. Thus, although semi-skilled and unskilled workers made up a substantial part of the population, only 19.3 per cent of the lieutenants were drawn from such lowly backgrounds. Moreover, to be the son of a lieutenant did entail considerable protection against rapid downward mobility. More sons of lieutenants obtained lieutenant jobs than sons from any other background. Further, those sons from this class who did not become top level managers, administrators etc. were likely to win other white collar positions. Lastly, the researchers emphasised that even the limited mobility to the lieutenant class '. . . does not extend to the key positions in the country's political and economic élite.'[68]

Outside of Scotland, research is also progressing under the Oxford Social Mobility Research Group. The initial publications are heavily concerned with a reformulation of concepts and methodology, while the findings are subject to various interpretations. However, Westergaard and Resler, who had access to the Group's early material, deduce that there is little sign of substantial increase in mobility.[69] A member of the research team has written that, although mobility between some occupations is increasing, '. . . the overall effect is if anything to increase the correlation of a father's and son's status (that is to reduce the amount of status mobility between generations)'.[70]

How can the studies and findings be summarised? The social structure of Britain is not static. People do move from one class to another and the extent of movement has probably risen over time. However, some of the mobility has arisen because of changes within the framework of occupations, involving an expansion in the number of white collar jobs. Consequently, some people will have moved up a job level without corresponding numbers having to drop down. Further, Bottomore explains

> ... that most social mobility takes place between social levels which are close together; for example, between the upper levels of the working class and the lower levels of the middle class.[71]

It follows that social mobility cannot be said to be widespread or extensive. Movement from social class v to social classes I or II (or vice versa) is not unknown but it is rare. Mass changes are certainly not happening. Bottomore comments crisply, 'the vast majority of people still remain in their class of origin',[72] a position which remains even when their capacities warrant change. Halsey, a member of the Oxford Group, stresses caution because of the complexities of concepts and methodologies. Nonetheless, he concludes:

> ... that mobility between generations has somewhat increased during this century ... But what is more remarkable is that the strong emphasis on egalitarian social policies in education and the social services ... have not led to unequivocal evidence of greater fluidity of movement between the classes.[73]

Enough evidence has now been presented to demonstrate that Britain is a stratified society. Whatever the degree of social mobility—and it seems surprisingly small—society can be said to be characterised by the existence of social classes and élites and by a distribution of resources which is grossly disproportionate to numbers. The extent and persistence of these divisions are such that it is difficult to see how discussions of social deprivation sometimes occur with so little mention of them. The contention here is that they are at the core of understanding the continuance of poverty. But, before proceeding to examine this matter, it should be observed that the existence of differing strata does not mean they possess different cultures. The varying strata are distinguished by their differing access to economic, social and political resources but they share the same basic values, aspirations and motivations. For instance, a lawyer in social class I and a labourer in social class V may be separated by thousands of pounds in terms of income, wealth and possessions, by differing vulnerabilities to illness and death, and by differing access to decision making. But they may share loyalty to, say, the institutions of marriage and the family, and they may both believe in the value of thrift and hard work (although, as will be shown, the latter's values may 'bend' under pressure). The explanation to be expounded rests on the existence of a stratified society, not on a culture of poverty.

## THE FUNCTIONS OF POVERTY

British society is a stratified one, with income, wealth and power unequally distributed between various sections. Moreover, these differences have been remarkably persistent, continuing through periods when national wealth has increased and while educational and social services have grown. The interpretation now offered is that poverty or social deprivation is not just the lowest expression of the stratified society but is functional to it—that is, it functions to uphold the differences, to maintain inequality. In this view, poverty is functional in that it maintains a social system, rather than dysfunctional which would imply stopping or arresting the present system. Thus poverty is not eliminated even when society has sufficient affluence to achieve this end, for it exists for reasons other than a total lack of resources. Three examples of the performance of this function will now be explained.

### The Justification of Poverty and Wealth

The poor are frequently held to blame for their poverty. Some of the explanations studied in this volume have explicitly or implicitly condemned the socially deprived. As pointed out, Friedman said that the poor choose not to save and thus must accept responsibility for their condition. Boyson described them as 'the idle, the failures and the feckless'. Clegg and Megson described those who could work but chose instead to draw social security, which they spent on themselves while neglecting their children. Research has underlined the limitations of these stereotypes but there can be little doubt that they express an element of widespread popular opinion.

If poverty exists and the poor are to blame, then a divided and stratified society is accepted as normal and just. It follows that if poverty justifies the existence of lower strata in society, then the position of higher strata is also legitimated. As Wilson puts it, 'The existence of poor people guarantees our status by providing evidence of what appears to be the result of personality pathology and makes us feel good.'[74] In a survey, Feagin found that affluence and poverty were justified in these terms and, interestingly, were justified by all income groups.[75] Rytina, Form and Pease also showed that this belief was widely held, but to a decreasing extent down the social scale.[76] In short, if poverty exists and the poor are held responsible, then their position is deserved. Similarly, the affluent are held responsible for, and deserving of, their position. The stratified society is justified.

To put the argument another way, if poverty existed but was generally considered unjust or undeserved, then the legitimacy of other gradings or rankings in society would be brought into question. An ideology is required which simultaneously justifies the existence of poverty and wealth. It is found by holding that income, wealth and social position depend wholly on hard work, ability, honesty and responsibility. Rytina and her colleagues conclude: 'Our data confirms the hypothesis that the support of an ideology is strongest among those who profit most from the system which the ideology explains and defends, the rich in this case'.[77]

If the favourable position of higher social classes and élites is to be legitimised, then not only are the poor required but it must be the poor who are held blameworthy, who are in their rightful position. Thus poverty cannot be understood or studied separately from affluence. Nor is it likely that poverty can be combated without affecting those holding higher positions in a stratified society.

*Lessening Prospects of Change*

It might be considered that the existence of social deprivation
would stimulate the disadvantaged forcibly to change the position
of the wealthy. Such revolutionary action might indeed occur
if society were divided into two clearly defined classes consisting
of a minority of resource holders and a large, poor working
class. However, as has been demonstrated, not only are the
poor in a minority in Britain but the system of stratification
is one of a number of classes and groupings which merge
into each other. In these conditions, poverty can function to
reduce the prospects of alterations to the nature of society.

Runciman has argued that social classes tend to use as their
reference groups, those classes or groupings which are close
to them.[78] The fact that some persons experience extreme social
deprivations means that those just above—the large number
of workers with around average or just below average earnings—
can regard their own lot as favourable by comparison. As
their position is not the worst in society there is less inducement
to agitate for political reform of a kind which would also
alter the income, wealth and power of those social groups
which hold the most favoured positions. A similar point is
made about American society by Reissman. He explains that
the bulk of working class people gain their status from the
fact that there is a more inferior group—the poor. Any radical
programme to change the poor would thereby threaten their
ranking in society: 'To do something about inequalities of poverty
... means, among other things, a threat to the working-class
person's position.'[79] If the poor did not exist as a minority,
the attention of the working class might be directed towards
lessening the distance between them and higher social groupings
rather than maintaining the gap with the poor.

Numerically speaking, social classes I and II, the élites or
the major holders of wealth, are in a minority. Their position
is safe as the remainder of society is not united in opposition
to them. This observation, of course, is by no means original.
Thane points to historical examples of higher social classes
combining with middle or lower ones in order to forestall the
lowest. In the 1890s Joseph Chamberlain articulated a policy
of winning over the 'respectable' working class to side with

the middle class so as to maintain their distance from the poor. Thane explains that as the working class at large shared the values of higher groups—particularly in regard to thrift, as shown in their mass support of Friendly Societies—so the oneness between them could be promoted, with the poor cast as the undeserving, feckless outsiders. In such circumstances, popular support would not be found for any measures threatening to alter society in any significant manner.[80]

Writing of contemporary society, Jordan also regards poverty as instrumental in creating a division within the working class. Jordan, who has worked with Claimants' Unions, describes the recent growth of what he calls 'the new claiming class'—the recipients of supplementary benefit. The working class are thus split into 'the sector represented by the worker who lives in a semi-detached house, earns £30 a week (including incentive bonuses) at his skilled trade, and pays rates and taxes: and the sector represented by the claimant, who earns £18 a week when he can get a job, and claims Family Income Supplement, rent rebates, free school meals and exemption from prescription charges'. The former sees the latter as 'a drain on the nation's hard pressed resources ... a scrounger or a layabout ... he will identify him as one of a class of such people which can be distinguished from his own class, whose members can be identified by behaviour which denotes inferiority'.[81] The former will not want social intervention of the kind that radically helps the latter. Instead, he will support economic and social policies which prosper skilled workers and middle class groupings. As Jordan implies, there will be no impetus to disturb the existing pattern of society.

Poverty, then, as a condition of a minority, functions to dampen down reforming notions of other social classes. In addition, since the poor are regarded as responsible for their plight, attention can be focused on them as a problem to be controlled instead of on changes to bring them out of poverty. Townsend makes this point in regard to the coloured poor. The growth of immigration, particularly to inner city areas, in the 1950s and 1960s, was accompanied by social commentators defining immigrants or colour as a problem. Consequently, less consideration was given to the need for housing, income and amenity reforms since solutions were couched in terms of controlling immigrants.[82] Similarly, it is commonplace for hostility to be expressed against 'problem families' on council estates. The result is that action is directed against the families and away from changes in other sections of society which are therefore left intact.

## The Dirty Workers

The poor are needed to undertake the least desirable jobs and positions implied in a stratified society. Middleton's documentation of the nineteenth and twentieth century poor law system shows that it did more than punish and disgrace the poor. It also produced the kind of workers fitted to undertake tasks essential to more affluent classes but which they would not do themselves. Children raised in poor law institutions were trained to function as servants and maids or to enter the lowest ranks of the armed services. Provision was also made for adults to act as seasonal workers on local farms where labour was scarce. In short, the poor supported society by filling its most menial positions.[83]

The workhouses—and most servants—have passed away. However, poverty is still required in order to provide a pool of workers prepared to accept the low wages and unhealthy and dirty jobs which serve higher social classes. Unless the poor existed, the job might not be undertaken. In addition, the poor are required to function as the group which is prepared to accept unemployment. Pruger draws upon economic data to show that the incomes and profits which place the affluent in their exalted position, stem from an economic system which can regulate progress by unemployment. The poor are the 'first fired and last hired'. As Pruger explains, the poor 'perform vital functions for the national economy. They bear the major costs of both technological progress and efforts to maintain price stability'.[84]

A related point is taken up by Rein in discussing Sundquist. He explains how a pool of unemployment can serve to hold wages down—by inhibiting wage claims—and so increase the profitability of industry.[85] If the poor did not exist as the body liable to unemployment, problems would be created for industry and government when wanting a means of regulating the economy. The threat of large scale unemployment might spread to higher classes, who might then question the present ordering of society.

Rousseau stated that 'moral or political inequality ... is established, or at least authorised, by the consent of men' and is not the inevitable result of nature.[86] The argument of this section is that poverty is not the inevitable fate of an unlucky few but that it continues by the consent of society because the latter profits by it. Poverty functions to justify inequalities, to lessen the prospects of alterations in the stratifications associated with inequality, and to provide a group of persons constrained to undertake the least favoured and most vulnerable positions in society.

### MECHANISMS OF A STRATIFIED SOCIETY

Poverty functions to uphold a stratified society. It is to be expected, therefore, that society's major institutions will contribute to both the maintenance of positions of privilege and the continuation of poverty. Three examples of such institutions will now be discussed, institutions which support the élites, the mass media and, perhaps surprisingly, the social services.

### Educational Institutions

Elites, it has already been explained, constitute a major element in the hierarchical nature of British society. The élites predominantly consist of persons educated at Oxbridge and/or fee paying private schools (public, independent and direct grant schools). The ethos and the aims of élites depend largely on those prevailing within the privileged sector of education.

As Halsey makes clear, it is easy to lampoon the public schools as the conveyors of 'snobbery and sodomy'.[87] It is easy to dismiss Oxford and Cambridge, as Maxton did, as 'those centres of snobbery and exclusiveness' which will wither away with the growth of socialism.[88] But their continuing domination of élite positions makes them of more importance than that. At the very least, the restriction of many posts to a narrow element means that the bulk of the population are excluded. As the latter will contain many able people, the nation is deprived of their capacities in key positions. The limitations of the present élite are often referred to. Roger Opie observes that the archetypal entrant to the higher civil service may be very well-mannered but 'know next to nothing of the modern world'.[89] However, it is not being argued here that the private schools and Oxbridge do not produce talented people. It is rather that ability is not limited to them and it is reasonable to expect that only a fraction of the nation's talent is found within the small percentage which attends these institutions.

In the context of this section, however, the importance of the 'feeders' of the élites is not just that they exclude talent but that they provide members who will uphold and maintain the present distribution of resources within society. The private schools cater not only for a small section of the populace but also for the children of the most wealthy. The General Household Survey referring to 1971 showed that only seven per cent of fathers earned over £3,000 a year but their children accounted for nearly half the pupils at independent and direct grant schools.[90] Thus at home and at school the children receive similar socialising experiences and tend to mix with children whose wealth and privilege are akin to their own. Moreover, the same schools predominate in controlling access to the older universities. The result is that the members of élites have had similar backgrounds so that their interests and aims will tend to coincide. As Westergaard and Resler make clear, their upbringings will provide them with similar core assumptions about the economy and society. Moreover '. . . the closeness of the links between them from common experience, often also personal associations and family ties . . .' will give a unity which inhibits any questioning of these assumptions.[91] Thus not only will it be in their economic self-interest to perpetuate society as it is, but their assumptions will convince them of the rightness of a society which is sharply stratified and in which resources are concentrated in the hands of minorities.

Being agreed on objectives, the élites can uphold them in two main directions. Firstly, they can preserve the hold of

the public schools and Oxbridge on the élite occupations themselves. As élites select their own recruits, they are likely to
assess suitable candidates as those from backgrounds akin to
their own. Thus Rex, in discussing the higher civil service, states:
'So far as the administrative apparatus is concerned, the astonish-
ing thing in Britain is the resilience of the system of recruitment
and socialization through Oxbridge'.[92] As was shown earlier
the same could be written of the public schools and of their
hold on the armed forces, the city, the professions and major
political parties. The unchanging membership of the élites means
there is little challenge to their prevailing objectives and beliefs.

Secondly, such élites can use their influential positions from
parliament, the pulpit, the courts, to persuade other sections
of the population that the present state of affairs serves the
interests of the nation as a whole. George and Wilding make
this point very strongly,

> The major social institutions are staffed and organised largely by
> members of the dominant social groups which successfully perpetuate
> themselves from generation to generation—e.g. the former Adminis-
> trative Class of the Home Civil Service. Their values are expressed
> and embodied in such institutions as the civil service, the law
> and the courts, in the public schools and in the state education
> system through its imitation of the private sector. Through their
> expression and embodiment in national institutions, class values
> become national values.[93]

In such a situation, there is less prospect of the position of
élites being questioned and, accordingly, less chance of any
impetus to change the condition of those at the bottom end
of a stratified society.

Apart from providing recruits to élite occupations, it should
be added that—as the Public Schools Commission baldly stated—
the privileged sector creates social divisiveness.[94] But, as its
members strongly influence public opinion, such divisiveness or
stratification becomes acceptable. As Bottomore explains: 'In
Britain, all manner of ancient institutions and modes of behaviour—the aristocracy, the public schools, Oxbridge, differences
of speech and accent, the relationships of the "old boy" network—
frustrate mobility and buttress the public conception of a rigidly

hierarchical society'.[95] It might be countered that social mobility does occur, that some educated in state schools and from non-privileged backgrounds do obtain positions of importance, including membership of the élites. However, the scale of such mobility is so small that the system is untouched. Moreover, only those recruits who accept the élites' objectives need be taken. Consequently, the limited mobility can appear to demonstrate the existence of an open society while not being sufficient to alter the interests or homogeneity of the privileged. Such mobility, George and Wilding claim, is 'a kind of political safety valve' which draws in able critics from lower down the system and 'gives them a firm stake in its continuance'.[96]

The public and independent schools, along with the universities of Oxford and Cambridge, may seem far removed from social deprivation. Yet they provide a homogeneous membership which dominates élite positions in a stratified society. From these vantage points they can prevent other sections of the population from gaining access and can convince the wider society that the present distribution of wealth, income and power is justified. As their positions in the strata are maintained, so too are those in lower grades, including the poor. It is worth recalling that Richard Tawney, that great advocate of equality, specified two reforms as essential to its attainment. One was the abolition of inherited wealth, the other was the abolition of the institutions of privileged education.[97]

## The Mass Media

The means of public communication—the press, television and radio—are now major social institutions with access to the eyes and ears of the bulk of the population. The extent to which the media do shape attitudes and behaviour is a matter of debate. Obviously, its recipients are also subject to the influence of home, school and class. Yet it can hardly be doubted that these organs of mass communication do have some impact. For instance, voting preferences are not subject to great change but Blumler and McQuail's research demonstrated that television does sway the voting intentions of some electors.[98] Advertisers have no doubts that the written and spoken word can change spending habits.

It could be argued—as Sampson does—that communicators are another élite. He calls them the 'new boy net' but also shows that the leading figures are drawn from similar backgrounds as other élites.[99] The governors and director generals of the BBC, the chairmen and members of the Independent Television Authority, the owners and editors of newspapers, even many leading TV personalities (especially in current affairs) are drawn from what Sampson calls 'the establishment'. They possess overlapping and interlocking upbringings and represent similar commercial interests. Of course, Sampson realises that most journalists and reporters (apart from the 'quality papers') do not possess élitist backgrounds. But he explains that journalists are in a weak position as 'the majority of newspapers, like their proprietors, are predominantly on the right. Licensed rebels can hold forth in Conservative newspapers ... but they are like eccentric radicals invited to amuse or provoke a Tory dinner party'.[100]

Sampson would appear to have over-simplified the situation. Nonetheless, the observations of this experienced journalist do support the contention that, in general, the mechanisms of public communication operate to uphold the prevailing distribution of wealth, income and power. This is not to say that at times the press or TV will fail to campaign for certain reforms but rather that the reforms pursued will not be ones which endanger the present structure of society. Again, as Westergaard and Resler point out, an air of neutrality is sometimes conveyed by presenting more than one side of an issue. Writing of TV and radio, they explain that it is a constrained 'neutrality' for

> ... the diversity of opinions and perspectives which find expression ... are broadly contained within the limits of a 'consensus' that allows little scope for more than spasmodic questioning of the society's core assumptions. Like the civil service, the broadcasting services in effect thus uphold continuity of the established order. But they do so discreetly. The limits of the 'consensus' to which they adhere are in the main unspoken, the way in which conformity to them is achieved is in the main indirect.[101]

Oddly enough, the authors continue, broadcasters and writers are sometimes attacked for undermining society by their permissive views. But the liberalism which is criticised is usually a defence of individual deviance, particularly sexual deviance, '...

the targets of its scepticism do not, and cannot, usually include the unspoken premises of the current economic order'.[102]

Academic studies made in the 1970s tend to support this line of argument. An investigation of TV news coverage of industrial matters concluded that news selection and presentation is not 'neutral' but is 'a sequence of socially manufactured messages which carry many of the culturally dominant assumptions of our society'. The study particularly noted how low income workers were cast in a poor light when threatening industrial action.[103] Similarly, a news content survey of Midlands newspapers revealed how they conveyed popular misconceptions about the life styles and behaviour of black people.[104] Again, the contributors to Cohen and Young's *The Manufacture of News* generally agree that the media tend to perpetuate the interests of the controlling groups in society.[105] It must be added that the authors are not painting a picture of a small core of communicators plotting together to find ways of harming the lower classes. Obviously the process is more complex than that and concerns the dominance of certain assumptions and attitudes which are taken for granted.

Studies of the media's handling of social deprivation are few but there is little reason to doubt that their coverage and focus follow a similar direction. Three points can be made with confidence. Firstly, the poor tend to be cast in an unfavourable light. The socially deprived rarely make the headlines but when they do the glare is usually on individuals who abuse the social security system. For instance, in 1976 the July 15th issue of the *Daily Express* devoted its front page lead and editorial to a man imprisoned for fraud against the Supplementary Benefits Commission. Within days an MP was stating—without foundation—that half the claimants were cheating the system.[106] Spotlights on scroungers also frequently appear in the Sunday populars. The abuse of the system should not be defended but the press frequently creates the impression that the poor as a body act in such ways. Further, it will rarely give adequate space to allow corrections or to present a more balanced account. Interestingly, a social work journal did make a study of the reaction of the press to a Mr Deevey who cheated social security by comparing it with coverage of the Lonhro affair in which a group of companies 'cheated their own shareholders'. The media allowed no defence of Mr Deevey but gave considerable coverage—and three minutes on TV news—to a well known politician who spoke in favour of the companies.[107]

If scroungers gain the headlines, it is worth noting which subjects do not. The working poor are rarely mentioned. Efforts by the unemployed to find jobs or create employment do not earn favourable headlines.[108] Cases of the poor who do not receive their benefits are rarely reported. Interestingly, a few weeks after the *Daily Express* drew attention to a case of social security fraud, an official report identified large numbers of claimants as not receiving their full benefits. The *Daily Express* issue (16 September 1976) gave the report neither front page mention nor an editorial. Again, middle class fraud of the inland revenue, which is far more costly than social security abuse, is not a regular subject for condemnation. Not least, what may be termed as work abuses against manual workers are not rated as scandals. Thus a report in 1973 that industrial accidents were causing an annual 1,000 deaths and 750,000 serious injuries earned hardly a paragraph in the dailies.[109]

Although exceptions occur, the overall tone of the media reinforces the view that the poor choose not to work, that they abuse the system and that they deserve their poverty. As an experienced journalist concluded, such selective reporting 'perpetuates myths and misunderstandings within the community'.[110] Goodwin sums up, '... middle class persons are reinforced continuously in their views about the poor by reports on the behaviour of lower class persons in the media'.[111] Consequently, any case for proposals to remove poverty by an extensive redistribution of resources is not likely to gain widespread support.

The subject of poverty is not totally ignored. On occasions, TV current affairs programmes will include a short discussion on how it can be alleviated. A commendable balance is maintained between speakers from Conservative and Labour, from right and left. But rarely are the poor represented. The very fact that apparently they cannot debate for themselves—indeed that their fate must be discussed by those privileged by birth, education and position—serves to strengthen the belief that the poor are inarticulate and inadequate. Again, they are cast in an unfavourable light.

Secondly, the financial differences between social groups (or classes) are not highlighted. The continuing concentration of wealth in the hands of a minority or the continuing income gap between the lowest ten per cent and the others is not plugged as a major issue. Indeed, if anything, the institutions of communication focus on the wage claims of trade unions, so creating the impression that the working class is gaining relative to the middle class. Consequently, support for increases to the latter rather than to the poor may be stimulated. Bottomore wryly comments:

> It is obvious ... that in some Western countries there is a great disproportion between the modest wage increases which many industrial workers have claimed in recent years, and the large increases of salary which some groups of professional workers have demanded. Those in the professions have many advantages ... their actions are usually interpreted more sympathetically by the mass media than are the similar actions of industrial workers.[112]

Speaking of television, Blumler and McQuail draw attention to its power of selecting certain issues and excluding others.[113] Attention being diverted away from the issue of financial differences, is therefore also diverted from the consideration of the narrowing of differences.

Thirdly, it follows that these mechanisms rarely challenge the existing stratified nature of society. Thus in a TV debate two politicians may discuss the level of child benefits but they will not question the hierarchical structure of society or question their own privileged position within it. To take another topical example, cases involving parents who do not provide acceptable care for their children will provoke considerable comment from the press, who suggest further powers for removing the children from their homes. Yet the same papers rarely comment on the established link between the poverty of parents and their inability to cope. To do so would raise issues of social class and extensive social change which could have implications for the privileged as well as for the poor.[114]

*The Social Services*

Ostensibly the social services were created to alleviate social deprivation. This section, however, will attempt to show that they can also contribute to the perpetuation of poverty. To cite Michael Meacher MP, 'But what is remarkable is the extent to which the GHS [General Household Survey] and a variety of other evidence indicates that public expenditure and public services are often geared, not to the reversal of these inequalities, but to their extension.'[115] Before proceeding on what may appear to be an attack on the social services, a qualification must be made. The argument is not only that they maintain poverty. They may also function to prevent and alleviate, being complex organisations with many roles, as will be explained at the end of this section.

How can the social services reinforce differences between social groups? One familiar argument, already mentioned, is that higher income groups actually receive greater financial benefits from the social services so that the gap is widened between them and the lower paid. For instance, it is well known that tax relief for owner occupiers—£755 million in 1974–5—most benefits those with higher incomes and expensive houses. Even the introduction of improvement grants for older property has, as Holmes summarises, frequently benefited

> ... well-off private owners or tenants on inter-war council estates already in reasonably good condition. They [the grants] were not concentrated at all on the tenanted properties in the worst condition. In addition, grants were being abused in potentially attractive neighbourhoods, especially of inner London, to speed up 'gentrification' and aggravate the shortage of cheaper rented accommodation.[116]

Meacher himself explains that the existence of private welfare services which qualify for tax relief, along with the expert utilisation of state social services by higher groups, does lead to figures which turn the usual image of the welfare state on its head. Again, despite popular views to the contrary, income tax takes from the pockets of many low-paid workers so that '... the cut taken by the state shows little variation as a fraction over most of the range [of income groups].'[117] At worst, the gap between the various income sections widens, at best, as Westergaard and Resler explain, money is redistributed between households at different stages of their life cycles while leaving unchanged the overall income distribution between different classes.[118] These themes need not be pursued here as they have been so admirably dealt with by Titmuss.[119]

Here attention will be directed at three other ways in which the social services provide the machinery for underlining social deprivation. Firstly, by supplying benefits or services at such low levels that problems are contained but not improved; secondly, and similarly, by running services in such a way as to reflect or reinforce the disadvantageous position in which society has cast the deprived; and thirdly, by conveying the services with attitudes and practices which imply blame and condemnation of the poor. The consequences are that the poor react with even less acceptable behaviour, the view that poverty is deserved is upheld, and the belief that a stratified society is both inevitable and just is strengthened. The three themes will now be illustrated in regard to education, housing and income maintenance services.

The twentieth century has witnessed a massive expansion of *educational services*, particularly in regard to secondary and tertiary education. Yet, in practice, they often maintain rather than reduce relative deprivation. Consider financial grants. Ostensibly, the means-tested benefits of welfare and school maintenance grants appear designed to enable poor parents to clothe their children for school attendance and to keep them there after compulsory school age. Presumably the children will benefit from educational opportunities in the same way as other children. However, several analyses by the Child Poverty Action Group have established not only that these grants have not kept pace with inflation but that their value is extremely low.[120] In some local authorities, the eligibility level for essential clothing grants is so low that even some parents in receipt of supplementary benefit do not qualify. The benefits, consequently, make little impact on keeping children at school yet their very existence and receipt advertises that 'something is being done' and directs any blame for failure at parents who cannot cope even with the aid of grants.

Whether children stay after compulsory leaving age or not, the overall effect of education does not appear to have equipped children to move out of poverty. The exhaustive national studies carried out by the National Children's Bureau have done much to tabulate the educational disadvantages of children in the lowest social class. The reason, its researchers explain, rests not in the children but rather in the educational machines which 'tend to be middle class institutions in which most of the pupils are working class'.[121] The upshot is that such children are turned out fitted to take their place at the bottom of the social scale. The schools therefore reflect rather than interrupt the existing processes and patterns of society.

Care must be taken not to confuse this argument with that of the defective institution as stated in a previous chapter. The implication there is that if only resources were available and teachers changed their methods then the children of the poor would be so educated as to allow them to move into well-paid jobs. The emphasis here is that, despite the commitment and devotion of some teachers, the schools support a divisive society by preparing some children for poverty. Townsend makes a similar point about a group especially liable to social deprivation—coloured immigrants. He explains that such immigrants have traditionally been assigned menial jobs and low incomes—even when their qualifications merited better. Many have no option but to live in socially deprived areas where 'the schools attended by their children have also been substandard ... (consequently) the second generation of immigrants is being reared in areas and in schools which fit them to occupy only the lowest levels in the occupational and social hierarchy'.[122]

Bernstein extends this theme. He argues that the term 'compensatory education' is misused when applied to children educated in slum areas. The children never received an initial 'adequate educational environment' so they cannot be compensated for something they failed to use. He argues that the term can be used to blame parents for educational failure—the children have to be compensated for bad parents—and can serve as a diversion from actually providing the extensive educational and other changes needed in such locations.[123] But such changes will not come, for the schools are fulfilling their role of maintaining a stratified society.

Educational services—for all their advantages—reinforce
poverty by providing inadequate grants and preparing children
for lowly positions. They may also contain elements which
strengthen the belief that the poor are a race apart deserving
of separate treatment. The best known example concerns children
in receipt of free school meals. Field documents that even in
the 1970s, many were deliberately identified by school systems
which made them eat at different tables, line up in different
queues or produce a special card. The children were liable
to stigmatisation by others with the result that some—or their
parents—declined to avail themselves of the benefit.[124] Children
whose parents were unable to afford school uniform or certain
sports equipment—such as cricket kit or football boots—were
publicly punished, made to pick up litter or banned from
games.[125]

By no means all schools adopt such practices but the point
being made is that education contains aspects which reinforce
the strongly held belief that the poor are so blameworthy as
to deserve public isolation as a means of punishment. Given
these elements, it becomes clearer why—despite the tremendous
growth of education in the past fifty years—it has made so
little impact on reducing inequalities.

Turning to *housing services*, mention can be made of but few
of the many studies. Attention will be drawn to three recent
research studies which record how particular local authorities
have dealt with the poor in relation to homelessness, eviction
and rehousing. Minns made a detailed four year study of a
council's treatment of the homeless.[126] Three local departments
had some responsibilities. The Welfare Department, under the
National Assistance Act (1948), had a duty to help those whose
plight arose from 'circumstances which could not reasonably
have been foreseen or in such circumstances the authority in
any particular case determine'. The Children's Department had
a duty, under the Children Act (1948) to receive into care
children whose parents could not provide home and care. The
Housing Department, in allocating tenures, had a duty under
the Housing Act (1957) to give 'a reasonable preference' to
people 'living under unsatisfactory conditions'. Obviously, the

legislation is subject to varying interpretations. What ensued?

The Children's Department, hoping to reduce the numbers of children received into care, urged the Welfare Department to increase its amount of temporary accommodation (the units reserved for the homeless) in order to keep families intact. However, Welfare—fearful of an influx of the homeless—provided only a small number of units, would not as policy accept families whose homelessness arose from any reason deemed to be their fault—such as rent arrears or family quarrels—and created low standards of comfort within the units so that residents would want to leave. The department's officers could recommend to the Housing Department for rehousing those families which 'showed a sufficiently improved and reasonable attitude'. However, Minns explains that the officers saw the problems only in terms of individual irresponsibility rather than in the context of structural pressures creating certain behaviour, and somehow expected them to perform as they (the officials) would do. Consequently, the Welfare Department did not take up the quota of houses set aside for its nominations. This attitude coincided with that of the Housing Department which—faced with many demands for housing—did not award preference to the homeless.

The housing services thus did nothing to solve the social deprivations of the homeless. The local authority could not tackle the low incomes which made rent payment difficult and eviction likely. Yet little impetus came to highlight this need, for the two departments refused to accept that a lack of a house was the real problem. The real difficulty, in their view, rested in the clients' personalities or in the fact that they were 'problem families' who should be insulated from ordinary tenants. If anything the plight of many grew worse. Treated harshly within the units or refused help altogether, the clients regarded the council as punitive and could respond with the very behaviour which further angered the officials. Minns sums up:

> . . . a borough which based its policies on assumptions of reprehensible behaviour on the part of homeless families established a control mechanism which narrowed the options the homeless could take in dealing with complicated problems and compelled them to act in accordance with the assumptions on which help was based.

Thus neither the housing nor income deprivations were solved
while the families' behaviour took directions which made effective
help even more unlikely.

Glasgow is termed 'the most intensively deprived British city'.
With over 11 per cent of its population in conditions officially
recognised as overcrowded, over 20 per cent of houses lacking
hot water and over 30 per cent wanting a fixed bath, it well
merited the attention of the voluntary housing agency, Shelter.
Shelter found that Glasgow corporation had made massive efforts
to help, building over 150,000 houses since 1918. Yet in the
1970s, 75,000 were officially deemed as being below a tolerable
standard, while 100,000 new or improved dwellings were required
by 1981. Despite the shortage, some tenancies were hard to
let. In particular, the far-flung overspill areas, with few local
amenities and involving long distances (and high fares) to work,
had proved as unpopular as the inner-ring slums. But what
particularly caught Shelter's attention was the figure of 2,737
tenant abscondences and 574 evictions in 1972. These former
tenants found themselves in a particularly vulnerable position
as the corporation would not house them again while the private
rented market was shrinking. Subsequently, Shelter took a sample
of those receiving eviction notices and studied their history.[127]

Not surprisingly, the study identified most of the sample
as having a low income, £19 per week per family. Moreover,
some 20 per cent were fatherless families while a further 20
per cent had a father who was disabled. Their major need
was for an adequate income with which to pay rent. As their
poverty was never officially recognised as a problem, the tenants
could well assume that they were inadequates, predestined to
a life of pauperism.

Given that the local authority had few if any powers to
increase incomes, Shelter still found that the tenants were subject
to hard treatment. After four weeks' rent arrears the tenants
were sent (although most claimed not to receive) a 'warning'
letter. If a satisfactory explanation was not offered after twenty
eight days, they were 'taken' to court. Here, in one morning,
upwards of 200 cases were rapidly authorised for eviction. Shelter
discovered that tenants then borrowed money to pay the arrears
(so placing themselves further in debt), absconded or were evicted.

Noticeably, few tenants appeared at court and legal representation was a rarity. The court, Shelter says, is little more than an extension of the Housing Department. Such tenants were deemed as problem families with no explanations or legal rights. If treated thus, it was not surprising that they fled from authority or got into debt to escape. In either case, local authority action, although understandable, only worsened the tenants' financial plight or reinforced the belief that they must act like irresponsible paupers.

Further, Shelter found that few efforts were made to facilitate payment. In only one case was the Social Work Department brought in to help a family. Moreover, the Housing Department was reluctant to accept rents on anything but a monthly basis although the families' incomes came in weekly. Obviously monthly payments are administratively more convenient and cheaper for the department. But, Shelter concluded, 'It is bureaucratic idiocy to expect families on the breadline to budget across four weeks, especially when there may be heavy quarterly bills of electricity and gas to pay.'[128] Even so, for families dependent on social security the rent problem could have been solved if the local offices would have paid the rent direct to the Housing Department. This was refused on grounds of 'pressure of work, or that it destroys a family's responsibility for paying rent'. The result was that the housing and income deprivations of the families, far from being alleviated, were actually made more intense.

The next study also concerns Glasgow but this time investigates how council houses are allocated to low income applicants. Many Housing Departments have used a system of judging applicants' personalities and—in conjunction with other factors such as length of residence—matching this with a comparable grade of house.[129] In Glasgow, Dr Sidney Jacobs worked with residents subject to this process. He describes how applicants in two tenements were visited by the investigators who, in the course of a short interview, judged them according to such criteria as 'type of people', 'cleanliness' and 'furniture'. The investigator specified the kind of area she considered they were suitable for and awarded them an overall grading on a 5 point scale from 'very good' to 'poor'.[130] Those receiving low gradings were offered property in poor conditions in undesirable neighbourhoods. Jacobs documented examples—flooded housing, completely undecorated, windows all smashed, rat infested, unwired, vandalised—which were worse than homes from which applicants were being removed due to demolition.[131] Yet many felt compelled to accept the offers for fear that no others would be made.

The Cullingworth Report on Council Housing pointed out that such a system leaves 'too much scope for personal prejudice and unconscious bias to be "acceptable"'.[132] It can be too readily assumed that low income persons in a district with a bad reputation should be given a low grading. Further, those unfortunate enough to be visited during a bout of untidiness, those experiencing a period of unemployment when money had not been spent on furnishings, those displaying aggression to the visitor, or those demoralised by grinding poverty, could receive a low grading. Not least, once rehoused in damp, over-crowded and cold conditions, the tenants found it difficult if not impossible to raise their standards to the point which justified a higher grading and better house.

This particular service obviously does not alleviate the social deprivations of certain residents, for their housing conditions were not substantially improved. In addition, as 'low graders' they were subjected to off-hand, rude treatment from investigators and clerks. The view was conveyed that they were persons whose wishes counted for little, who were not seriously consulted about their future and who had no rights to decent housing. Their position stood in stark contrast to owner-occupiers who can choose their residence and have legal rights to their property. Consequently, the social differences between the low grades and other income groups were made clear with the implication that the former were of little value compared with those in private property or more adequate council housing.

One other housing study can be mentioned, Glastonbury's investigation of homelessness in South Wales and the West of England. An important finding was 'the degree to which local authority officials—and in the social services at that—set themselves up to judge morality, and punish the accused by depriving her (usually) and her family of the kind of welfare assistance needed'.[133] Thus some housing managers felt that 'deadlegs' were not worth helping while 'One family had been refused re-housing when the housing burnt down because the mother was felt to be immoral'.[134] The allocation of houses (and the quality of houses) depended on subjective judgements about the behaviour and character of a group of socially deprived families. The consequences were severe. Some families were refused help and their children taken into care. As many of those rehoused were awarded only sub-standard property, Glastonbury documents that their housing improved very little.[135] Moreover, even this aid could be surrounded by conditions which deeply humiliated the poor in ways not experienced by other members of the community. For instance, one woman had been separated from her husband who had left some rent arrears. After three years, they wanted a reconciliation but the housing manager made her sign an agreement that she would lose her tenancy if he returned.[136]

The third complex of services to be considered are *income maintenance services*, i.e. those which provide or supplement incomes. In Britain they include National Insurance benefits (such as unemployment pay and pensions), child benefits, Family Income Supplement and supplementary benefit. Earlier, evidence was presented of the low levels of supplementary benefit, levels which mean that some recipients remain in poverty. It was also argued that the overall effect of the income maintenance services has not been to reduce greatly the resources gap between the lowest income categories and the rest of society. Indeed, it may now be that government overtly accepts that such services should so act. Over the last ten years, state pension schemes have been so framed as to award larger pensions to the wealthier sections of society. The White Paper *Strategy for Pensions* (1971) was intended to encourage private occupational pensions while leaving an inferior state scheme for the poor. A change of government meant a new scheme with less emphasis on occupational pensions but still with different grades of pension. This income scheme would thus continue rather than abate the condition of the poor. Overall, the concessions made through cash benefits do not reduce inequality or radically reduce poverty. However, they do create the impression that extensive government intervention is occurring on behalf of the poor and that no further action is necessary. Consequently, the stratified nature of society is untouched.

Cloward and Piven develop the theme by arguing that governments use cash benefits directly (even only) as a means of 'regulating the poor'. They claim that cash benefits are raised in times of unemployment solely to damp down any revolutionary discontent: 'The purpose of relief-giving at such times is not to ease hunger and want but to deal with civil disorder among the unemployed.' They continue that the gains are 'then abolished or contracted when political stability is restored' and that there- fore income services should not be regarded as 'responsible, humane and generous'.[137] Their thesis is over-simplified and has been strongly criticised by the late Gordon Rose concerning Britain[138] and by Kristol concerning the USA.[139] Cloward and Piven's account does not explain why benefits may also rise in times of full employment and does not give sufficient credit to the view that services can have numerous, even conflicting objectives. Yet there is little doubt that governments do use benefits as a tool of social order. Turnbull, having access to government archives, establishes that in Britain during the 1930s, marches by the unemployed were seen both as a threat to public order and a demonstration of the failure of the govern- ment's policies. The government's subsequent actions were 'based on the use of the press and the manipulation of the unemployment insurance and the poor law administration'.[140] The government was prepared either to reduce or abolish relief or to concede extra discretionary help as a means of avoiding radical change. Certainly, at this point, the abolition or even the alleviation of suffering was not seen as the primary aim.

During the post-war years, public order has not been threatened to the same extent. But Jordan also argues that the income maintenance services are a means of control. By keeping benefits at a very low level and even cutting off benefits to those who refuse 'reasonable' offers of jobs, governments compel workers to take low-paid employment. Poverty is thus maintained, for the industries concerned do not have to raise wages in order to obtain labour.[141]

Whether or not contemporary governments deliberately use income maintenance services as a means of control will have to be established by future historians. But there can be little doubt that, of all social services, those involving means-tested benefits are most open to criticism for sometimes treating the poor in humiliating ways. Supplementary benefit in particular—

but also rate and rent rebates, free prescriptions and optical treatment, to mention a few—are awarded only after a close examination of the applicants. Kay in a penetrating study concludes that the test involves an evaluation not just of means but of character.[142] The documentary evidence is overwhelming that many applicants are subjected by officials to attitudes and behaviour experienced by few other members of society. Kay's analysis and Colin's autobiography depict the aggressive cross-examination tactics used by officers who assume that applicants are dishonest.[143] Jordan reports difficulties in getting payments, long delays and uncooperative manners.[144] Marsden's research found unsupported mothers who were assumed to be immoral and against whom the cohabitation rule—the reduction of benefit on suspicion of sleeping with a man—was rigidly applied.[145] Bond's investigation found that officials frequently failed to inform the poor of certain discretionary payments for which they were eligible.[146]

Such treatment, Kay points out, conveys a stigma on those who receive means-tested benefits. They are marked out as persons to be treated with reserve and suspicion. The stigma affects the poor themselves. Many refuse state benefits rather than subject themselves to humiliation.[147] Bond found that of those in receipt of supplementary benefit, many failed to insist on their full entitlements. The mechanisms thus kept them even poorer than was necessary. Next, Kay explains how the stigma conveys messages to other officials and institutions. School teachers, the police and employers may assume that the poor or their children are unreliable, dishonest and immoral and treat them accordingly. Lastly, the stigma is carried to society at large. Officials assume applicants to be scroungers. 'Abuse and fraud are thus taken to be the norms among the poor: honesty and frankness among the better-off'.[148] The view that the poor deserve poverty and that society should remain unchanged is thereby strengthened. If the poor are to blame then social intervention should concentrate on changing them while leaving the rest of the population untouched.

The foregoing analysis of the social services is not meant to convey the impression that all officials act in the ways described, or that those who do, always act with malicious intent or that social services only function to maintain social deprivation. As stated before, social services are complex organisations which can simultaneously prevent, alleviate and promote poverty. It is thus as well that the following qualifications be made. Firstly, similar kinds of social services may treat their clients in very different ways. For instance, although there is a great deal of documented criticism of social security officials, Stevenson points out that their behaviour is not necessarily typical and that the Supplementary Benefits Commission recognises the need to promote improvements.[149] The present writer would record that, although some social security officials with whom he has worked have been brusque, off-hand and punitive, others have displayed considerable concern for and patience with claimants. However, it is the rude brush-offs, the hours of waiting, the insulting innuendoes and the general unhelpfulness that claimants remember and repeat to others. Again, although some Housing Departments have discriminated against low-income lone mothers, this is not the practice of all.[150] Secondly, an agency's humane act towards one client may entail harming another. As explained, the decision to give priority to removing a child from a family may be at the cost of refusing to give material and environmental support to deal with the parents' social deprivations. The decision is understandable but it leaves the parents without help and feeling rejected and to blame for what has happened. Thirdly, social service employees may act from kindly and sincere motives and yet still act as a mechanism of poverty. Beresford studied agencies—staffed by devoted workers—aiming to help the single homeless. The agencies rarely offered low-priced flats or bed-sits. Instead it was assumed that the homeless were inadequates and vagrants to be referred to doss houses, day centres and government reception centres. Once in this world, they had little chance of moving out. Yet Beresford records that some had not been vagrants—indeed some were in full-time employment—but were persons lacking adequate income and housing. The result was to intensify their social deprivations: 'Homelessness puts people like these at real risk of drifting into vagrancy. It can endanger their jobs and personal relations and put their whole way of life and security at risk.'[151] Fourthly, the apparently harsh attitudes and practices, although damaging to the deprived, may stem from the agencies' own lack of resources. Jacobs is a trenchant critic of the practices of Glasgow's Housing Department which allocates poor-quality housing to those applicants graded as 'poor'. Yet Jacobs himself makes plain the impossible position of an agency which simply lacks sufficient good-quality housing to go round. 'Essentially, a local authority must bully, threaten, misinform and force people into accepting houses which they do not want and which they would not choose for themselves.'[152]

The poor would be worse off without the social services. The services act collectively to protect them from an even more extreme fate if nothing was offered. Some agencies and their officials act in humane and dedicated ways. But having made these qualifications, two points must be re-emphasised. Firstly, the social services have not removed social deprivations. At best, they have stopped the position from deteriorating further. Secondly, the services contain elements which uphold poverty and therefore maintain the hierarchical divisions of society. Some years ago, George and Wilding put forward the proposition that the social services were '. . . a series of well-regulated compromises that provide short term benefits to the working class and long term benefits to the upper classes.'[153] They over-simplified the situation but an analysis of available studies does confirm the main thrust of their argument—social services function not just to relieve suffering but to bolster inequality.

## The Mechanisms

The argument to date is that poverty is an essential part of a stratified, divided Britain. In turn, this section has described three of the mechanisms which uphold poverty. There is a danger in such an analysis of stereotyping the mechanisms and presenting them as the embodiment of evil. This is not the intention. It is recognised, for instance, that the public schools and Oxbridge may educate talented and humane persons (some of whom are committed to eliminate poverty!). Yet it is also recognised that these institutions are the main sources for élites whose interests are bound up with perpetuating a society in which resources are grossly and unevenly divided. Similarly, the mass media and social services may contain individuals opposed to poverty while, as institutions, they do much to cast the poor in an unfavourable position. For poverty is essential to the prevailing structure of society. The question which then arises is: what effect does poverty have on the poor?

## POVERTY AND THE POOR

Poverty is functional in legitimising and promoting a stratified society. The implication is that the poor must continue in their poverty. Major social institutions—education, the media, the social services—operate as the mechanisms by which the structures are upheld, by which poverty is maintained. What, then, happens to those condemned to poverty, who face socially depriving conditions and mechanisms which humiliate and fail to help? This section will consider, firstly, studies which examine the effects of poverty on the course of family life and growth and, secondly, those which depict reactions of individuals to prolonged and extensive deprivations.

### The Effects of Poverty

The various explanations of poverty agree that a person's capacities to earn money and take a place in society are shaped by his experiences within the family, school and work. The structural explanation put forward in this chapter would concur but argues that it is the prior existence of social deprivations that militates against the poor having the experiences and advantages available to the rest of the population.

A major illustration can be taken from *child-rearing practices*. As was explained in chapter 3, some authors attribute poverty to the personalities developed in children by the inferior child care methods used by their inadequate parents. Recent research, while not disputing the adverse effects of certain child care patterns, attributes their employment not to inherently inadequate parents but to conditions of poverty which leave parents no alternatives but to resort to such practices. In Britain, Harriett Wilson has been in the forefront of such research and her findings are of such importance that they must be described.[154]

Wilson and her colleague, Herbert, studied a sample of low income families with five or more children. All families were below, on or just above the official poverty line while 79 per cent were in conditions of statutory overcrowding. A control group was matched for family size and composition. Information was obtained by psychological, educational and medical testing and by a series of interviews within the homes. In regard to child-rearing patterns, Wilson also compared the families with the methods used by the sample of all families as recorded in the work of the Newsons.[155] Amongst the low income group, many parents did not pursue methods associated with developing the social, intellectual and future occupational skills of children. Only 25 per cent of mothers fully participated in play with their younger children. Two thirds of parents never took the children out together, while family holidays were almost unknown. Although some parents, as will be mentioned, curtailed certain activities of their children, it was common for them to be permissive in the sense of not checking them. For instance, mothers would not necessarily insist that they went to school or helped with household tasks.

The lack of parental involvement, however, did not stem from personal inadequacy in the sense of not caring about children or of being unsure of good practice. The parents made valiant efforts to find time to spend with the children and did share the wider values of society in wanting them to succeed, be honest, etc. In particular, Wilson recorded that the parents did 'play a consistent role as protector: the occasional humorous remark, the fatalistic accepting attitude, the demonstration of affection, the expression of confidence that things will not get worse, all protect the children.'

The explanation for the child-rearing practices, Wilson continues, rests not in inadequate parents but in the depriving circumstances in which children had to be raised. The lack of involvement in play was related to an inability to afford toys and play equipment. 'Most of the families had very few or no toys' and there was a significant relationship between their possession and parental participation. Similarly, the inability to own books, cameras, sports equipment, created a milieu which militated against families developing joint activities. As

Wilson puts it, 'even such simple activities as knitting or regular
reading of a newspaper are outside the reach of those on a
poverty income'. Of course, even amongst the poor there are
degrees of poverty and participation. All the parents found
their relationships with their children constrained by the effects
of 'bad diet, lack of sleep, polluted air, untreated conditions
of ill-health'. But some had the extra stresses of financial harass-
ment, unemployment and invalid children which were inhibiting
their family's growth to an even greater extent.

The over-permissiveness was also related to the extent of
social deprivation. In overcrowded, terraced homes where movement and noise can easily disturb others the 'main objective
is to keep peace in the family, and to avoid noisy arguments
that neighbours on the other side of both walls would hear'.
In such circumstances mothers are more likely to give way
to children. Yet notwithstanding this permissiveness, and remem-
bering that younger children were sometimes encouraged to
play in the street in order to relieve overcrowding, Wilson
also found that some parents did insist on older children spending
much time indoors. For in order to reduce the chance of delinquency, these parents tried to stop their children mixing with
known offenders, especially after dark. The research concluded
that such an approach was successful—and was essential in
a deprived area—but at the cost of restricting the children's
activities, of holding back any desires to explore and of promoting
a suspiciousness of other people.

Wilson's contention that poverty leaves parents with little
choice in the methods they adopt to raise children confirms
the findings of other studies. Mintrum and Lambert's cross-cul-
tural study found what they call 'situational' constraints more
influential than psychodynamic factors or beliefs. Overcrowded
and materially stressful conditions were particularly significant
in reducing the amount of affection and warmth mothers could
show to children.[156] Danzinger's authoritative review concludes
that parents' child-rearing methods 'will be limited by a host
of extraneous circumstances which determine the time and the
resources at the disposal of the parent. For example, the relative
material poverty of the parent makes it difficult or impossible
to provide certain kinds of support for the children's demands'.[157]

These studies, then, are in agreement that the socialisation experiences of the children do not equip them with the characteristics which lead to success at school and work. Wilson explains that children's language is less likely to be developed when they have to spend much time out of their parents' company because of the constraints of overcrowding and time spent on the struggle to survive. The lack of toys, the absence of constructive play experiences, the non-availability of books, all can retard the development of social and intellectual skills which are prerequisites for success at school. It is not that the children are innately less intelligent than others but rather that they lack the cues and stances which outside institutions will interpret as meaning the possession of ability. Consequently, the children have little prospect of breaking away from the life of poverty in which they are raised.

The study by Wilson, to which attention has been directed, deals mainly with the way young children are treated at home. It is now timely to consider what happens at *school*. Educational success is often regarded as the escape route from poverty. Yet the children of the poor do not generally do well at school. In the past, these failures have often been attributed solely to lack of parental stimulation and interest as though they deliberately withheld their support. Yet, as the longitudinal study *Born to Fail* makes clear, there is a direct correlation between low attainment and depriving circumstances.[158] As just explained, poverty leads to child-rearing methods which place the children at a disadvantage at school when compared with those from more affluent backgrounds. Further, children may have difficulties in completing homework in overcrowded and noisy homes. There is evidence that parents, although interested in education, may keep their children at home if they cannot afford clothing or bus fares.[159] In these ways, the existence of poverty becomes the barrier to educational advancement. The children's performances can be regarded—sometimes wrongly—by teachers as meaning a lack of ability and interest. In turn the children underestimate themselves and behave accordingly.[160] Children and parents become progressively disillusioned with education.

A present tendency is to exhort parents to improve their children's attainment by changing their child-rearing methods. But the structural analysis shows that such changes are unlikely unless the social deprivations are first tackled. This point has been recently underlined by a study of unsupported mothers. The finding that their children tended to fare badly at school could have led to the accusation that the mothers lacked the capacities to stimulate and motivate their offspring. Yet a further statistical analysis by the researchers revealed that if social deprivations were held constant then the children's performance was on a par with others. In other words, the mothers' poverty was the cause of their children's lack of attainment.[161]

After school, the children of the poor seek an *occupation*. Obviously, the range of jobs open to them is limited by their lack of achievement at school. Even so, the continuing influence of social deprivation poses yet further disadvantages. For instance, the ill-health which afflicts the poor more heavily than other groups can tell against job security, performance and advancement. Askham, whose work will shortly be considered in more detail, identified a cumulative process at work. After a record of non-achievement at school, the poor tend to obtain unskilled jobs. Ill-health, boredom and redundancies can lead to a high turnover rate of jobs.[162] Yet the very record of many jobs makes it more difficult to obtain a better position.

The researches have been cited to give the order of how poverty affects childhood, school performance, job attainment. Finally, in this section, attention will be directed at the poor when they marry and have families. How does poverty affect *family life*? An important investigation was carried out by Askham whose starting point was to discover why families in social class v tended to be larger than in other social classes. There is a view, mentioned several times in this book, that such families possess values and attitudes quite distinct from the rest of society. According to this particular school, the irresponsibility, inability to plan ahead and instability of lower class families mean that no consideration is given to family size and thus they breed quickly and prolifically. Large families mean more mouths to feed and so poverty follows. Askham used such views to formulate the hypothesis that the different behaviour of large families sprang from a cultural difference.[163] She then tested the hypothesis by comparing the attitudes and behaviour of large and small families in social classes v and III.

At the end of her investigation, Askham concluded that the

hypothesis could not be upheld. The lower class large families, although poorer than the rest of the sample, did not differ in their fundamental values, wishes and aspirations. They did have definite 'ideas about the number of children they wanted at different times in their marriage'.[164] Most respondents had hopes for and valued thinking about the future. 'Similarly, most respondents appeared to value material well-being, had aspirations for themselves and their children.'[165] She summarised her findings: 'the cultural differences between the groups were not great, except with regard to the beliefs about what it was possible for people in certain circumstances to achieve'.[166]

Yet although values were similar, behaviour was not. The parents of poor large families had tended to marry young, moved often, changed jobs more and had less stable marriages. Why was there such a contrast between values and behaviour? Like Wilson, Askham's explanation rests on the effects of social deprivation on families and individuals (rather than vice-versa),

> ... where deprivation is low, orientations will develop which stress thought for the future, planning of one's life, and concern for material achievement. When deprivation is extensive the type of orientations which develop, and which guide behaviour, are a concern with the present, rather than with the future, a sense of the individual's lack of control over his own life and therefore a passive acceptance of events rather than the use of individual initiative, and a relative lack of striving for material achievement.[167]

Whatever their basic values and wishes, the poor had to react to their social deprivations by adopting actions or orientations which enabled them to cope—even though the results of such actions did nothing to improve their situation. For instance, many couples married early (without saving for a deposit on a house) and quickly had children. These patterns of behaviour, Askham stresses, were 'not normatively reinforced'; instead they were seen 'as the only possible ways of acting given their circumstances'.[168] The decision to marry early and quickly could spring from the desire to move out of overcrowded home conditions. There seemed little point in waiting for children because financial circumstances were never likely to improve. Their orientation was thus adapted to the present not the future. As Askham states, '. . . deprivation or insecurity produces lower-working class orientations which in turn lead to the building of large families'.[169] Again, the instability of domicile arose from circumstances which were not of their choosing. The inability to pay rent, landlords wanting the property, the demolition of the dwelling and disagreements while living with other relatives were prominent reasons for moving home. The result could be that not only did the family become regarded as unstable and fickle but its members themselves could accept the judgement as valid.

The insecure and unsettled pattern of life identified by Askham was amongst families who generally stayed together. More extreme instability is sometimes reflected in marital break-ups. Of course, family separations sometimes result from psychological interactions which have nothing to do with material circumstances. However, it is worth mentioning that in an authoritative review of the literature, Chilman concludes that poverty creates conditions of family stress which threaten the life of a marriage.[170] The stress can produce tensions which are harmful to children or, ultimately, lead to the separation of husband and wife. Unsupported mothers or lone fathers are particularly liable to poverty.[171] Thus the initial social deprivations provoke a situation which only intensifies poverty.

The studies cited in this section have demonstrated that the poor frequently exhibit patterns of child care, attitudes towards education and employment, and family behaviour which will alienate teachers, employers and even society at large. Consequently, their poverty is made more intense, the prospects of improvement less likely. Yet the explanation being put forward is not to be confused with, say, those of Lewis and Joseph who regard inadequate cultures or inadequate families as the starting point which then leads to poverty. The structural interpretation sees poverty existing in order to justify and uphold a stratified, unequal society. Those families placed in poverty, although a part of the wider culture, have to adapt to their depriving environments. Their methods of coping, of adjusting to the present, entail the very behaviour described in the preceding paragraphs, behaviour which only serves to reinforce their poverty.

*Reactions to Prolonged Deprivation*

Most poor people will experience something of the adverse effects of social deprivations as just described. In addition, a number are subjected to even more extreme experiences which entail almost complete dependence on state support and harsh condemnation from officials. Where this occurs for prolonged periods, authors are agreed, individuals react by extreme kinds of behaviour ranging from almost complete withdrawal or apathy to pronounced aggression and hostility.

Haggstrom has drawn together a number of empirical studies of the functioning of the poor. He explains that western society makes the basic assumption that 'anyone, given enough time and enough effort, could achieve success', should be independent and able to support themselves and their families.[172] But what of those whose poverty means they cannot give their families the kind of life enjoyed by most other people, who are dependent on state income for many years, and, as Haggstrom puts it, have 'very little scope for action, in the sense of behaviour under their own control which is central to their needs and values'?[173] A common reaction is to withdraw, to resign oneself to a lowly position, to take flight to apathy and depression. Some may avoid the reminder of their 'failure' by actually refusing to ask for help. Others will accept state benefits but in a withdrawn manner which never asks for more. Goodwin's more recent study has similar findings. He establishes how those persons in receipt of long-term (as against short-term) welfare benefits so lost confidence in themselves that eventually they accepted the inevitability of unemployment and the impossibility of improvement.[174] Liebow, in his moving account of black men condemned to the street corner as a result of their poverty, sees their withdrawal as almost the destruction of their personality. He writes,

> The kind of job he can get—and frequently only after fighting for it, if then—steadily confirms his fears, depresses his self-confidence and self-esteem until finally, terrified of an opportunity even if one presents itself, he stands defeated by his experiences, his belief in his own self-worth destroyed and his fears a confirmed reality.[175]

These American studies are in accord with recent British ones. Coates and Silburn noted 'a basic sense of helplessness or powerlessness, underlying, and at the same time reinforced by, people's fatalistic acceptance of their situation'.[176] Wilson's investigation of low income families detected that it was those facing extra burdens, such as long-term unemployment, who were most liable to apathy and depression.

If withdrawal or flight is one reaction, then aggression or attack is another. Haggstrom states that 'people tend either to retreat from or to attack forces controlling their lives which they cannot affect'.[177] Ways are sought of hitting back at society. In some cases, social security claimants appear to reason that if they are made the objects of suspicion then they will act vigorously to confirm it. Goldring describes how officials who consistently refuse to make discretionary payments to those in need may provoke them into making false claims.[178] Similarly, Parker's fascinating portrayal of under- and unemployed youngsters in the inner city shows how they can hit back at a condemning authority by 'fiddling'.[179] However, it should not be thought that illegal abuse of the welfare state is a common occurrence. Indeed, a government investigation reported to the contrary.[180] Aggression and hostility are more likely to be shown in overt behaviour towards officials. Kemeny and Popplestone summarise:

> Such clients may be militant in social security departments and demand attention by sheer persistence. They may put social workers in embarrassing positions or use past remarks to show some inconsistency in the caseworker's behaviour. Such manipulation may have the aim of putting the agency or worker sufficiently at a disadvantage to accede to the client's own requests.[181]

Instead of showing gratitude, clients may ask why social workers have done so little and accuse social security officials of deliberately withholding payments. Advice may be defiantly ignored as a gesture of independence.

Extreme though these patterns of behaviour are, they are to be regarded as the means by which individuals cope with overwhelming social deprivations. The humiliation and sense of failure, the loss of self-esteem, can have 'a destructive impact on ... personal functioning' so great as to generate complete 'personal disorganization'.[182] Withdrawal or aggression are ways of preventing collapse. By withdrawal, the poor cut themselves off from society and from the unfair competition with others. By aggression, they attack those who remind them of their own failures. As Kemeny and Popplestone put it in their perceptive work:

> A person experiencing a depriving world spends his life perfecting his adaption to it, striving to protect himself in that world, and in squeezing out of it whatever gratifications he can. Thus he will adopt strategies that are based on the need for survival or coping with this incomprehensible world.[183]

The 'catch 22' situation for the most deprived is that although their behaviour is a means of surviving, it is counterproductive in terms of alleviating their poverty. Withdrawal does not lead to a higher income. Aggression to officials only leads to harsher treatment. Social workers may be so puzzled by apathy or hurt by a spurning of their help that they may conclude that the clients are beyond help. Indeed, the behaviour may serve to confirm the belief that the poor are to blame for their own plight and that they do not deserve any form of relief.

Again, it will be noted that the reactions to depriving circumstances may involve behaviour and attitudes which, on the surface, appear to support certain psychological or cultural explanations. Thus Wilson acknowledges that the mental and emotional troubles of some of the women she studied might be used to argue that their mental instability led to their poverty. The defeatism and apathy of the men in Liebow's study could be taken as evidence of a separate culture characterised by laziness and lack of motivation which resulted in unemployment and poverty. But both authors are at pains to reject such interpretations. Wilson makes clear that her sample had a normal distribution of personality types while the study also revealed some women's mental state gradually deteriorating as a response to prolonged poverty. Similarly, Liebow argues that

> The street corner man does not appear as the carrier of an independent cultural tradition. His behaviour ... [is] his way of trying to achieve many of the goals and values of the larger society, of failing to

do this, and of concealing his failure from others and from himself as best he can.[184]

In short, the prior existence of poverty compels its victims to act in ways which may be at variance with their own basic values. They may outwardly reject work although they believe all should work. They may accept dependence on state handouts while believing that all should be independent. A few may swindle welfare agencies while exhorting their children to be honest. Rodman has conceptualised this process as 'value stretch'. He explains that the poor do share the values of society at large, but under great pressures they cope by 'stretching' their own values and codes to allow behaviour for themselves of which they do not approve. Their deviant behaviour stemmed from poverty rather than caused poverty.[185]

The structural explanation of poverty is now complete. Britain consists of a stratified society within which resources, in terms of income, wealth and power, are unequally divided. Poverty functions to service and justify these divisions. The existence of the poor, who are held responsible for their poverty, implies that the position of the more affluent should be left unchallenged. In addition, the socially deprived provide society with a pool of workers who have no choice but to undertake the state's most unattractive occupations. Further, they are so powerless that they cannot oppose being used as the 'regulators' by which the economic system can be controlled. Poverty is thus essential to maintaining the present shape of society. In turn, certain social mechanisms have developed both to maintain and continue the positions of the affluent and the poor. Lastly, poverty itself, far from stimulating motivation for change, only makes change less likely. The poor are constrained to employ child-rearing methods, attitudes to education and work, family behaviour patterns and individual reactions which both further disadvantage their children's development and also appear to prove that they are fit for nothing else except poverty.

## THE STRUCTURAL–ADAPTIVE EXPLANATION

Up to now, the explanation has been entitled 'structural' in that poverty's main function is regarded as upholding prevailing social and economic structures. Yet it also explains how poverty compels behaviour and provokes adaptations which reinforce the social deprivations of the poor. It might, therefore, be more aptly called the structural–adaptive explanation.

## Some Qualifications

Before proceeding to discuss the advantages of the structural–adaptive approach, it is worth while clarifying what it does not say. A class analysis of society is used but it is not a Marxist explanation. Society is discerned as stratified into a number of interlocking classes, not into the twofold division of capital and labour. Moreover, social service agencies are not seen as part of the capitalist apparatus whose only functions are to exercise social control and to persuade the poor that all is well.[186] Instead, these services are regarded as possessing varying and conflicting purposes. In part they do reinforce poverty but they may also alleviate, help and act from humane and altruistic motivations.

Next, the structural–adaptive approach does not claim to be fully comprehensive. An illustration may be borrowed from Askham. Her data shows that the tendency for the lower income group to have large families stems from attitudes and behaviour resulting from the experience of poverty. Yet exceptions occurred. Some poor couples did not have large families, some affluent couples did. Other factors were at work, such as sub-fecundity or religious beliefs, which thus intervened 'in the process of situational deprivation'. Nonetheless, these exceptions 'do not contradict the major hypothesis' which generally was in the direction of Askham's explanation.[187] Similarly, it is not denied that, for instance, harmful psychological experiences can promote poverty independent of other factors. Yet the studies consulted do suggest that structural forces constitute a major explanation of poverty.

Finally, the explanation should not be branded as structural determinism. Authors who contend that external factors—such as accommodation, social-class position, occupation—strongly influence behaviour are sometimes accused of conceiving man as having no individuality, as being a puppet whose whole past, present and future is determined for him so that no change can occur whatever he does. They are charged with reducing man to the point where knowledge of externals means his whole life course can be predicted. Incidentally, such accusations might also be made of all other explanations, be they genetic, cultural deprivation, culture of poverty or whatever. The structural–adaptive thesis certainly does hold that the poor have been placed in poverty and that they have little power in controlling their life styles and environments. However, the following arguments show that this outlook is not completely deterministic. Firstly, although structures may influence the development of a group or class as a whole, they cannot be used to predict exactly what happens to every individual. As a comparison, consider the process of ageing. Harwood points out that knowledge of how organisms cease to function is now well advanced and statistical predictions can be made about the general age of death. But it is not possible to use this knowledge to predict accurately the age of death of each individual. Similarly, structural explanations are not deterministic in claiming to predict the exact wealth or poverty of particular individuals. Secondly, exceptions occur to usual patterns. Harwood, again, reports that scientists have detailed knowledge of what may be called the structure of the weather, of the state of the atmosphere and of some of the rules governing the ways in which the atmospheric state changes. Short-term predictions about the weather can therefore be made with some accuracy. Nonetheless, exceptions occur and predictions for particular areas are sometimes wrong.[188] Similarly, exceptions occur in the world of poverty and, although whole groups may follow the expected path, individuals will escape. The structural explanation does not, for instance, argue that all children born into poverty in socially deprived areas and raised in inadequate housing will inevitably be poor themselves. But it does contend that, whatever their innate ability, the constraints of their environments mean that they are much more likely than other children to spend their lives as the poor. Thirdly, the structural–adaptive view is not deterministic in claiming that men cannot alter their environment. Certainly, it concedes that individuals are frequently caught in the grip of structures more powerful than themselves. But, as will shortly be shown, it also claims that individuals can act together to promote meaningful change.

*Some Advantages*

The structural–adaptive explanation will be criticised and, hope-fully, expanded and improved. As an analysis of social deprivation it does have certain advantages. It does not exclude all other interpretations but rather offers a framework in which they can be placed. For instance, it does not dispute that genetic processes mould human behaviour. Yet the genetic explanation of poverty as the result of inherited low intelligence fails to show why some individuals and groups fail to reach their potential ability or why society does not allocate more resources to those with less ability. The structural approach, however, demonstrates why poverty has to be maintained, why some groups have to be kept at a disadvantage. Again, there is agreement with the cultural views that inadequate child-rearing methods are a major carrier of social disadvantage. But the structural analysis draws upon studies to show that social deprivation promotes these child-rearing practices. A cycle of deprivation does exist but the pedals are pushed not by a breed of inferior parents but by structural forces.

By putting these explanations into a structural framework, some light is thrown on previous attempts to abolish social deprivation. Bronfenbrenner has described the extensive American attempts to reduce poverty by persuading parents to improve their attitudes, attempts which have had such disappointing results. He concludes: 'Once again we find ourselves confronted with the conclusion that the powerful forces which inhibit and warp the development of children, at least in the United States, lie neither within the child nor within his family but in the larger social context in which the family lives.'[189] The structural interpretation expects failures from such approaches, for they attempt to alter human behaviour without changing the external constraints on behaviour.

Not the least advantage of the structural analysis is that it places poverty in the context of wealth. Too many studies of social deprivation have simply studied the poor and have deduced that the characteristics which distinguish the poor are therefore the cause of poverty. A structural approach, by contrast, involves an examination of the distribution of resources through-out society and then of the mechanisms which uphold that distribution. From this it is concluded that poverty plays a part in preserving the stratified nature of society. As Goldthorpe puts it, it is not possible to give a satisfactory explanation for the persistence of large-scale inequalities 'without reference to the purposive exercise of their power and advantage by more privileged groups and strata. In other words, it has not proved possible to explain social inequality otherwise than as a structure with important self-maintaining properties.'[190] Poverty thus becomes meaningful in the context of overall structure. The implications therefore are that poverty can only be approached by reducing inequality, and inequality by modifying the structures of society.

REFERENCES

1 See R. Lewis and A. Maude *The English Middle Classes* Penguin Books (1953). A more recent statement about the decline of the prosperous is by P. Hutber *The Decline And Fall Of The Middle Classes* Penguin Books (1977)
2 B. Heraud *Sociology and Social Work* Pergamon Press (1970) p. 102
3 Cited in T. Bottomore *Classes in Modern Society* Allen and Unwin Fourth Impression (1969) p. 25
4 J. Westergaard and H. Resler *Class in a Capitalist Society* Heinemann (1975) p. 27
5 *ibid.* pp. 92–5
6 G. Cole *Studies in Class Structure* Routledge (1955) c.1
7 J. Goldthorpe and D. Lockwood 'Affluence and the British Class Structure' *The Sociological Review* vol. 11, no. 2 (1963)
8 W. Runciman *Relative Deprivation and Social Justice* Penguin Books (1972) parts 3 and 4
9 Westergaard and Resler *op. cit.*
10 F. Zweig *The Worker in Affluent Society* Heinemann (1961). See also H. Kahan, O. Butler and D. Stokes 'On the Analytical Division of Social Class' *British Journal of Sociology* vol. 17, no. 2 (1966)
11 Zweig *op. cit.* p. 134
12 Bottomore *op. cit.* pp. 66 and 11
13 Westergaard and Resler *op. cit.* pp. 92, 346
14 *ibid.*
15 *ibid.*
16 *ibid.* pp. 95–6, 350
17 *ibid.* pp. 93–5, 348
18 J. Askham 'Delineation of the Lowest Social Class' *Journal of Biosocial Science* vol. 1 discussed by Askham in her *Fertility and Deprivation* Cambridge University Press (1975)
19 *Social Trends No 6* HMSO (1975) table 1.1 p. 11

20 *ibid.* table 3.5 p. 19
21 *ibid.* fig. 3.1 table 3.4 pp. 17–19
22 *ibid.* table 5.2 p. 22
23 *ibid.* tables 5.5, 5.6
24 *ibid.* table 6.2 pp. 23–5
25 D. Wedderburn and C. Craig 'Relative Deprivation in Work' in D. Wedderburn (ed.) *Poverty, Inequality and Class Structure* Cambridge University Press (1974)
26 *Social Trends op. cit.* p. 28
27 Westergaard and Resler *op. cit.* p. 343
28 *Social Trends op. cit.* p. 29
29 J. Askham *Fertility and Deprivation op. cit.* pp. 2–3
30 *Social Trends op. cit.* pp. 28–29
31 R. Titmuss *Income Distribution and Social Change* Allen and Unwin (1962)
32 A. Atkinson 'Poverty and Income Inequality in Britain' in Wedderburn (ed.) *op. cit.* p. 62
33 *ibid.* p. 64
34 *The Royal Commission on the Distribution of Income and Wealth* Cmnd. 6171 HMSO (1975)
35 H. Lydall and D. Tipping 'The Distribution of Personal Wealth in Britain' *Bulletin of the Oxford University of Statistics* (1961) cited in Runciman *op. cit.* p. 104
36 A. Atkinson *Unequal Shares: Wealth in Britain* Penguin Books (1972) p. 24
37 R. Jenkins *What Matters Now* Collins (1972) pp. 20–22
38 Westergaard and Resler *op. cit.* p. 115
39 *ibid.* p. 407. See also B. Hindness *The Decline of Working Class Politics* Macgibbon and Kee (1971)
40 R. Rose 'Class and Party Divisions: Britain, a Test Case' *Sociology* vol. 2 (1968) pp. 129–62
41 K. Newton and D. Morris 'The Social Composition of a City Council: Birmingham 1825–1966' *Social & Economic Administration* vol. 5 (January 1971)
42 P. Chamberlain 'The Coming of a New Type of Member' *Municipal Review* vol. 46, no. 544 (April 1975) pp. 6–7
43 Runciman *op. cit.* p. 145
44 For a fuller discussion of élites see I. Crewe (ed.) *Elites in Western Democracy* Croom Helm (1974) and P. Stanworth and A. Giddens *Elites .and Power in British Society* Cambridge University Press (1974)
45 D. Boyd *Elites and their Education* NFER (1973) pp. 16–37
46 See C. Hood 'The Rise of the British Quango' *New Society* vol. 25, no. 567 (16 August 1973)
47 R. Kelsall *Higher Civil Servants in Britain* Routledge (1955)
48 R. Johnson 'The Political Elite' *New Society* vol. 27, no. 590 (24 January 1974)
49 Boyd *op. cit.* p. 54
50 Johnson *op. cit.*
51 Westergaard and Resler *op. cit.* p. 254
52 A. Halsey and I. Crewe 'Surveys and Investigations. Social Survey of the Civil Service' vol. 3 in Lord Fulton (chairman) *The Civil Service* HMSO (1969)
53 A. Sampson 'The New Mandarins' *Observer Review* (28 February 1971)
54 Boyd *op. cit.* tables 15, 18, 19, pp. 88–92

55 *ibid.* p. 66
56 *ibid.*
57 Johnson *op. cit.*
58 T. May 'A Government of Meritocrats' *New Society* vol. 40, no. 762 (12 May 1977)
59 Preface to Boyd *op. cit.* p. 13
60 Bottomore *op. cit.* p. 56
61 A. Halsey (ed.) *Trends in British Society Since 1900* Macmillan (1974) chapter 4
62 D. Glass (ed.) *Social Mobility in Britain* Routledge (1954)
63 *ibid.* p. 188
64 See Westergaard and Resler *op. cit.* p. 299
65 Boyd *op. cit.* pp. 93, 111
66 See P. Blau and O. Duncan *The American Occupational Structure* Wiley (1967)
67 A. Harris and R. Clausen *Labour Mobility in Great Britain* Government Social Survey (1962) cited in Westergaard and Resler *op. cit.* p. 303
68 G. Payne and G. Ford 'The Lieutenant Class' *New Society* vol. 41, no. 772 (21 July 1977)
69 Westergaard and Resler *op. cit.* p. 318
70 J. Ridge (ed.) *Mobility in Britain Reconsidered* Clarendon Press (1974) p. 41
71 Bottomore *op. cit.* p. 38
72 *ibid.* pp. 16, 40
73 Halsey *op. cit.* p. 13
74 H. Wilson 'Some Observations on the Relevance of the Environment' paper read to British Association of Social Workers (1975)
75 J. Feagin 'American Attitudes Towards Poverty and Anti-Poverty' (mimeo) (1971) cited in L. Reissman *Inequality in American Society* Scott, Foresman (1973) p. 69
76 J. Rytina, W. Form and J. Pease 'Income and Stratification Ideology' *American Journal of Sociology* 75 (January 1970)
77 *ibid.*
78 Runciman *op. cit.* chapter 4
79 Reissman *op. cit.* pp. 42–3
80 P. Thane 'The History of Social Welfare' *New Society* vol. 29, no. 621 (29 August 1974)
81 B. Jordan *Paupers* Routledge (1973) p. 69
82 P. Townsend *The Social Minority* Allen Lane (1973) p. 100
83 N. Middleton *When Family Failed* Gollancz (1971) chapter 4 and p. 276
84 R. Pruger 'Social Policy: Unilateral Transfer or Reciprocal Exchange' *Social Policy* vol. 2, part 4 (October 1973)
85 M. Rein *Social Policy* Random House (1970) p. 307
86 Cited by Bottomore *op. cit.* p. 15
87 A. H. Halsey 'The Public School Debacle' *New Society* vol. 12, no. 304 (25 July 1968)
88 Cited in Runciman *op. cit.* p. 270 note 1
89 R. Opie in H. Thomas (ed.) *Crisis in the Civil Service* Anthony Blond (1968)
90 Social Survey Division of the Office of Population Census and Surveys *General Household Survey* HMSO (1973)
91 Westergaard and Resler *op. cit.* p. 254
92 J. Res 'Power' *New Society* vol. 22, no. 522 (5 October 1972)
93 V. George and P. Wilding 'Social Values, Social Class and Social Policy' *Social and Economic Administration* vol. 6, no. 3 (September 1972)

94 The Public Schools Commission *First Report* vol. 1 HMSO (1968)
95 Bottomore *op. cit.* p. 40
96 George and Wilding *op. cit.*
97 See his *Equality* Allen and Unwin (1931) 4th revised edition (1952)
98 J. Blumler and D. McQuail *Television in Politics* Faber (1968) see especially pp. 263, 271
99 A. Sampson *Anatomy of Britain Today* Hodder and Stoughton (1965) pp. 666–7 and A. Sampson *The New Anatomy of Britain* Hodder and Stoughton (1971) chapters 21 and 24
100 A. Sampson *The New Anatomy of Britain op. cit.* p. 403
101 Westergaard and Resler *op. cit.* p. 262
102 *ibid.* p. 272
103 Glasgow University Media Group *Bad News* vol. 1 Routledge (1976)
104 M. Parker *et al. Race in the West Midlands Press* Centre for Contemporary Cultural Studies University of Birmingham (1976)
105 J. Cohen and J. Young (eds) *The Manufacture of News* Constable (1972)
106 Mr Ian Sproat MP reported in the *Guardian* (26 July 1976)
107 *Social Work Today* vol. 7, no. 9 (5 August 1976)
108 For an example of the press handling the work initiatives of a Claimants' Union see Jordan *Paupers op. cit.* especially p. 62
109 See R. Lewis and G. Latta 'Industrially Injured' *New Society* vol. 27 no. 587 (3 January 1974)
110 *Social Work Today op. cit.*
111 L. Goodwin 'How Suburban Families View the Work Orientations of the Welfare Poor' *Social Problems* vol. 19, no. 3 (Winter 1972)
112 Bottomore *op. cit.* p. 75
113 Blumler and McQuail *op. cit.* p. 266
114 For a fuller discussion see R. Holman *Inequality in Child Care* Child Poverty Action Group (1976)
115 M. Meacher 'The Coming Class Struggle' *New Statesman* (4 January 1974)
116 C. Holmes 'Contradictions in Housing' in P. Wilmott (ed.) *Sharing Inflation? Poverty Report 1976* Temple Smith (1976) p. 109
117 Westergaard and Resler *op. cit.* p. 62
118 *ibid.* p. 68
119 See R. Titmuss *Essays On the Welfare State* Allen and Unwin (1958) chapter 2
120 See *Poverty* no. 24 (1972) and no. 25 (1973) and no. 33 (1975/6)
121 P. Wedge and H. Prosser *Born to Fail* Arrow Books (1973) p. 55
122 P. Townsend *The Social Minority* Allen Lane (1973) p. 100
123 B. Bernstein 'Critique of the Concept of Compensatory Education' in Wedderburn (ed.) *op. cit.*
124 F. Field *The Stigma of Free School Meals* Child Poverty Action Group (1974)
125 See *Poverty* no. 25 (1973)
126 R. Minns 'Homeless Families and Some Organisational Determinants of Deviancy' *Policy and Politics* vol. 1, no. 1 (September 1972). Minns' research took place before the unified Social Service Depts took over both Welfare and Children's Depts.
127 SHAC *Report* Shelter (1973)
128 *ibid.* p. 3
129 See S. Damer and R. Madigan 'The Housing Investigator' *New Society* vol. 29, no. 6 (25 July 1974)
130 S. Jacobs *The Right to a Decent House* Routledge (1976) pp. 77–8
131 *ibid.* pp. 56–7

132 Cited in Jacobs *op. cit.* p. 79
133 B. Glastonbury *Homeless Near A Thousand Homes* Allen and Unwin (1971) p. 11
134 *ibid.* p. 101
135 *ibid.* chapter 6
136 *ibid.* pp. 106–7
137 F. Piven and R. Cloward *Regulating the Poor* Tavistock Publications (1972) pp. xiii–xvii
138 G. Rose 'Regulating the Poor: An Essay Review' *Social Service Review* vol. 45, no. 4 (1971)
139 I. Kristol 'Welfare: The Best of Intentions, the Worst of Results' in P. Weinberger (ed.) *Perspectives on Social Welfare* Collier Macmillan 2nd edition (1974) pp. 237–42
140 M. Turnbull 'Attitude of Government and Administration to the Hunger Marches of the 1920s and 1930s' *Journal of Social Policy* vol. 2, part 2 (April 1973) pp. 131–42
141 Jordan *Paupers op. cit.*
142 S. Kay 'Problems of Accepting Means-Tested Benefits' in D. Bull (ed.) *Family Poverty* Duckworth (1971)
143 J. Colin *Never Had It So Good* Gollancz (1974)
144 B. Jordan *Poor Parents* Routledge (1974) pp. 126–31
145 D. Marsden *Mothers Alone* Allen and Unwin (1969)
146 N. Bond *Knowledge of Rights and Extent of Unmet Need Amongst Recipients of Supplementary Benefit* Coventry Community Development Project (1972) pp. 1–9
147 See R. Holman (ed.) *Socially Deprived Families in Britain* Bedford Square Press (1970) pp. 187–91
148 Jordan *Poor Parents* p. 183
149 O. Stevenson *Claimant or Client?* Allen and Unwin (1973) chapter 8
150 See Marsden *op. cit.* chapters 2 and 8 and M. Young (ed.) *Poverty Report 1974* Temple Smith (1974) pp. 117–8
151 P. Beresford 'Homelessness: A New Approach' *Social Work Today* vol. 4, no. 24 (7 March 1974)
152 Jacobs *op. cit.* p. 146
153 George and Wilding *op. cit.*
154 Dr Wilson's study is fully given in a forthcoming book. In addition she has already published 'Parenting in Poverty' *British Journal of Social Work* vol. 4, no. 3 (1974); (with G. Herbert) 'Hazards of Environment' *New Society* vol. 29, no. 506 (June 8th 1972); (with G. Herbert) 'Social Deprivation and Performance at School' *Policy and Politics* vol. 3, no. 2 (December 1974); 'Some Observations on the Relevance of the Environment' paper read to the British Association of Social Workers (1975)
155 J. and E. Newson *Infant Care in an Urban Community* Allen and Unwin (1968)
156 L. Mintrum and W. Lambert *Mothers in Six Cultures* Wiley (1964) cited in V. Allen (ed.) *Psychological Factors in Poverty* Markham (1970) p. 375
157 K. Danzinger *Socialization* Penguin Books (1971) p. 76
158 Wedge and Prosser *op. cit.*
159 M. Brown and F. Field *Poverty and Inflation* Child Poverty Action Group (1974)
160 See R. Wiley 'Children's Estimates of their Schoolwork Ability as a Function of Sex, Race and Socio-Economic Level' *Journal of Personality* no. 31 (1963) pp. 203–224 cited in Allen *op. cit.* p. 69

161 National Children's Bureau *Growing Up In a One Parent Family* National Foundation for Educational Research (1975)
162 J. Askham *Fertility and Deprivation op. cit.* p. 153
163 *ibid.* p. 166
164 *ibid.* p. 163
165 *ibid.* p. 166
166 *ibid.*
167 *ibid.* p. 168
168 *ibid.* p. 127
169 *ibid.* p. 160
170 C. Chilman 'Families in Poverty in the Early 1970s' *Journal of Marriage and the Family* (February 1975)
171 See Marsden *op. cit.*, V. George and P. Wilding *Motherless Families* Routledge (1972)
172 W. Haggstrom 'The Power of the Poor' in F. Riessman (ed.) *Mental Health of the Poor* Collier Macmillan (1964) p. 210
173 *ibid.* p. 213
174 Goodwin *op. cit.*
175 E. Liebow *Tally's Corner* Little Brown (1967) p. 71
176 K. Coates and R. Silburn *Poverty: the Forgotten Englishman* Penguin Books (1970) p. 137
177 Haggstrom *op. cit.* p. 216
178 P. Goldring *Friend of the Family* David and Charles (1973)
179 H. Parker *View From the Boys* David and Charles (1974)
180 Fisher Committee *Report of the Committee on Abuse of Social Security Benefits* Cmnd. 5228 HMSO (1973)
181 P. Kemeny and G. Popplestone 'Client Discrimination in Social Welfare Organisations' *Social Work* vol. 27, no. 2 (1970)
182 J. Roach and O. Gurslin 'An Evaluation of the Concept "Culture of Poverty"' *Social Forces* vol. 45, no. 3 (1967)
183 Kemeny and Popplestone *op. cit.*
184 Liebow *op. cit.* p. 222
185 H. Rodman 'The Lower Class Value Stretch' *Social Forces* vol. 42 (1963)
186 Professor Peter Leonard is a Marxist who does not share this approach but he admits that it is a common Marxist belief. See his helpful, 'Marx: the Class Perspective' *Community Care* no. 123 (11 August 1976)
187 Askham *Fertility and Deprivation op. cit.* pp. 175, 180
188 I am grateful to Dr David Millard of Oxford University for sending me R. Harwood's paper 'Determinism and Predictability in Physical Systems'
189 U. Bronfenbrenner 'Children, Families and Social Policy: An American Perspective' in DHSS *The Family in Society: Dimensions of Parenthood* HMSO (1974) p. 99
190 J. Goldthorpe 'Social Inequality and Social Integration' in Wedderburn (ed.) *op. cit.* p. 229

# CHAPTER 6

# Combating Social Deprivation

The major intention of this book has been to discuss explanations of social deprivation rather than possible solutions. However, I cannot forbear presenting a final chapter which does consider the relevance of the structural analysis to means of combating social deprivation.

In discussing the various explanations, it has been possible to draw upon and evaluate a number of relevant research studies. These pointers begin to disappear when talking of possible future changes. Consequently, I must make an interpretation—sometimes a very hopeful one—based on present trends. The interpretation will be coloured by my own commitment towards promoting greater social equality and, no doubt, by my other personal values. It is appropriate, therefore, that throughout this chapter I make my own values quite explicit.

## WHY OPPOSE POVERTY?

Social deprivation was defined in chapter 1 in relative terms. It was regarded as the lack of access to certain resources which is suffered by a section of the population by comparison with others. Any commitment towards countering relative deprivations will involve a commitment towards social equality. Equality is sometimes derided as wanting to make all people identical. Obviously, individuals cannot be exactly the same in terms of their personalities, appearance, talents and needs. This is not what is meant by equality. Nor is it the mere legal *right* to, say, a fair trial or a place at university if eligible, for some persons are so socially deprived that they are much more vulnerable to the pressures which can provoke criminal behaviour or much less likely to enjoy the environments which stimulate the development of their educational capacities. Rather, equality implies the situation in which social conditions enjoyed by the state's various members are not so vastly different that they make it impossible for certain members to attain the advantages accruing to others. As Richard Tawney, author of a masterpiece on equality, pointed out, equality entails the promotion of each individual's uniqueness 'without regard to the vulgar irrelevancies of class and income'.[1] As long as vast differences exist in terms of income, wealth, environmental conditions and power, then the socially deprived are unequal by virtue of their lack of material resources, their lack of the means to obtain redress, their lack of educational attainment and occupational choice, and their lack of control over the constraints which shape their responses and behaviour.

Probably social equality can never be attained but I believe the end is worth pursuing. The attempt would involve a significant attack on social deprivation and hence on the structures which uphold it. But the question remains, why? What is the objection to a grossly unequal society? Far from objecting, some people would argue that the state of poverty is desirable, even beneficial. They point out that the poor are in the happy position of avoiding the worries of mortgages and the weight of possessions. Certainly, affluence does not necessarily bring happiness but anyone close to the poor knows that their condition brings anxieties about debts, insecurity about eviction and endless worries about the health of family members. Social deprivation cannot be defended on the grounds that it brings happiness.

Turning from the moral argument for the continuance of poverty, Runciman puts the case for a more equal society by drawing upon the contractual theory of justice as expounded by Rawls. Rawls debated what principles would be established by rational people as the basis on which claims for resources should be made and conceded. He argued that their major guidelines would be the principles they would have laid down if they had been ignorant of what aptitudes and position in society they were to possess. The conclusion drawn is that such men would draw up rules to protect themselves should they occupy the lowest position in society. They would want a society in which resources were distributed according to need, merit and contribution to the common good. They would not desire a society in which they were distributed according to the accident of birth or social background, in case they were unfortunate enough to be born in a lowly position. These criteria would lead not to an equal society (for people's needs differ) but to one which is more equal than at present. In a moving passage, Runciman argues that the application of such principles would mean the 'just society', which would

> be neither an inchoate and undisciplined rat-race nor an army of sullen and mediocre conformists. In such a society, there would be less inequality of wealth; there would be no inherited privilege; there would be some specialized educational institutions, but none to which admission was based on any social or economic advantage or attribute; there would be no unearned income except that allotted on the basis of need to those unable to earn a sufficient sum; the allocation of rewards would be conducted on a basis whereby any differential from the lowest not only in money but in all conditions of work would have to be justified by the . . . principles agreed upon.[2]

Runciman's vision appeals. It constitutes an ideal for which to strive. Nonetheless, Rawls' theory does contain certain difficulties. Men and women do not consistently behave as rational creatures. Further, how is 'need, merit and contribution to the common good' to be assessed? As Campbell points out, it might be argued that some persons have little merit, and do not contribute to the common good. Are they to be awarded just enough to meet physical needs? A sounder base for the caring society, Campbell continues 'is to identify the obligation to relieve distress, whatever its origin, as one of humanity'.[3]

Yet still the question must be pursued. What is the basis or source of what Campbell calls 'humanity'? The discussion now moves into the realm of individual beliefs and assumptions.

People justify equality for various religious, humanistic and political reasons, some of which have been discussed by Donnison.[4] My personal values derive from the Christian faith. I believe that God created man in the image of Himself and that He created the earth for man's benefit.[5] Three deductions follow. Firstly, men and women are valued by God and hence should be valued by each other. Social deprivation—because it means distress and disadvantage for valued people—should not be tolerated. Secondly, having a common source, men and women are in a family relationship with each other. Tawney used the beautiful word 'fellowship' to describe the commitment, concern and solidarity which could exist between people. He added that great economic and social differences served to create divisions between people, served to destroy the attempt to build fellowship. Thirdly, as the earth is given to all, there is no justification for restricting so much of its abundance to one section of society while denying it to others. I agree with Tawney that equality is 'the necessary corollary of the Christian conception of man'.[6] Thus the case for equality rests partly on the regard people should have for each other. The very fact that they come from a common source, that all are of value, means that none should be condemned to poverty, to a denial of the earth's fruits. Yet there is another side. Christianity teaches that men and women possess the capacity not only for doing good but also for evil. It follows, as Tawney again argued, that power should be dispersed, should not be concentrated in the hands of what could be an evil minority. Power as well as material resources should be more evenly distributed throughout society.

Equality, the drive to end social deprivations, is not the only value I hold. I believe in democracy, the right to elect alternative political parties. I desire a stable society which, I imagine, is likely to be promoted by the observance of the law, by reliance on non-violent means of change and by the existence of the institutions of the family, marriage and work. Within this society, freedom of expression is another desirable end. The attainment of these objectives does not guarantee a perfect society for, no doubt, greed, envy and selfishness will always exist to a certain extent. But I believe that a more equal society, a stable society, in which all people had greater access to the machinery of democracy and in which they were allowed to develop their family and occupational lives, would be a better society than the one we now have.

The holding of a variety of objectives and values, however, produces complications. At times they are in conflict, the attainment of one endangering the grip on another. For instance, it might be considered that a totalitarian government could abolish poverty. But the price to pay in terms of losing democracy and freedom of expression would, in my view, be too high. Of course, it must be interjected, as two modern writers make clear, that totalitarian governments do not necessarily even reduce social deprivation.[7] Lane shows that élitism and inequality remain as institutionalised features in communist countries. Mishra states: 'In the communist countries . . . distribution has not necessarily become need-based following the socialisation of the means of production.' Again, whatever the form of government it is hoped to attain, it might be argued that equality can only be reached by means of a violent revolution. This appears to be Coates' conclusion in his analysis of the failures of the British Labour Party.[8] Yet this, too, is unacceptable as it conflicts with the premise that change should be wrought by peaceful means. There would be little gain if one value was promoted at the cost of destroying another. My hope is that the search for social equality will be made and achieved within the boundaries which maintain and promote the other aspects of the kind of society described in these paragraphs.

### PROPOSALS FOR CHANGE

A number of other writers—probably for very different reasons—share the commitment to a more equal society. They have put forward proposals which, they believe, could greatly reduce and even abolish poverty. Many years ago, Tawney concluded that the inequalities of income, wealth and power would not be seriously challenged until the private inheritance of wealth was severely modified and the stranglehold which the public schools and older universities hold on the membership of élite occupations was broken. Titmuss shared Tawney's analysis of

these educational institutions and considered that their domination held back other members of society while the influence
of their graduates retarded '. . . the moral conviction to search
more intensively and more widely for greater equality in all
spheres of our national life'.[9] A recent annual series of *Poverty
Reports* is attempting to hammer out more comprehensive blue-
prints.[10] In one, Michael Young calls for higher family allowances, a new benefit for unsupported mothers, increased pensions,
automatic rises in social security rates to keep pace with inflation,
new methods of encouraging greater take-up of available services,
and an administrative simplification of the maze of means-tested
benefits. His colleague Peter Willmott makes the threefold plea
that the working poor be guaranteed a minimum wage of two-
thirds of average earnings; that this level be maintained so
that gaps between them and the rest of society would not
grow; that higher benefits for non-workers—children, the retired,
the unemployed—be also guaranteed at a fixed ratio to average
earnings. Wilson finished her explanation of poverty by arguing
that the behaviour of the poor could change only if their social
conditions were improved:

> The families in the slums need help urgently if their children are
> to live more abundantly, but the help they need is not retraining.
> They need large scale fiscal measures to speed up slum-clearance
> and housing schemes, to improve local amenities, to boost family
> income by generous family allowances, to improve the job market
> in the inner city, especially for the unskilled and the disabled,
> and to implement the proposed expansion of nursery provisions.
> Combined with these measures the abolition of all means-tested
> support schemes would help parents to find or regain their self-res-
> pect.[11]

Finally, the Child Poverty Action Group has put forward many
suggestions. Recently, its director expounded four major proposals. Firstly, that low earners should benefit from a new and
reduced level of income tax. Secondly, that the government's
new child benefit should be related to average earnings,
say at $6\frac{1}{2}$ per cent. Thirdly, that the unemployed should be
continuously eligible for national insurance benefits—rather than
means-tested supplementary benefits—and that rates should be

set at a reasonable ratio to average earnings. Fourthly, that the rates of all social security benefits should be reviewed three to four times a year in order to keep pace with inflation.[12]

The above proposals, if implemented, would certainly alleviate poverty and, in some instances, would lead to greater social equality. Unfortunately, the writers do not tackle the major question: *how* can their proposals be implemented? It is not enough to present research findings and a shopping list of ideas. Reports on the poor have been available since the nineteenth century but the availability has not resulted in the countering of relative social deprivation. Some consideration must be given to the means of change.

## The Means of Change

The extreme difficulty of instigating profound social change is highlighted when the structural explanation of social deprivation is brought into play. As poverty functions to uphold existing differences between social groupings, any effective counteraction would involve some alteration in the structure of society. Obviously, if the gap between the poor and the rest of society is to close, then the material resources and powers of some sections would either have to be directly reduced or not allowed to develop at the same rate as those of the poor. Moreover, the abolition of poverty would remove the reference group—the poor—against whom others had compared themselves favourably and who had provided a convenient scapegoat for many of the ills of society. It follows that any changes to alter the position of the poor would necessitate changes in other sections of the population as well.

As the poor serve functions which benefit others, it is doubtful whether the latter will easily concede changes so substantial that their own position in society is affected. They might agree to more educational resources being directed towards the deprived—provided that the distance between themselves and the poor is maintained. They might concede that social security rates are raised—provided that their own advantages in terms of income, wealth and power are untouched. As Young put it, 'The people above the line have seldom been willing to surrender some of their excesses to those below without a struggle.'[13] If greater equality is to be attained, a position must be reached where poverty is no longer necessary, indeed where society is not prepared to tolerate it. This position might conceivably be reached by humane individuals converting the rest of the population to their views, by social reforms carried through by organisations made up of persons already in places of influence, or by the efforts of the poor themselves.

## Personal Influence

One approach concerns those individuals who are not poor but—for humanistic, religious or political reasons—are committed to the end of social deprivation. If they can live lives which do not reinforce poverty, then it is hoped that their influence would move society in general to act in a similar fashion. Such individuals would not make the personal acquisition of wealth, income and power the major objective of their lives but, rather, would be concerned with the well-being of others; those from prestigious educational institutions would refuse to enter those élite occupations which were heavily biased towards applicants from such backgrounds; they would not separate themselves by geographical distance from the socially deprived; they would be akin to Tawney who made friends at all levels, who did not condemn the poor and yet did not over-romanticise them.[14] If substantial numbers of people did possess these characteristics then, no doubt, resources would be willingly redistributed.

The call to the individual to live the caring and sharing life is appealing. Unfortunately, the numbers who respond appear few in number. Even where they do exist their influence in regard to persuading others to act in similar fashion seems very limited. While not denying the need for individual behaviour of the kind just described, it cannot be relied upon as the means of reaching social equality.

## Middle-Class Reform

Individual altruists have often sought greater effectiveness by forming voluntary societies. During the last two centuries, middle-class pressure groups have established an impressive record of trying to improve the lot of the poor. Marxists tend to dismiss their efforts as no more than an attempt by the privileged to damp down revolutionary ardour by conceding minimal reforms. But, as Mishra points out concerning nineteenth-century evangelical reformers, their promotion of reform was a consistent theme and sprang from Christian compassion for the deprived. Even Marx conceded that genuine reforms can occur within the capitalist system and he welcomed the Factory Acts in the first half of the nineteenth century.[15]

This said, it is still true that much of the success of the pressure groups is attributable to the fact that their objectives could be conceived as benefiting the nation as a whole and not just the poor. For instance, those societies arguing for universal state education or state provision of health care could point out that Victorian industries were short of educated workers or that the army was having difficulty in recruiting healthy soldiers. Moreover, their objectives were acceptable in that their implementation would not alter the structure of society, would not adversely touch the affluent.

The arguments which were so compelling during the last 150 years have less force now. Today even some educated and skilled workers cannot obtain jobs. The army is able to turn away healthy applicants. Pinker concludes that 'It is the exhaustion of these traditional welfare imperatives which explains the persistence of residual poverty amongst minority groups. There are no longer any good non-welfare reasons for easing their lot.'[16]

If minority pressure groups can no longer call upon non-welfare reasons to convince others of the need for measures to aid the poor, is it possible that they will be persuaded by altruistic reasons? Is there any sign of a large-scale movement which finds poverty so unacceptable that it will sanction a redistribution of resources? It is sometimes hoped that social workers can educate society to such an extent that it will accept much greater equality. However, empirical evidence tends to support Pinker's other conclusion that '. . . there does not seem to be any ethical concept of welfare which is sufficiently articulated or popular to provide a moral justification for doing so.'[17]

Surveys amongst the middle class suggest that many of its members, far from having sympathy for the socially deprived, blame them for their poverty and see no reasons for taking action to alleviate their condition.[18] Middle-class organisations will continue to contribute to the attack on poverty. But there is little evidence to suggest that they are having a large-scale effect of convincing their fellows that society should be drastically changed in order to eliminate social deprivation.

### Politics and the Poor

Unless the unlikely happened, with the more affluent voluntarily giving away their resources, it seems inescapable that any major attack on social deprivation must come by political means. Goldthorpe, after conceding that 'structures of social inequality are inherently highly resistant to change', adds

> This is not, of course, to suggest that change in stratification systems cannot, or does not, occur; but rather that any significant reduction in the degree of inequality will require purposive, well-designed and politically forceful action to this end—that is unlikely to come about *simply* as the unsought-for consequence of technological advance, economic growth, or any such-like secular trends.[19]

Certainly, history contains examples of sections of society using political power, which Goldthorpe defines '. . . as the capacity to mobilise resources (human and non-human) in order to bring about a desired state of affairs', to improve their position relative to others. For instance, in the last century, skilled workers united in the trade union movement to forge a weapon—the withdrawal of labour—which could be used to win wage increases and the improvement of work conditions. They thus used political—to employ the term broadly—power. Subsequently, the trade union movement became the backbone of the Labour Party, which began to exercise more direct political power through local and central government on behalf of its supporters. Again, Mishra points out that historical and statistical studies do uphold the contention that the development of welfare

services and the improvement of social conditions more favourable to working men are associated with the rise of organisations
of working men.[20]

The deduction, then, is that the poor also need the political
strength to carry through the kind of reforms which would
alter their position in society. But it is precisely this kind of
power which they lack. Miliband scathingly remarks that their
powerlessness is most acutely shown when, in times of economic
crisis, they are unable to stop governments cutting social services.
In such times, '. . . the poor stand by far the best chance of
being sacrificed on the altar of the "national interest"; whoever
else may not suffer, they do'.[21] The poor—unskilled workers,
the unemployed, the elderly, unsupported mothers and others—
are not a large grouping when placed against the rest of the
population. Numerically they could not win an election. They
rarely if ever control a vital industry, such as the coal mines
or docks, as do more skilled workers. Thus the sanction of
'holding the country to ransom' does not belong to their armoury.
They are not a single, united political force.

It might be thought that the political power of the poor
would be expressed through the Labour Party. Yet, as was
explained in the last chapter, the Labour Party, particularly
in the composition of its cabinets, has become decreasingly
representative of the lower social groupings and increasingly
controlled by members of traditional élites. Consequently, it
does not now appear to be a party committed towards the
abolition of relative poverty if the cost involves changes in
social structure. In this respect it is similar to the Conservative
Party. Indeed, it is now not unusual to read of the political
consensus between the two major parties. Potter explains that
although politicians may disagree vehemently over immigration
controls, trade unions, the level of income tax, etc., their disagreements mask a fundamental similarity:

> . . . both parties have sought to pursue economic growth and
> incomes policies which have differed somewhat with maintaining
> or adjusting the present patterns of income distribution but which
> are at one in taking for granted the main features of the present
> distribution of wealth . . . they show decreasing interest in policies
> of radical structural reform.[22]

Partridge comes to a similar conclusion, arguing that few advocate any systematic alternative to the present basic political assumptions and arrangements.[23] Potter attributes much of the consensus to the increasing dominance of Oxbridge graduates over both the political parties and the civil service. Their common background '. . . gives something of a common mental cast in grasping problems, deciding what sorts of arguments and evidence are relevant, and judging what are appropriate solutions.'[24] Yet it must also be added that the reluctance to tackle inequality is reinforced by the lack of sympathy which skilled working-class supporters of both parties may display towards the poor.

Britain has a parliamentary system of government, a major political party traditionally regarded as the voice of the working class, and strong trade unions. The illusion is created of a participatory democracy. Yet the poor play little part in politics, in negotiating wage levels, or influencing the distribution of goods. The conclusion is that although the abolition of social deprivation requires political action, neither major party is prepared for structural changes in society, while the poor—as distinct from other members of the working class—play little part in the political and economic bargaining processes. The crucial issue becomes whether it is possible for the poor to increase their political weight.

COMMUNITY ACTION

So far, the analysis suggests that a serious attack on social deprivation requires more than a programme to improve child-rearing practices, more than agency reform to improve the efficiency of the social services. Rather, it requires a redistribution of social resources which will both free the poor from the constraints placed on their behaviour by depriving conditions and will also change their position within the social structure as a whole. Yet the social structure itself is made up of social groupings whose interests are served by the perpetuation of poverty. It follows that political action is necessary directed at one or more of the following ends:

(a)  to persuade what might be called the collective middle-class conscience that substantial structural changes are desirable even if they result in some losses to themselves;

(b)  to persuade those sections of the working class which do carry some political punch that the poor do not deserve to be left in poverty;

(c)  to develop a political voice of the poor themselves;

The dilemma is that until now the poor have lacked the power to attain any of these ends. Yet in recent years a phenomenon in Britain has been the rapid growth of community action. As community action does involve the poor, this section will examine whether it has a contribution to make.

### What Is Community Action?

Bryant, an academic and a community worker, has published an authoritative paper which defines community action as

> . . . a particular approach to organizing local groups and welfare publics; an approach in which the political impotence or powerlessness of these groups is defined as a central problem and strategies are employed to mobilize them for the representation and promotion of their collective interests.[25]

Writing in the same year as Bryant, Smith and Anderson took community action to be

> Collective action by people who live near each other who experience either common or similar problems, which are usually those giving rise to a common sense of deprivation.[26]

The meaning of community action may become clearer if three of its main characteristics are identified. Firstly, a major objective is for the socially deprived to gain greater control over their environment, their neighbourhood, their patterns of living. In practice this involves a greater contribution to, say, the manner in which their locality is developed, to what happens to their children, to the kind of housing they obtain, to the way in which they are treated by officials, to any changes within the local social services. With reference to the social services, the emphasis is not simply on improvement but on improvements made at the instigation of those the services are supposed to serve. Secondly, the greater control is associated with action by the deprived themselves. Community action usually occurs outside of statutory bodies. It involves the socially deprived themselves—local residents, welfare recipients, the low-paid—defining their own needs, problems and solutions. This contrasts with the usual practice of their wants being defined by those above them in the social structure. The fact that the poor are contributors does not mean that full-time workers are excluded. At times, community action groups employ professional workers, but the terms of their appointment rest in the hands of the community activists.

Thirdly, the greater control and grassroots involvement is associated with collective action. As individual tenants, clients, claimants, residents and applicants, the deprived have very little influence when negotiating with landlords, local authorities, government departments and politicians. Action is therefore rooted in the belief that only by working collectively can progress be made. For instance, it was reasoned in one project (which will be described later) that one tenant refusing to be rehoused into slum property by the local authority would have very little impact. But a hundred tenants declining to move would cause the authority to take notice.

Community action is not a new phenomenon but, as the Gulbenkian report on community work pointed out, it is more widespread than ever before.[27] The report accounted for the growth by reference to the apparent inability of central and local government to provide radical solutions to poverty, to disillusionment with party politics and to an increasing realisation by the socially deprived that by acting together they might count for something more than at present.

The nature of community action may be further explained by listing some examples and then describing a few in more detail. Homeless families, at times, have acted together to protest at administrators who have not only confined them to slum conditions but have insisted on separating husbands and wives. The housing focus has also been evidenced in the formation of tenants' associations who have attempted to improve physical standards, obtain repairs, peg rent rises, and gain rehousing.

Local inhabitants have run welfare rights organisations which both inform people of their entitlements and act with them to obtain their supplementary benefits, rent rebates, free school meals and so on. Within inner-ring areas and council estates, residents have formed and maintained advice centres, adventure playgrounds and day-care centres. In addition there has been a rapid expansion of organisations made up of particular categories in need, such as claimants, the disabled, and unsupported mothers. Accounts of various kinds of community action are now being documented.[28]

In Chapter 5, mention was made of Jacobs' study of the plight of low-income families in two Glasgow tenements which were due to be demolished. The residents faced many of the problems common to those of low status. They were provided with little or no information as to if, when and how they would be rehoused. Landlords, private and local authority, slowed down maintenance and repairs—in the face of impending demolition—with the result that tenants had to live with even more unblocked drains, damp patches, fires and vandalism. Not least, as described previously, they faced the grading system of housing investigators. When offered, often rudely and sharply, alternative accommodation in inadequate repair in districts to which they did not want to go, many tenants felt they had no choice but to accept. It was in these circumstances that a number of residents formed an action committee to which a local youth worker offered his services. Initially, the committee reminded landlords of their legal obligations to maintain property, while complaints were bombarded at councillors. In emergencies, the members of the new organisation mended burst pipes, put out fires and boarded up empty property. The demoralising decline of morale was arrested and gave members the strength to refuse unsuitable offers of rehousing. Public meetings and skilful use of media meant that councillors had to make a public response in which it was admitted that the grading system was indefensible and that tenants did not have to accept unsuitable offers. A restrained demonstration outside the Housing Department presented the tenants' case to the public at large. The expertise, which members were acquiring, enabled them more adequately to cope with interviews with officials.[29]

Claimants' unions have mushroomed since their origin in Birmingham in 1969. Controlled by claimants, they pursue aggressively the interests of members as perceived by themselves. Their attention has focussed on the attitudes of officials towards claimants, the time people are kept waiting in offices, the grim conditions of some offices, delays in receiving payments and, of course, the actual entitlements of claimants. If unsatisfied with decisions, the unions have been ready to take cases to Supplementary Benefit Appeals Tribunals. Emphasis is given to collectivity, with members helping each other rather than just pursuing individual interests.[30]

It should be added that community action in Britain has some similarity with events in the USA. The action and writings of Saul Alinsky have long been based on the belief that success stems from the oppressed acting together. In particular, the Woodlawn Organization in Chicago involved numerous low-income residents in large-scale operations which have swayed voting patterns, persuaded slum landlords to improve conditions, caused public health and building codes to be enforced, and influenced the practices of educational institutions.[31] The American National Welfare Rights Organization pioneered some of the approaches now used by claimants' unions.[32] Even more significantly, the civil rights movement attempted to demonstrate that the politically weak could use their numbers to achieve peaceful change. It largely directed attention at political discrimination but, during this period, deprived members of the black community were also making welfare agencies more responsive to their needs.[33]

## Failure and Success

There is no comprehensive evaluation of community action in Britain. No doubt many projects never get off the ground, others fail to win support and soon collapse. However, it is clear that a considerable number have thrived and from existing descriptive and analytical case studies it is possible to make some comments.[34]

Community action groups have successfully acquired community, administrative and political skills. Establishing groups, raising resources, maintaining services have necessitated organisational abilities of no mean order. Once established, they have been adept at assessing need and then exposing it by skilful use of publicity. Members have built up expertise in dealing with councillors, officials and the press. At times, when negotiations with resource-holders have reached an impasse, groups have resorted to tactics—demonstrations, boycotts, sit-ins, occupation of under-used property, the withholding of rent—which highlight the conflict of interests and values dividing them. Conflict and confrontation make for an uncomfortable life, and their employment is sometimes condemned as irresponsible or melodramatic. Such criticisms do not appreciate that the poor do not enjoy the access to decision-makers available to more prestigious organisations and that conflict may be one of the few effective tools at their disposal. Moreover, as Brager and Specht point out, social change will involve some degree of conflict '. . . since those who benefit from existing allocations of power and resources can be expected to resent and resist the challenge to them.'[35] Whatever the justification, it can be concluded that community action has equipped some members with skills, tactics and strategies which they did not previously possess.

It should not be thought that community action groups have been run by professionals aided by the poor. Not the least of the achievements of community action has been its success in involving some of the most deprived members of the community. Low-income workers, the unemployed, unsupported mothers, residents of low-status estates and so-called 'problem families' have not just been recruited, they have organised local groups. Indeed, some make a point of excluding from full membership any who are not *bona fide* residents or who do not fit into the category served by the organisation.

Community action has afforded protection to individuals and neighbourhoods who had appeared defenceless. Individuals have been saved from housing eviction and localities from redevelopments planned without their consent or even knowledge. Local authority tenants have frequently found that in tenants' associations they possess a collective means through which to negotiate about the upkeep of their property. Interestingly, there are also examples of private tenants doing the same.[36]

Community action has resulted in improved services or the expression of more civilised attitudes towards the socially deprived. Claimants' unions, along with other organisations, have enabled members to receive their full financial entitlements. In addition, they have had some success in persuading some agencies to improve the facilities in their waiting rooms. The committee in Glasgow is not untypical of housing groups which have arrested local decline, ensured that fuller information is circulated, obtained better offers of accommodation, won more choice in which districts they would live and gained greater respect from officials and councillors. Similarly, groups like the Housing Action Centre in North London have persuaded councils to accept responsibility for rehousing tenants in furnished accommodation in a redevelopment area.[37] Residents of hostels for the homeless have successfully negotiated to obtain improved conditions.[38] As well as improving the response of statutory social services, community action has frequently initiated and run its own services. The provision of adventure playgrounds, day-care centres, advice centres, workshops, community newspapers, etc., has made their neighbourhoods more acceptable places in which to dwell. An evaluation of a locally run advice centre in Batley, for example, concluded that it was reaching and involving the very people not helped by the social services.[39]

Lastly, it is worth mentioning that, although the essence of community action is collective involvement, case studies often throw up instances of individuals who translated the lessons learned from the collective experience into their individual functioning. To cite a person known to me:

A passive, poverty-stricken woman dwelt in slum council property with a mentally-ill husband and a large young family. She had no prospects of re-housing in better accommodation because of her 'low' housekeeping standards. The dwelling's toilet, an outdoor one, was unusable in wet weather due to holes in the roof which the council, despite her many requests, did not repair. The woman felt there was nothing she could do but accept the council's decisions. She became a committee member of a local neighbourhood group and ran one of its playgroups. Here she saw members handling officials in a different manner. She realised that she did not always have to bow meekly to the off-putting responses of clerks in the Housing Department. She thus adopted a more forceful pose and insisted on seeing the housing manager, refusing to leave the building until she did so. This achieved, she threatened to go to the press unless the repairs were made. The toilet was speedily mended.

Such individuals are exercising more control over their lives. They are beginning to have more choice about the way they are treated. Their victories, minor in themselves, raise their expectations and valuations of themselves and help them to function differently. Officials then begin to regard them more as human beings with the same dignity, feelings and rights as more affluent inhabitants. Community action is about collective operations but ultimately it is also to do with how individuals function and how they treat each other.

It should not be thought that community action is a sweeping success. Obviously, its achievements to date are of a limited and piecemeal nature. Community action is stimulated locally and its influence so far has not been felt at the national level. It may have improved local procedures, enabled more people to use existing services, gained extra resources for some deprived areas, but it has not altered national policies. Nonetheless, it may be moulding an approach which the socially deprived will be able to develop towards more significant social changes.

Further, it must be recognised that, at times, community action has been associated with attitudes and methods which undermine some of the values stated earlier in this chapter. Three examples stand out. Firstly, on occasions recourse has been had to stirring up extreme hostility, even hatred, against the police, housing officials, social security staff, capitalists and anyone whose political or social stance does not coincide with that of the activists. This practice is seen as a means of gaining solidarity amongst the deprived by united feeling against a hated outsider. Secondly, there is—again infrequently—the view that ends justify means, that the aim of social equality warrants illegal actions, half-truths and even violence. Thirdly, there is the occasional desertion from what may be called democratic practice—the refusal to listen to the other side, the shouting down of opposition, the misrepresentation of what others say, the out-of-hand dismissal of other people's views. I am opposed to these trends which, even if initially successful, would lead to a society in which equality and justice were absent. Certainly, they would not encourage a system in which all persons are held to be of value. The outcome would be a society in which violence and falsehoods became accepted practice. Freire's wise words are worth repeating,

. . . the oppressed must not, in seeking to regain their humanity become in turn oppressors, but rather restorers of the humanity of both.

This, then, is the great and historical task of the oppressed: to liberate themselves and their oppressors as well . . . . Only power that springs from the weakness of the oppressed will be sufficiently strong to free both.[40]

Fortunately, the documentation of community action suggests that examples of such dangers are exceptional rather than general. The attraction of community action to me is that it presents the possibility of collective action by the socially deprived towards the end of social equality within a framework of a democratic, lawful society.

## Combating Poverty

Community action has numerous limitations and dangers. Nonetheless, my belief is that *if* it continues to grow, then it comprises one of the few potentially effective attacks on social deprivation.

Community action serves as a political weapon of the kind the poor have lacked in the past. It is not the political weapon that possesses parliamentary seats or local government majorities. It is not the political power that can bring industrial production to a halt. But it is political in the following ways. Community action, as a collective force with access to publicity and self-defence, can bring harsh and unfair treatment into the open. As has been shown, such exposure can persuade authorities to reform their attitudes and practices towards the socially deprived. Further, if community action multiplies, it will make the political point that the issues they raise, although local in expression, are national in their coverage. As Jacobs said of the tenants in Glasgow, their small project touched upon the universal issue of '. . . the right of working class families to live and bring up their children in surroundings of their choosing.'[41] Jacobs points out, too, that local action also highlights the need for national action everytime it shows that local authorities cannot solve the problems on their own doorsteps.

He explains that the harsh allocation practices employed by the Housing Department stemmed not from a fundamental desire to do down the tenants but from the local authority's own lack of housing resources, which meant that some tenants had to be directed into inferior property. If the same lesson is drawn from many pieces of community action, then clearly the poor are evolving a means for showing that the resolution of poverty requires political action to redistribute resources in favour of the socially deprived.

Next, community action can challenge the belief that the poor, as a category, are irresponsible inadequates. To recall the research of Askham, she explained that extreme social deprivations led to the poor possessing orientations characterised by '. . . a concern with the present rather than with the future, a sense of the individual's lack of control over his own life and therefore a passive acceptance of events rather than the use of individual initiative . . . .'[42] These orientations are reinforced by the condemning attitudes of other sections of society, who regard the poor as the dregs, fully deserving of their plight. Successful community action teaches the deprived that they do not have to play the role of apathetic spongers into which they are cast. On the contrary, the deduction to be made is that not only are they not deserving of poverty but that in community action they may have found a lever for creating some change. It follows that the sense of hopelessness and withdrawal which frequently accompanies poverty can be averted and the motivation to act be stimulated. Haggstrom, after giving examples of how long-term poverty instils into the poor a bad self-image of themselves, then proceeds to demonstrate that '. . . their behaviour may be remarkably transformed when, as has happened through social action, they begin to acquire a sense of power, of ability to realise their aspirations.'[43] Further, the aspirations themselves are raised by community action. Successful outcomes, though small and local, will intensify the poor's sense of injustice that they are relegated to an inferior position. As Runciman's study made clear, the poor are least likely to take action when they accept the inevitability and rightfulness of their place; '. . . aspirations will be least disquieting when expectations are low'.[44] Community action appears to show the poor what might be achieved, it begins to involve them in negotiations with, or action against, those whose affluence contrasts with their own deprivations. Thus a cumulative process can be expected with small gains giving confidence for further action and with aspirations being heightened as the injustice of their own position is made more obvious.

Even more important may be the effects of community action on those who are not poor. Firstly, those who already possess some sympathy for the socially deprived. Freire contends that social reformers who work *for* the poor but are socially and physically distant from them, who proclaim solutions without having 'communion with the people', may actually contribute to social deprivation.[45] By assuming that they must act for and decide for the poor, they bolster the myth that the poor are inadequates, not capable of any action themselves. This trend is arrested when community action testifies that the socially deprived can think, organise and act. In effect, the activists are telling the sympathisers to listen to them. Freire puts it that authentic action can only be '. . . action with the oppressed'.[46] It must be *with*, not *for*. Community action, although as yet apparently insignificant, could constitute the base from which 'authentic action', to use Freire's term again, could stem.

Secondly, there is the effect on the affluent. Interestingly, Freire, drawing upon his experiences in Latin America, and Goodwin, using his extensive research survey, make similar observations concerning the relationship between the affluent middle class and the poor. Goodwin concludes that 'middle class persons tend to locate the problems of lower class poverty in the psychology of the poor', so that any alleviation is seen in terms of improving the behaviour of the poor rather than in any profound redistribution of resources:

> There is little opportunity for middle class persons to be confronted with data challenging their projections about the psychology of the poor, much less to be confronted with poor people. . . . Only through such confrontations is there likely to be an improvement in the accuracy of middle class perceptions . . . .[47]

Freire, in similar vein but with a different vocabulary, wrote:

The oppressed are regarded as the pathology of the healthy society, which must therefore adjust these 'incompetent and lazy folk' to its own patterns, by changing their mentality. These marginals need to be integrated, incorporated into the healthy society that they have 'forsaken'.

The truth is, however, that the oppressed are not marginals, are not men living 'outside' society. They have always been inside—inside the structure which made them 'beings for others'. The solution is not to 'integrate' them into the structure of oppression but to transform the structure so that they can become 'beings for themselves'.[48]

Community action appears one of the few peaceful means by which the middle class can have their assumptions challenged. It publicly portrays the poor, not as an inferior species but as humane and as able as other members of the community. Consequently, the pathology thesis, the acceptance of poverty as the just reward of the lazy, is shaken. To use Goodwin's terminology, community action does present a confrontation which challenges middle-class perceptions and undermines the assumptions with which poverty is upheld.

Thirdly, if the poor can no longer be regarded as inadequates, what of that group, those working-class persons who are neither rich nor poor, whose own contentment has been founded upon the belief that at least they were, and always would be, superior to the socially deprived. Through community action, the poor may show that they too are human and hence can no longer serve as the despised, inferior group. Moreover, their collective action may suggest that the poor are going to alter their position and that the security of the old *status quo* is threatened. In such circumstances, the eyes of those who act as a buffer between the poor and the affluent may be redirected towards the latter. If they are then spurred towards improving their own position relative to the affluent then the very structure of society—and its associated inequalities—is brought into question. In an interesting study of Sweden, a country with less inequality than Britain, Scase explains that workers have a more active awareness of inequalities because they select wider reference groups, i.e. they do not use only those below them for this purpose. He attributes this to the part played by Swedish trade unions in '. . . translating the everyday experience of Swedish workers into a broader ideological context'.[49] Community action may play a similar role in Britain. By undermining the beliefs by which the poor have been condemned to poverty, it may cause not only the poor but also other members of the working class to compare their lot unfavourably with more affluent groups and, finding an unfavourable situation, may motivate them towards change.

If far-reaching, then, community action could have a significant effect on the non-poor as well as the poor. It was argued that poverty functions to uphold the stratified nature of society. It does so by making poverty—and thereby affluence—appear merited, by lessening the prospects of average-income earners pressing for reform, and by providing a pool of 'dirty workers' prepared to undertake society's most menial jobs. Community action could undermine these functions. If the poor are shown not to be the lazy, work-shy breed, then the non-poor cannot so easily justify their refusal to grant them a greater share of income, wealth and power. Again, as just explained, those who stand between the poor and the privileged may have their focus diverted towards challenging the position of those above them instead of holding down those below. The poor whose aspirations and self-respect are raised through collective endeavour may no longer be ready to take menial jobs on menial terms. It follows that community action if (and it is a big 'if') it expands, could challenge the mechanisms which legitimate poverty and, in so doing, could question the stratified make-up of our society.

## The Expansion of Community Action

The condition *if* has been continually stressed. Can and will community action expand? Obviously, if community action is questioning the structures of society, it can expect opposition from those powerful sections which profit most from the present distribution of power, wealth and income. Local authorities often appear to disapprove of both the aims and aggressive stance of community action groups. The response of officials and councillors who oppose them has been discussed by the second Gulbenkian Report and by the present writer.[50] Further, when the joint government/local-authority Community Development Projects moved to a structural analysis of poverty and supported community action, the chances of their tenure being renewed disappeared. Again, the Labour Party has not been marked by any enthusiastic support for collective action by the poor.

For all the opposition—and it is considerable—it is still possible that community action may flourish. Indeed, it may do so within the very framework of those bodies which express opposition. For instance, government-sponsored projects may lead to community action even where this was not the original intention. Mention has been made of the Community Development Projects which were mounted upon cultural and agency explanations of poverty but in which a number of workers adopted a structural explanation as they experienced the problems at first hand. The result was the coexistence of a number of different approaches. Thus Crawforth, in a study of the Liverpool CDP, points out that the team was simultaneously working to improve the efficiency of local social services and also promoting community action at the neighbourhood level.[51] In Coventry, the CDP team eventually decided to fund local community action groups while working themselves to share a structural analysis with administrators, planners and other professionals. Although the CDP experiment is to end, the indications are that the government will sponsor other means of intervention into deprived areas. As has happened before, it is likely that support for local groups will be an unintended spin-off, with the community action continuing long after the official projects have closed.

At times, local authorities also back community action groups. Their support has stemmed, not from a desire to build up the collective voice of the poor but because certain shared interests are perceived. Community action, by involving the poor, improving their self-image and providing additional services may lead to fewer unhappy homes, less vandalism and a drop in delinquency.[52] It is sometimes appreciated that adventure playgrounds and day-care centres run by local residents may serve those whom officials are unable to reach. The representatives of local authorities may have disliked the tactics employed by activists but, on occasions, they have recognised that both sides are opposed to violence, pollution and broken homes. Of course, councillors and officials may remain hostile when community action entails fierce criticism of local government, when it leads to greater demands on the social services and when a shift is threatened in the seat of power. But in a complex situation, local authorities, in order to serve their own purposes, may financially back local groups who can then develop community action towards their objectives.

Coates and Silburn have stated that problems of poverty, although experienced locally, are not amenable to a local solution.[53] While agreeing, I would add that the pressure for structural change will still have to be generated locally. They then proceed to argue that, in order to obtain such change, community action must at some stage ally itself with some major political institution. Despite the lack of support from the Labour Party, they believe that community action will need to be accepted by the organised socialist movement and they reckon that the tide is now moving in favour of some acceptance. Certainly, there are some signs of trade union interest—particularly concerning the elderly—in supporting the poor whether or not they are members of a trade union. Again, the TUC approved of the statutory limit to wage increases of £6 a week on the grounds—mistaken as it turned out—that it would benefit low wage earners.[54] It is possible that the next stage of community action development will be towards joining local Labour Parties in an effort to influence policy and to reverse the trends which have made the party uphold rather than challenge the present structural shape of society. To put it grandly, the hope would be that local pressure would make the Labour movement more representative of the interests of the poor. In other words, even if the Labour Party shows little interest in community action, there may be scope for activists to move into the party. As Miliband says,

> . . . the effectiveness of efforts on their [the poor's] behalf depends, in part at least, on the pressure generated by the poor. In this respect too, one of the few general laws of politics holds, namely that those who do not speak for themselves are not likely to be effectively spoken for by others.[55]

There may well be scope for the growth of community action within the existing framework of local government, central government and the Labour movement despite their conflicting functions. But the strongest feature of community action will remain its capacity to act as a base for the poor even when all other hands are raised in opposition. The knowledge that community action is happening may in itself encourage multiplication in the way that claimants' unions have flourished, with claimants in one town quickly following the lead of claimants elsewhere. If many groups demonstrate that the poor can act, that they can mould political organisations, then the hope is that the attack on poverty will intensify in the directions already outlined.

## *The Only Approach?*

Community action has still to prove itself on a large scale. The case put forward here is not that it is the assured way to utopia but rather that it appears to contain elements which could constitute an effective attack on the structure and mechanisms of social deprivation. Further, it may be the means whereby the position of the poor can be relatively improved without recourse to violence or to the threat of a totalitarian society. But whatever the attraction of community action, it is not claimed that all other approaches should be rejected. For instance, consider attempts to improve the running of the social services. The social services are complex organisations which may both perpetuate and alleviate poverty. Studies show that certain housing practices do reinforce the social deprivations of a minority. Yet it would be foolish to ignore the beneficial effect of the provision of good standard council housing to many of the population. Thus I cannot concur with the radical views of Galper who claims that contemporary services 'do not and cannot be of great service to clients or to social welfare in general'.[56] Elements within the welfare state do prevent the condition of the poor from deteriorating and it serves no useful purpose to dismiss them *in toto*, to denigrate consistently all the efforts of officials, social workers and pressure groups who aim to raise the standards of agencies.

Far from leading to a complete rejection of other approaches, the structural understanding of poverty and the recognition of the value of community action can be used to inform developments within them. For instance, various proposals are put forward for tax reforms and new forms of social security benefits. From the point of view influencing this chapter, they must be assessed not just in terms of whether they raise the incomes of the poor but, overall, whether they improve their position relative to other sections of society. Again, proposals for improving the social services can be evaluated according to whether or not they diminish the processes whereby clients are treated as inadequates, whether they facilitate their gaining more control over their own lives.

If the social services can be evaluated according to their impact on the socially deprived, what of social workers? This book will conclude with a discussion of the role of social workers in regard to poverty. I have focussed on social work for three major reasons. Firstly, the number of social workers has increased rapidly in recent years.[57] Secondly, social workers (and their critics) are concerned about the issue. Thirdly, I have a close association with social work and so have a personal interest in assessing the relationship between poverty and social work.

## SOCIAL WORK AND POVERTY

If the structural–adaptive explanation is correct, what part can social work play in countering poverty? Various trends of thought within social work believe it cannot and should not be active in this direction. It is pointed out, quite accurately, that the personal social services, that is the agencies which employ most social workers, simply do not possess the resources or powers to remedy the problem of poverty. In England and Wales, the local-authority Social Service Departments have responsibilities towards a large range of clients whose difficulties impair the functioning of their lives. These services spend much on dealing with difficulties once they arise, with a considerable proportion going to residential institutions. But for the year ending March 1973, expenditure on preventive and supportive work came to a mere £1,431,000 out of a total budget of over £355 million. In the same year in Scotland, the Social Work Departments spent only £236,000 as direct material help to 20,316 clients.[58] The personal social services have few resources to allocate directly to the poor, while they are not the bodies with a statutory right to meet housing or income maintenance needs. Hence, some writers contend that social workers should not regard poverty as a major concern for their occupational activities.

Despite the paucity of social work resources, the British Association of Social Workers has pointed out that Social Service Departments are increasingly giving financial aid to clients in the form of contributions towards fuel bills, making grants or loans for furniture, clothes and food, and paying for bed and breakfast as a means of shelter for the homeless.[59] The trend is regretted on two grounds. Firstly, it is feared that Social Service Departments are inadequately taking over responsibilities which properly rest with the Supplementary Benefits Commission and Housing Departments. Secondly, it is contended that social workers are undertaking tasks which are not really social-work ones. Jordan, a radical social-work author, has called for Social Service Departments which are clearly not involved in relieving material poverty:

> A personal social service department which had no connection with poor relief would not be in danger of selecting its clients according to their need for financial assistance. It could then concentrate on human deprivation, on the emotional traumas of childhood and the conflicts of family life in all strata of society. . . .[60]

In short, poverty is not regarded as within the province of social workers, who should be free to apply their therapeutic and psychological skills to problems of the emotions.

The above views are scattered throughout the social-work literature and have been brought together and lucidly presented by Meyer. She agrees that '. . . it is primarily society and not the individual that is responsible for the social problems in our world'.[61] She accepts that '. . . the solution to poverty is a more equitable distribution of money; the solution to unemployment is jobs; the solution to illiteracy is education; and the solution to discrimination is more opportunity.'[62] Moreover, she acknowledges that the solutions will result only from political decisions. But, in her view, social workers cannot and should not contribute to radical change. They *cannot* because professions possess technical expertise but not '. . . the power to effect basic social change'.[63] Social work is small, weak and impotent even when compared with other professions. It *should not* because social work has not been briefed to do so, the employers of social workers do not pay them for that purpose. She states:

> Social work . . . is a reflection of the forces in society. When those forces are forward looking, so is social work. Of course, when those forces turn inward and become reactionary, social work as one of society's institutions will also follow that course.[64]

Society tends to be conservative, there is not going to be revolutionary change in the Western world, so social workers must reflect the wishes of society. Meyer adds: '. . . organised society will not be the source of support for forces that will overthrow it.'[65] She thus concludes that social workers cannot, should not and will not be allowed to promote the profound changes needed to counter poverty.

What, in Meyer's view, can social workers do? She is a persuasive and humane writer, one who deplores the ravages of urban deprivation. The role of social work is to 'individualize', to enable even the poor to realise that they are still unique individuals despite the complexity of urban living. The social worker must aim '. . . to enable people to command their own lives and destinies to the greatest extent possible in light of the isolating, technological, specialized, and hopelessly complex world in which we live . . .'.[66]

## The Grounds for Social Work Involvement

Social workers have been severely criticised for their apparent lack of involvement with the poor. Sinfield, in a powerful and influential Fabian pamphlet, castigated them for doling out therapy rather than resources. He accused social workers of ignoring material need because its relief brought little professional status, whereas a concentration on psychological problems facilitated the development of casework, the skill which provided them with an identity quite separate from other occupations. In short, he contended that they were more concerned with building a profession and extending administrative empires than in taking political action on behalf of the poor. He concluded that many social workers were '. . . faced with the task of persuading people to tolerate the intolerable. They became agents of control or "social tranquillizers"'.[67] A cartoon in *Cas Con*, the magazine for revolutionary social workers, catches the mood of Sinfield's attack. It shows a poverty-stricken woman facing her social worker who enquires, 'Well, Mrs Bloggs, how do you feel about your rats?'[68]

These barbs have contained sufficient truth to hurt. But there are other, more substantial grounds for arguing that social workers should accept involvement in combating poverty. Firstly, social workers daily meet persons whose distress and suffering spring from or are multiplied by social deprivations. For instance, numbers of children have to be received into public care because of the devastating effect poverty has on their home lives. I have summarised the relevant data elsewhere,[69] and here it is sufficient to cite Thorpe's conclusion: 'The evidence from this research points to the lamentable conclusion that poverty and deprivation are still closely associated with reception and committal to care.'[70]

Turning to mental disorders, George Brown and his colleagues have established that threatening social deprivations—inability to move from a slum, unemployment, redundancy, etc.—are frequently linked with depressions and abnormal anxieties in women.[71] Again, there is evidence that a substantial proportion of approaches to the personal social services in both England[72] and Scotland[73] come from persons in financial difficulties. In Glasgow, it is estimated that 80 per cent of initial enquiries are related to financial need.[74] Clearly, poverty shapes the number of clients calling for social-work help and influences the very personal problems which social workers are expected to treat. To 'individualise' clients is a worthy end but it is hardly sufficient. If social workers desire to meet the needs of their socially deprived clients, then they must also commit themselves to alleviating poverty in the short term and reducing or abolishing it in the long term.

Secondly, social workers cannot regard social work as an activity quite separate from social deprivations, for there are elements within it which may reinforce poverty. In the last chapter, it was explained that certain social mechanisms uphold poverty by casting the poor in the role of the cause of social deprivation. Social work is not always free from this tendency. For instance, a woman experiencing depression after years of struggling in a slum may be offered some financial assistance on condition that she improves her personal behaviour. The problem is thus located in the woman herself, and her sense of failure is intensified. Jordan cites one client as resenting the intimate questions which had to be answered before any material aid could be considered.[75] In such cases, social workers are wrongly diagnosing the reasons for the behaviour of the poor, they are failing to recognise that social conditions as well as innate personality disorders can promote personal difficulties. Haggstrom comments on social workers who define the poor as paranoid:

> It is easy to see the poor as paranoid since they are so often hostile to and suspicious of powerful objects which they may perceive in distorted fashion. However, paranoia presumably requires origins in early childhood, while the hostility and suspicion of the poor naturally arise from their social position. . . . .[76]

The poor who are so diagnosed find the causal finger pointed at their internal deficiencies. Consequently, their sense of inadequacy and powerlessness is increased, while nothing is done to alter their relationship to poverty. If the social workers' approach makes the poor feel more blameworthy, more inadequate, then they have allied themselves to the mechanisms which keep the poor at the bottom of a structured society.

Of course, it must be acknowledged that social workers do also deal with emotional and psychological difficulties—amongst the poor and others—whose origins and manifestations are not connected with poverty. One of the major challenges facing social work is to develop the skill to distinguish between the various causes of personal difficulties.

Thirdly, if social workers regard themselves as political neutrals, they may be reinforcing poverty in another way. Meyer rightly claims that social workers cannot regard themselves primarily as politicians. But if 'political' means not just party politics but any organized activities which contribute to the values and mechanisms underpinning the allocation of resources, then social workers cannot claim to be without political influence. Bitensky explains that during the period when psychoanalytic-style case-work strongly moulded social work practice, it was taken that social work was non-political. Yet it exercised a political influence, howbeit a negative one, in the sense that many social workers colluded with the prevailing assumption that personal problems would not be alleviated by a redistribution of power, wealth and income.[77] Indeed, social workers using such approaches have been accused of making poverty acceptable to the poor as well as the rest of society.[78] Social workers cannot completely remove themselves from the issue of poverty. Their emphases, their methods, their doctrines, will either lend support to its present extent or will be seen as wanting to change it. Either way, the direction is towards political decisions.

The tenor of the argument is that social workers have a responsibility towards combating poverty. But how? Three ways will be briefly discussed. In the short term, they can attempt to alleviate or modify the financial condition of some of their clients. In the mid term, they can attempt to make their agencies more sensitive to the needs of the poor. In the long term, they can—if their own values support the notion of a more equal society—contribute to the political forces which may alter the position of the poor.

## Modifying Poverty

In the immediate situation, social workers can modify the impact of poverty by informing clients of their entitlements to certain welfare benefits, by advocating as a means of obtaining their dues, and by acting as 'brokers'. These three activities are discussed in the social-work literature, and only brief mention need be made here.

Welfare rights is usually taken to cover the entitlement of

low-income persons to statutory financial or material provisions (or exemption from making payment for them). Best known is entitlement to supplementary benefit—both its basic rates and various 'discretionary payments'—while other important benefits are family income supplement, educational maintenance grants, rent and rate rebates, free school meals, and exemption from certain health and dental charges. Evidence abounds to prove that many poor persons do not take up the very services for which they are eligible.[79] Welfare rights activity essays to improve take-up by systematically informing people of their rights and encouraging them to apply. Some notable successes are on record. Bond tells of action in Coventry which led to many recipients of supplementary benefit gaining additional resources from special needs grants, weekly additions, and the rectification of official mistakes.[80] Similar successes are reported by a number of social workers.[81]

The giving of information about, even the application for, benefits does not always mean they are gained. Where it is felt that requests have been unfairly refused, the role of advocacy comes into play. The term 'advocate' can be used in a wider sense[82] but generally, as Terrell explains, an advocate is taken to be one who 'acts on behalf of a client against an adversary'.[83] An advocate is not an objective neutral but has a primary commitment towards his client. An increasing number of social workers appear with and for clients at Supplementary Benefit Appeals Tribunals where, for instance, they may try to reverse a decision not to grant a discretionary benefit or to raise the level of a weekly payment. In other fields, the advocate may call for reductions in rent or rates, appeal for greater compensation for a work injury, or insist on the right to a war or occupational pension. It is worth noting that organisations of the poor also perform as advocates. In the future, the contribution of the social worker may be to refer their clients to bodies which will advocate for them or equip them to act for themselves.

Services are not always rights, and the path to them is not always easy to follow. The social worker takes on a 'broker-age' role when he negotiates between individuals and organisations. Jacobs, in his study of rehousing, demonstrated that one of the greatest difficulties faced by the socially deprived is how to penetrate vast and complex bureaucracies.[84] The procedures necessary to obtain day care, accommodation, repairs to property—from statutory or private sources—may be so baffling and time-consuming that applicants eventually withdraw. Social workers, however, frequently know which agency can provide the goods, what information is required, what are the short-cuts. In brief, they are able to bring the needs of the applicant into direct contact with those who make decisions about the allocation of agency services. Social workers who broker for the poor offer a modest but significant contribution. They provide the disadvantaged with some of the 'know-how' which more affluent citizens take for granted.

The now substantial literature on welfare rights, advocacy and, to a lesser extent, brokerage reflects its increased practice. Sinfield could not now criticise social workers in the blanket way he did in 1969. These approaches do not abolish poverty. Even when the poor obtain their full entitlements and win appeals, they still remain in poverty. Nonetheless, to ignore such activities is to dismiss a means of modifying poverty and serves only to increase distress. As Bull claimed at the close of a welfare rights exercise, the families concerned may still be poor but at least they are 'a pound or two better off each week'.[85]

## Agency Reform

If welfare rights activities modify poverty in the short term, social workers can also work, in what might be called the mid term, to make their agencies more responsive to the socially deprived. In chapters 4 and 5, it was made plain that welfare agencies do not always adequately help those in greatest need and that room for improvement existed. Social workers—at the field level—may not be in the administrative, managerial or elected positions which are usually associated with directing agency changes. Nonetheless, Patti and Resnick urge that their allegiance to social-work values and the well-being of clients still places upon them an obligation to labour for internal reform.[86] Three areas in which change may be advanced come to mind.

Firstly, agencies are continually making decisions about the allocation of their resources. Social workers, as those in closest contact with clients, are well placed to argue which clients and neighbourhoods most need aid. To take another example. Social workers might insist that money be diverted towards improving the reception facilities of agencies—both the physical surroundings and attitudes of receptionists—in order to dignify the treatment of clients instead of strengthening the belief that the poor deserve third-class conditions.

Secondly, there are the roles of social workers. Consider welfare rights again. If clients are to obtain their dues, then ideally all social workers should possess welfare rights expertise. However, the British Association of Social Workers has stated that the range of benefits is now so extensive that it is questionable whether a single social worker can cope with them all as well as their many statutory duties.[87] While recognising that all social workers should possess some basic knowledge of entitlements, it has been proposed that Social Service Departments should create a new post, of welfare rights officer.[88] A few departments have now appointed such officers who keep social workers abreast of new information and advocate in difficult cases. Their arrival is an example of change within a welfare agency in order more fully to help the material position of the socially deprived.

Thirdly, there is the interpretation of legislation. Although local authorities have statutory obligations placed upon them, the legislation is frequently so vague or permissive that great variety occurs in practice. The granting (or not) of material aid is a well-known example. The Children and Young Persons Act (1963) permitted local authorities to render aid to individuals to prevent children being received into care or brought before the courts. Subsequently, the Social Work (Scotland) Act of 1968 widened the brief of authorities north of the border to do so in order 'to promote social welfare'. Studies in England[89] and Scotland[90] have discovered that authorities vary enormously in their interpretation of these powers. Clients in one area may receive material aid which is not offered to similar clients elsewhere. The use made of the powers appears to depend partly on the pressures exerted by social workers. It has now been suggested that they should persuade their departments to establish guidelines to ensure that their clients are not deprived even by comparison with the needy in other authorities.[91]

It might be rejoined that decisions about the policies of agencies are beyond the scope of social workers. This depends on the social workers. As the only employees with continuous direct contact with clients, they determine the kind of information and demands which are initially fed into the communications network. Further, the interpretation of decisions at ground level is their domain. Thus, case studies do suggest that social workers influence agency decisions. In studying agency developments, Donnison suggested that the providers of services are major initiators of change, especially when they are '. . . trained and skilled, when they are given considerable discretion in the practice of their own work, and when the services they provide depend largely on their own direct contacts with those served'.[92] This description, of course, aptly covers social workers. In an American examination of practice, Patti and Resnick looked at an agency which in ten years changed from a service based on '. . . ego-orientated casework treatment to one providing a broad array of services including short-term crisis-orientated treatment, client advocacy and institutional intervention'.[93] They explain that agency bureaucracies often resist external reforms unless they are counterbalanced by internal influences. Social workers can be that force. Taking up this matter in a subsequent paper, Patti and Resnick outlined the stages involved in instigating agency change—goal formulation, resource mobilisation and intervention. They also discuss whether social workers should use collaborative or adversary strategies and the limits placed on action by the social workers' values, agency loyalty and personal vulnerability to recriminations.[94]

Agency reforms will not abolish poverty. As was explained in chapter 4, agencies work within the constraints of their resources and duties. These limitations, however, do not constitute a reason why social workers should not attempt to alleviate poverty by making their organisations more responsive to and of more use to the socially deprived.

*Politicising the Poor*

Welfare rights activity and agency reforms will not, on their own, counter poverty. Indeed, these approaches have all the limitations of those put forward in earlier chapters. How can social workers contribute to the long-term political processes which may challenge the effects of a socially stratified society? The part, if any, which professional social-work organisations may play in swaying government decisions has been discussed by Lees.[95] Here, attention will dwell on social workers' interactions with individual clients and with community action groups.

Leonard has forcibly expounded—from a Marxist standpoint—the direction in which social workers could politicise their clients. During interviews, they could clarify the structural rather than the personal nature of their distress. He says, speaking of the social worker's role:

> Paramount will be a determination to confront in every available context the dominant definitions of problems which emphasise individual and community pathology . . . .[96]

> The social worker's task is to counteract dominant cultural definitions of poverty, to re-inforce and support resistance to those definitions.[97]

One reason that steps are rarely taken against poverty, it was argued in the last chapter, is that poverty is attributed to individual shortcomings. Indeed, the poor themselves sometimes accept this definition and are thus inhibited from action. Leonard therefore urges social workers to encourage clients to refute this definition. Once the poor refuse to see themselves as the cause of poverty, they are more likely to consider collective action against an unequal and unjust society. For Leonard, this means the classic Marxist confrontation between the ruling and subordinate classes. He says that the social worker is to transform

> . . . a private experience of poverty and exploitation into a manifest expression of class consciousness.[98]

> . . . the purpose of a marxist-based social work practice would be to bring the class struggle more clearly into the state apparatus . . .[99]

As will be indicated, I believe social workers, in some situations, can politically influence the poor. But first some reservations about Leonard's wide-ranging exhortations must be expressed. Integral to a Marxist analysis is a final reliance on violence, class warfare, the overthrow of law and the end of democracy. By now it will be obvious that my personal values do not accord with these means and ends nor with their conveyance to clients. Further, if political messages are scattered in an indiscriminate manner, there is a danger of raising clients' expectations to an unrealistic level. They can be led to believe that agitation will immediately and fundamentally alter their standing. Their resultant disappointment may engender deep disillusion. Lastly, it must be emphasised (and Leonard makes the point) that not all individual problems spring from structural causes and that the social workers' skills are needed with difficulties which are not political in origin.

Even where problems clearly do spring from structural poverty, clients should not be regarded as objects to be used simply to further the social workers' political dreams—no more than simply as objects on which to practise casework skills. A major responsibility of the social worker is to offer the services of his agency. Any attempt to enable clients to redefine their problems must be within the context of helping the immediate difficulties which brought him to the agency. Thus the social worker must attempt to balance his duty to enlist immediately his agency's resources to aid the client with his knowledge that the long-term resolution of the problems requires changes in the nature of society. Within this context and with regard to the limitations, I would suggest three directions in which the social worker might increase the political awareness and involvement of socially deprived clients.

Firstly, social workers should acknowledge to the clients that they are socially deprived. Poverty continues, partly because the poor are led to believe that their lot is not so bad. The media make much of the claim that today's poor may possess a TV set or even visit pubs, that the welfare state is doing much for them, that they should be grateful and passive. The truth is that extensive relative differences of income, wealth and power exist. The poor, as this book has striven to portray, have far greater likelihood than others of experiencing educational disadvantage, occupational under-achievement, unemployment, sickness and, ultimately, an earlier death. In discussing a client's position, the social worker should be prepared to identify the former's position at the very bottom of an unequal society.

Secondly, in working with those whose problems stem from their socially depriving conditions, social workers can avoid the temptation to treat them in such a fashion that poverty is reinforced. This occurs when clients are cast into a therapeutic relationship implying that their difficulties spring from personal or moral defects which the skilled worker will remedy. Appropriate as this approach may be to some clients, it does not help the poor. A more helpful stance entails a greater degree of equality between social worker and client. Of course, the former will still possess skills, powers and agency responsibilities not shared by the latter. The greater equality would issue from social worker and client perceiving that they are both attempting to counter external forces. In this relationship, the client does not have to see himself as an inferior person who has to be treated, who is to blame, who can only take but cannot contribute. Instead, he would see the possibilities of working with others against those forces which maintain poverty.

Thirdly, if it is helpful to clients, social workers could discuss the structural causes of their condition and the adaptive responses which shape their behaviour. If oppressive social conditions drive clients to violent despair, crush them into depression, push them into debts, make them unable to provide for their children, then the social worker is as justified in pointing to that explanation as when problems are explained by reference to childhood emotional disorders. However, social workers who do accept the structural explanation should not conclude that the skills of working with individuals are not required. Clients should not be denied the support, comfort and empathy to uphold them through their distressing experiences. The distinctive feature is not that the social worker dismisses one-to-one relationships but that through them he is prepared to point to the client's enforced position in a society in which the poor are functional. He is also ready to acknowledge that long-term solutions will be found not in social work but in collective, political action.

Within such relationships, there is a danger, as Leonard highlights, of social workers arrogantly assuming themselves to be the sole holders of truth which they now reveal to the poor.[100] Yet often the clients have already made deductions about their position. Their complaints about the odds against them, the injustice of their lot, their efforts coming to nothing, the futility of job-hunting, are often dismissed out-and-out. Yet they may be the expressions of those who perceive that an unequal society means that some must suffer. The social worker's intervention, in such circumstances, would be aimed at discussing further these topics which hitherto clients have felt did not come into their relationship. Together they might then discuss what form of action, if any, is feasible.

If social workers relate in these directions, then certain benefits may accrue. Clients may be strengthened by the realisation that their social workers accept that forces other than their own inadequacies explain their plight. A brake may be applied to those agency practices which support the political process of encouraging clients to accept their social deprivations as deserved and inevitable. Not least, clients may be more likely to challenge the system which, for instance, promotes unemployment, blames the poor for not working, and accuses them of preferring the dole to paid employment.

In some cases, clients will wish to participate more actively in attempts to counter poverty. This leads to the main point. The discussion to date has looked at the political content of the relationship between social workers and individual clients. Yet the theme of the earlier part of the chapter centred on the collective action of the poor. Can social workers help community action? They do have contact with some clients who are socially deprived. They are also likely to know of the existence of local groups. It follows that social workers are strategically well-placed to link the two. They might put clients in touch with a community action group because it is better equipped to deal with their welfare rights problem, because it is composed of members similar to themselves, or because it operates in their neighbourhood.

If linkage is likely to be the social worker's most frequent contribution, there may also be times when they actually stimulate the formation of organisations made up of the poor. As Gulper tells, some social workers did just this during the American 'War on Poverty'.[101] Their role, of course, was not to dominate or lead community action groups but to use their contacts to bring individuals together in order to examine the possibility of joint action. Lastly, social workers can use their knowledge and expertise in the service of community action. They can sometimes influence statutory and voluntary grant-giving bodies to support the collective poor or can advise groups to whom to apply for money. Gulper records social workers in Philadelphia who exposed the unwillingness of a fund to aid the local Welfare Rights Organization. One result was the creation of a fund to finance the movement.[102] Through these various contributions, community action groups could be helped to grow numerically and financially while the individuals with whom they are put in contact would benefit from the expertise, protection and fellowship of the groups.

*Implications for Social Workers*

Social workers who act as described, sometimes meet opposition from within their own agencies and local authorities. As well as unofficial 'frowning' upon social workers, it is not unknown for departments to forbid contact with, say, claimants' unions. The reasons for the hostility from seniors and councillors can readily be appreciated. The social workers are injecting an explicit political content into their work—rather than the implicit one of accepting poverty. Moreover, they associate with community action, groups which can be unpopular by virtue of their abrasive stances, their demands on services and the adverse publicity they stimulate. The situation could be ripe for employee/employer confrontation at the local level. Although necessary at times, engagements of this kind are to be regretted, for their immediate effect may be to disrupt the services which are offered to clients. A more profitable approach is for social workers to labour within their occupational organisations to obtain legitimisation for their activities. The vexed question then arises—which organisation? The British Association of Social Workers remains the major representative of social workers. Radical social workers have accused it of, and condemned it for, aspiring to be a profession. Professions, in turn, are slammed for being conservative, élitist and for having a preoccupation with the advancement of members rather than clients. BASW can hardly win, for it is also criticised for inadequately pushing members' interests when compared with trade unions. Whatever the reasons, a number of social workers have preferred to join the National Association of Local Government Officers, the National Union of Public Employees or the National Union of Social Workers. Thankfully, lack of space forbids entry here into this particular controversy, but one comment can be made. It is a mistake to assume that professional standards and a commitment to a more equal society cannot go together. Social work may not, perhaps should not, develop as a profession in the sense that medicine and law are professions. But it is feasible and desirable to have an organisation of social workers which insists on certain levels of practice and is also prepared to protect members who work for a different kind of society. If the organisation accepts that support for community action groups is an integral part of social work, then workers would have strong grounds for undertaking such work within their agencies.

## Social Workers and Poverty

Social work cannot abolish social deprivation. Indeed, its impact may be but small. As Carmichael points out, not only are the resources of social work agencies insufficient to meet income needs but, even although *many* poor families do approach Social Service Departments, '. . . *most* poor families don't have a social worker' (my italics).[103] Moreover, Meyer is probably right in arguing that any effective societal change is more likely to be created by '. . . the poor, the black community and youth, than by social workers in their roles as practitioners'.[104]

The limitations of social work in regard to redressing poverty, however, should not be used as grounds for dismissing its value. Social work can be justified on other grounds. Among its contributions, three are of particular importance. Firstly, social work does prevent the break-up of some families. As conceded, it does not remove the social deprivations which handicap certain parents in coping with their children. But social-work skills and resources have been used to stop the process at the point where removal or abandonment is unavoidable. An obvious example is where social workers find day-care facilities to keep children at home rather than in institutions, while casework skills are used to enable parents to understand and control their attitudes towards their offspring.[105] Social workers have contained delinquents within the community rather than in residential schools while, in regard to adults, they have lowered the re-conviction rates of ex-prisoners.[106]

Secondly, social work does alleviate some of the destructive impact of poverty. The support and sympathy offered to those condemned to long-term unemployment, the counselling given to the broken family, the holiday to the over-burdened mother, the play-groups arranged for the large family, may not touch the causes of their difficulties but they do make life easier. I agree with Meyer that social workers should help people survive and come through the immediate and worst effects of poverty. It is easy to dismiss their efforts as palliatives, yet the alternative may be to do nothing.

Thirdly, social work serves to humanise the meeting of human need. Social work within the social services has replaced many of the functions of the old poor law. Instead of harshness, coldness and deterrence, it emphasises empathy, consideration and prevention. Instead of a policy of disposing of the members of needy families into separate, forbidding buildings, social work has, in general, advocated the keeping of families together in the community. Where receptions do occur—into children's homes, mental hospitals, old people's homes—social workers have striven to arrange them in a non-traumatic fashion into institutions which welcome and respect their residents. Certainly, these standards are not always attained. Nonetheless, social workers have made progress in establishing that statutory services can be conveyed to those in need in a dignified and skilful manner.

At its best, social work helps to maintain family life, promotes a concern for individuals and engenders care about the distress of others. Simultaneously, as argued in this chapter, it can do something to modify poverty and a little towards stimulating the political development of the poor themselves. To my mind, these contributions are of value, and reflect to the credit of social work.

## CONCLUSION

Social work has been used as the occupation which I know best. Obviously members of other occupations and professions will contribute as well. In their workplace and neighbourhood they can oppose those attitudes and practices which serve to uphold poverty and also offer support to the movements of the poor. For the burden of this chapter is that their role will be secondary to the collective action of the socially deprived themselves.

Whatever the means of instigating change, those who advocate a more equal society are sometimes charged with paying too much attention to material matters, of regarding possessions as more important than people. The opposite is true. It is realised that the quality of people's relationships underlie a satisfactory life. To end on the personal note of this chapter, I reckon that my deepest needs are met through relationships— with the members of my family, with friends, with neighbours, with workmates and, I believe, with God. Most people seek mutually satisfying contacts with others. Yet these relationships cannot be entirely separated from material matters. Concern, love, compassion, feelings, must be expressed through the sharing of resources. This book has attempted to show that when great disparities occur, then not only are distress and disadvantage created but so are behaviour patterns which can lead to apathy, extreme aggression and the inability to survive in modern society. In short, grossly unequal conditions are likely to promote those features which inhibit the growth of happy relationships. I believe in seeking those structural changes which will lead to a society in which the distribution of resources will facilitate concern for others, tolerance and sharing.

REFERENCES

1 See R. Tawney *Equality* Allen and Unwin (4th ed, 1952)
2 W. G. Runciman *Relative Deprivation and Social Justice* Penguin Books (1972) p. 343
3 T. Campbell 'Humanity Before Justice' *British Journal of Political Science* vol. 4, pt 1 (1974)
4 D. Donnison 'Equality' *New Society* vol. 34, no. 685 (20 Nov. 1975)
5 Genesis i 26–30
6 Cited by R. Terrill *R. H. Tawney and His Times* Deutsch, 1973
7 D. Lane *The End of Equality* Penguin Books (1971); R. Mishra 'Marx and Welfare' *Sociological Review* vol. 23, no. 2 (1975)
8 D. Coates *The Labour Party and the Struggle for Socialism* Cambridge University Press (1975)
9 R. Titmuss 'The Social Division of Welfare' in A. Lochhead (ed.) *A Reader in Social Administration* Constable (1968) pp. 313–14
10 M. Young (ed.) *Poverty Report 1974* Temple Smith (1974) pp. 13–18; P. Willmott (ed.) *Poverty Report 1976, Sharing Inflation?* Temple Smith (1976) pp. 12–15
11 H. Wilson 'Parenting in Poverty' *British Journal of Social Work* vol. 4, no. 3 (autumn 1974)
12 F. Field *The New Corporate Interest* Child Poverty Action Group (1976)
13 Young *op. cit.* p. 4
14 See Terrill, *op. cit.*
15 Mishra *op. cit.*
16 R. Pinker 'Social Policy and Social Justice' *Journal of Social Policy* vol. 3, pt 1 (1974)
17 Pinker *op. cit.*
18 L. Goodwin 'How Suburban Families View the Work Orientations of the Welfare Poor' *Social Problems* vol. 19, no. 3 (winter, 1972)
19 J. Goldthorpe 'Social Inequality and Social Integration in Modern Britain' in D. Wedderburn (ed.) *Poverty, Inequality and Class Structure* Cambridge University Press (1974) p. 218
20 Mishra *op. cit.*
21 R. Miliband 'Politics and Poverty' in Wedderburn *op. cit.* pp. 189–90
22 A. Potter 'The Political Consensus' *New Society* vol. 7, no. 182 (24 March 1966)
23 P. Partridge 'Politics, Philosophy, Ideology' in W. Birrell *et al.* (eds) *Social Administration* Penguin Books (1973) p. 374
24 Potter *op. cit.*
25 R. Bryant 'Community Action' *British Journal of Social Work* vol. 2, no. 2 (1972)
26 C. Smith and B. Anderson 'Political Participation through Community Action' in G. Parry (ed.) *Participation in Politics* Manchester University Press (1972)
27 Community Work Group, Gulbenkian Foundation *Current Issues in Community Work* Routledge (1973) p. 41
28 Adult Education Department *Case Studies in Community Work* vol. 1, University of Manchester (1974)
29 S. Jacobs *The Right to a Decent House* Routledge (1976)
30 See H. Rose 'Up Against the Welfare State: the Claimants' Unions' in R. Miliband and J. Saville (eds) *The Socialist Register 1973* Merlin (1974); and East London Claimants' Union 'East London Claimants' Union and

the Concept of Self-Management' in D. Jones and M. Mayo (eds) *Community Work One* Routledge (1974)

31 See J. Hall Fish *Black Power, White Control* Princeton University Press (1973)
32 See L. Jackson and W. Johnson *Protest By The Poor* Lexington Books (1974); and R. Holman 'Changes in American Welfare Rights' *New Society* vol. 21, no. 520 (21 Sept. 1972)
33 See e.g. A. Billingsley and J. Giovannoni *Children of the Storm* Harcourt Brace (1972)
34 For a fuller discussion, see Community Work Group, Gulbenkian Foundation *op. cit.* pp. 51–62
35 G. Brager and H. Specht *Community Organizing* Columbia University Press (1973) p. 335
36 G. Popplestone 'Collective Action among Private Tenants' *British Journal of Social Work* vol. 2, no. 3 (1972)
37 A. Power *I Woke Up This Morning* British Council of Churches (1972)
38 See R. Means 'Social Work and the Undeserving Poor' Ph.d thesis, University of Birmingham (1976) ch. 11
39 R. Lees *Research Strategies for Social Welfare* Routledge (1975) ch.5
40 P. Freire *Pedagogy of the Oppressed* Penguin Books (1972) p. 21
41 Jacobs *op. cit.* p. 8
42 J. Askham *Fertility and Deprivation* Cambridge University Press (1975) p. 168
43 W. Haggstrom 'The Power of the Poor' in F. Riessman (ed.) *Mental Health of the Poor* Collier Macmillan (1964) p. 216
44 W. G. Runciman 'Deprivation and Social Justice' in A. Lochhead (ed.) *A Reader in Social Administration* Constable (1968) p. 295
45 Freire *op. cit.* p. 37
46 ibid. p. 42
47 Goodwin *op. cit.*
48 Freire *op. cit.* p. 48
49 R. Scase 'Relative Deprivation: a Comparison of English and Swedish Manual Workers' in Wedderburn *op. cit.* and cited by Wedderburn, p. 9.
50 Community Work Group, Gulbenkian Foundation *op. cit.* pp. 62–4; R. Holman 'Why Community Action?' *Municipal Journal* vol. 82, nos. 14, 15 (5 and 12 April 1974)
51 The Community Development Projects were initiated in the 1960s for a fixed period but with a view to developing more permanent ways of fighting poverty. However, in 1976 the government decided not to extend the experiment. A number of studies of the twelve CDPs have been made, one of which is J. Crawforth 'Community Work and Social Deprivation' in Department of Applied Social Science *Social Work Studies No. 1, Working in the Community* University of Nottingham (1975)
52 E. Maccoby *et al.* 'Community Integration and the Social Control of Delinquency' *Journal of Social Issues* vol. 14, no. 3 (1958)
53 K. Coates and R. Silburn *Poverty: the Forgotten Englishman* Penguin Books (1970)
54 See Willmott *op. cit.* pt 1
55 Miliband *op. cit.* p. 191
56 J. Galper *The Politics of Social Services* Prentice-Hall (1975). It must be added that Galper modifies this view in ch. 11
57 The annual report of the DHSS revealed that, at the end of 1972, local-authority

social service departments employed over 15,000 social workers. This number excludes those employed by central government and voluntary agencies

58 DHSS *Health and Personal Social Service Statistics* HMSO (1974) p. 26

59 British Association of Social Workers *Survey in the London Boroughs of Section I Children and Young Persons Act 1963 Payments* (1974)

60 B. Jordan *Poor Parents* Routledge (1974) p. 181

61 C. Meyer *Social Work Practice* Collier Macmillan (1970) p. 18

62 *ibid.* p. 14

63 *ibid.* p. 19

64 *ibid.* p. 3

65 *ibid.* p. 18

66 *ibid.* p. 106

67 A. Sinfield *Which Way for Social Work?* Fabian Society (1969), repr. in part in E. Butterworth and R. Holman (eds) *Social Welfare in Modern Britain* Fontana (1975) p. 170

68 Cited by Jordan *op. cit.* p. 100

69 R. Holman *Child Care and Inequality* Child Poverty Action Group (1976)

70 R. Thorpe 'Mum and Mrs So-and-So' (article based on doctoral thesis) *Social Work Today* vol. 4, no. 22 (7 Feb. 1974)

71 G. Brown, M. Ni Bhrolchain and T. Harris 'Social Class and Psychiatric Disturbance among Women in an Urban Population' *Sociology* vol. 9 (1975)

72 See J. Heywood and B. Allen *Financial Help in Social Work* Manchester University Press (1971)

73 M. Jackson and B. Valencia 'Financial Aid Through Loans' *Social Work Today* vol. 7, no. 3 (26 April 1976)

74 Figure given by C. Carmichael 'The Relationship between Social Work Departments and the Department of Health and Social Security' in N. Newman (ed.) *The Place of Financial Assistance in Social Work* University of Edinburgh (1974) p. 57

75 Jordan *op. cit.* p. 118

76 Haggstrom *op. cit.* p. 216

77 R. Bitensky 'The Influence of Political Power in Determining the Theoretical Development of Social Work' *Journal of Social Policy* vol. 2, pt. 2 (1973)

78 See L. Rainwater 'The Revolt of the Dirty Workers' *Transaction* vol. 5, no. 1 (Nov. 1967)

79 See R. Holman (ed.) *Socially Deprived Families in Britain* Bedford Square Press (1970) pp. 187–91

80 N. Bond *Knowledge of Rights and Extent of Unmet Need amongst Recipients of Supplementary Benefit* Coventry Community Development Project (1972)

81 See P. Sharkey 'Welfare Rights and Social Service Depts' *Social Work Today* vol. 4, no. 13 (1973); P. Burgess *The Welfare Rights Service in Manchester* Manchester Social Services Department (1973)

82 Occasionally, 'advocate' is used to cover any promotion of change within any agency or within society. For a review of some of the literature, see R. Baker 'The Multirole Practitioner in the Generic Orientation to Social Work Practice' *British Journal of Social Work* vol. 6, no. 3 (1976)

83 P. Terrell 'The Social Worker as Radical:Roles of Advocacy' in P. Weinberger (ed.) *Perspectives on Social Welfare* Collier Macmillan (1974)

84 Jacobs *op. cit.*

85 D. Bull *Action for Welfare Rights* Fabian Society (1970) p. 23

86 R. Patti and H. Resnick 'Changing the Agency from Within' *Social Work* vol. 17, no. 4 (July 1972)

87 Statement by British Association of Social Workers in *Social Work Today* vol. 3, no. 21 (25 Jan. 1973)
88 See J. Streather 'Welfare Rights and the Social Worker' *Social Work Today* vol. 3, no. 13 (5 Oct. 1972)
89 J. Heywood and M. Allen *op. cit.*
90 See Newman (ed.) *op. cit.*
91 M. Adler 'Financial Assistance and the Social Worker's Exercise of Discretion' in Newman (ed.) *op. cit.*
92 D. Donnison *et al. Social Policy and Administration Re-visited* Allen and Unwin (1975) p. 291
93 Patti and H. Resnick *op. cit.*
94 R. Patti and H. Resnick 'The Dynamics of Agency Change' *Social Casework* vol 53, no. 4 (1972)
95 R. Lees *Politics and Social Work* Routledge (1972)
96 P. Leonard 'Marx: the Class Perspective' *Community Care* no. 123 (11 Aug. 1976)
97 P. Leonard *Poverty, Consciousness and Action* British Association of Social Workers (1975) p. 8
98 *ibid.* p. 8
99 Leonard 'Marx: the Class Perspective' *op. cit.*
100 Leonard *Poverty, Consciousness and Action, op. cit.*
101 Gulper *op. cit.* p. 205
102 *ibid.*
103 Carmichael *op. cit.* p. 59
104 Meyer *op. cit.* p. 24
105 See Holman *Inequality in Child Care, op. cit.* for a discussion of the preventive potential of social workers
106 M. Shaw *Social Work in Prison* HMSO (1974)

# Index